CROOKED PATHS
MADE STRAIGHT

CROOKED PATHS MADE STRAIGHT

A Blind Teacher's Adventures
Traveling around the World

ISABELLE L. D. GRANT

Edited and with an Introduction and
Afterword by Deborah Kent

CROOKED PATHS MADE STRAIGHT
A BLIND TEACHER'S ADVENTURES TRAVELING AROUND THE WORLD

iUniverse books may be ordered through booksellers or by contacting:

iUniverse
1663 Liberty Drive
Bloomington, IN 47403
www.iuniverse.com
1-800-Authors (1-800-288-4677)

ISBN: 978-1-4917-7035-1 (sc)
ISBN: 978-1-4917-7027-6 (e)

Library of Congress Control Number: 2015918083

Print information available on the last page.

iUniverse rev. date: 1/11/2016

And I will bring the blind by a way they know not;
I will lead them in paths that they have not known;
I will make darkness light before them,
And crooked things straight.

—Isaiah 42:16

CONTENTS

PART IV. HOMEWARD BOUND

INTRODUCTION
by Deborah Kent

When Dr. Isabelle Grant retired from teaching in June 1962, her colleagues at Irving Junior High School hosted a gala farewell celebration. Dr. Grant had taught in the Los Angeles public schools for thirty-two years, and her fellow teachers showed their love and respect by presenting her with a book of letters and tributes. "We love you very much and shall miss you as a vibrant part of our daily lives," wrote a teacher named Beverly Walker. "Happy school retirement to you, Dr. Isabelle Grant, the epitome of the student, the scholar, the great teacher, the marvelous person."[1]

At the time of her retirement, Dr. Grant completed a short questionnaire, listing her degrees and the teaching positions she had held. The form concluded with a few personal questions. Where it inquired about special interests, Dr. Grant responded, "None out of the ordinary." When asked about ambitions, she replied, "None in particular." To the question about future plans, she answered, "At this time it is good to have no particular plans. Time will take care of them."[2]

These self-effacing comments reflect Dr. Grant's modesty, combined with her ironic sense of humor. Just two months after her retirement party, she set out for Pakistan on a Hayes-Fulbright Fellowship to train teachers of blind children. The trip launched her into a new career as international ambassador, working to promote the rights of blind people throughout the world. Ten years later, her work brought her a nomination for the Nobel Peace Prize.

Dr. Grant had begun her world travels two years before her

retirement. During the 1959/60 school year, she took a sabbatical leave from teaching and embarked upon a round-the-world expedition. *Crooked Paths Made Straight* is her memoir of this journey (or safari, as she calls it), during which she visited twenty-three countries from Great Britain to Fiji. She traveled alone, accompanied only by Oscar. Oscar was her long white cane. At the time of her journey, Dr. Grant had been totally blind for twelve years.

In 1965, Dr. Grant completed the writing of *Crooked Paths Made Straight*. She found writing to be an arduous process. She struggled to decipher Braille notes that had been flattened by the dampness of the tropics, and she battled endlessly with an uncooperative typewriter. Often she was ready to give up the endeavor, but her friends encouraged her to carry on. "My blind friends urged me to tell the story," she wrote in her postscript to the book. "Young blind people were especially insistent. If an old lady could do it, then they, too, could do it in due time. My sighted friends also insisted that I tell my story. They were reluctant to believe that I had made the circuit of the globe. They said it could not be done, even after I had done it."[3]

Dr. Grant tried several times to find a publisher for *Crooked Paths*, but none of the houses she approached showed much interest. After her death in 1977, the manuscript lay untouched for nearly thirty years. In 2007, Allen Calhoun, one of Dr. Grant's grandsons, donated several cartons of her papers to the Jacobus tenBroek Library at the headquarters of the National Federation of the Blind in Baltimore, Maryland. Among the papers was the manuscript of *Crooked Paths Made Straight*, as well as *Africa Passbook*, another unpublished book about Dr. Grant's travels, which she completed in 1970. (A second collection of Dr. Grant's papers is housed at the Bancroft Library at the University of California–Berkeley.)

Isabelle Grant was a dedicated member of the National Federation of the Blind, and she is honored as one of its early leaders. Her life and work were an inspiration to the blind people of the United States, but her impact reached beyond any borders. She is best remembered as a woman who worked tirelessly to empower the blind of the world.

•   •   •

In her later years, Isabelle Grant adhered to the philosophy that it is rude to inquire about a woman's age, and she was closemouthed about her date of birth. Immigration records at Ellis Island reveal that she was born Isabelle Lyon Dean in 1896 in Lossiemouth, Morayshire, a fishing village on the northern coast of Scotland, about seventy miles from Aberdeen. Isabelle (known to her family and friends as Ella) was one of four children of Jane and William Dean. Three of her father's brothers were the captains of schooners that "sailed the world round." Though her father never took to the sea, Isabelle grew up with his stories of the explorer Captain James Cook. She reflected later, "The life of this intrepid seaman, scientific explorer, and skillful navigator had always been a link of understanding between my father and me."[4] Her father also instilled in her a deep respect for education. His cherished copy of *The Three Voyages of Captain Cook*, awarded to him as a school prize in 1884, served to remind her of the high academic standard she herself sought to achieve.

Isabelle attended the public school in Lossiemouth and continued her studies at Elgin Academy. She earned a degree in English and French at Aberdeen University in 1917 and taught school in Scotland and England for the next five years.

At the age of twenty-eight, Isabelle Dean Grant left Scotland to make a new home in the United States. She and her husband, Dr. Alexander Lewis Grant, crossed the Atlantic on the *Californian*. (Isabelle almost surely knew the role of the *Californian* in the tragic story of the *Titanic*. On the fateful night of April 14, 1912, members of the *Californian*'s crew failed to respond to distress flares from the foundering ship eight miles away, assuming that the "unsinkable" *Titanic* was celebrating its maiden voyage with fireworks.)

Although she adjusted quickly to life in her adopted country, Isabelle Grant never lost her Scottish burr or her love for her homeland. In a journal entry dated October 18 (no year is given), she describes "chasing accents" as she rode a northbound train during a visit to the UK sometime in the late 1960s. She writes of hearing "unintelligible Cockney" followed by "the singsong of Midlanders." Then, she exults, "York and Arlington becoming broader and less clipped as Newcastle approaches. Then [an] overwhelming cataract of burrs, achs and ochs, announcing unalterably, unquestionably, and gloriously, Scotland!"[5]

Isabelle crossed the Atlantic again in 1928 to study at the University of Madrid. The following year she studied at the Sorbonne. She became fluent in Spanish and acquired what she jokingly referred to as "twenty words of French." In 1940 she received a PhD in comparative literature from the University of Southern California in Los Angeles.

Isabelle's knowledge of Spanish served her well as a teacher in the Los Angeles County schools, where a high proportion of students came from Spanish-speaking families. She began teaching in Los Angeles in 1927 and soon became a vocal advocate for her Mexican American students. She spoke to school officials on their behalf, went with them to court when they got into trouble, and encouraged them to stay in school.

Isabelle had one daughter, Jane Susannah Hermione Grant, known as Hermione, who was born in 1930. Alexander Grant, twenty years his wife's senior, died in 1946. Soon after, Isabelle learned that she was losing her sight due to glaucoma. Desperate to save her vision, she visited one doctor after another and underwent eight painful surgeries, all to no avail. By the fall of 1948, she was totally blind.

In general, Isabelle Grant was not one to talk about her personal life. The story of her adjustment to blindness was a rare exception; she told it often when she lectured to build support for her efforts in the international blind community. In her first months without sight, she often declared, she felt utterly helpless. She believed that she couldn't cook, couldn't sew, and certainly couldn't teach. Most of the people around her concurred. They treated her as though she had lost her wits as well as her eyesight.

Isabelle turned for help to a local agency for the blind, the Braille Institute of America, but received little encouragement. Then, as longtime friend Hazel tenBroek recalled, "When she returned to the care of the friend who had driven her [to the agency], she was ready to give way to the dejection she felt, and to quit. The [friend], however, had another idea. She knew a blind man with a zest for living who did many things most people thought required sight. Dr. Grant must meet him immediately. They drove to his home without more ado."[6]

The blind man was James Garfield, an active member of the National Federation of the Blind. Although Isabelle arrived at his door unannounced, he invited her in, listened to her story, and delivered a pep talk that changed her life. "You have hit bottom," he told her, "and there is nowhere to go but up. Don't feel sorry for yourself, because that won't do you any good or get you any place."[7] He urged her to become proficient in the use of Braille, to learn to travel with a long white cane, and to get to know blind people who were active and independent.

Isabelle embraced Garfield's message. She flung herself into an effort to master a set of new skills that would allow her to live independently and with dignity. She was proficient in Braille within a few months, and she became a confident cane traveler. She began to attend meetings of the California Council of the Blind, an affiliate of the National Federation of the Blind. She formed a deep and lasting friendship with the organization's founding president, Dr. Jacobus tenBroek, and his wife, Hazel.

•   •   •

Among legal scholars, Jacobus tenBroek is remembered for his pioneering work on constitutional law and civil rights. In *Antislavery Origins of the Fourteenth Amendment* (1951) and *Prejudice, War, and the Constitution* (1955) he demonstrated how the tenets of the US Constitution upheld the rights of all citizens, regardless of race or ethnic heritage. Breaking new ground, tenBroek also identified discrimination against people with disabilities as a civil rights issue. His essay "The Right to Live in the World: The Disabled in the Law of Torts," published in the *California Law Review* in 1966, helped prepare the way for the disability rights movement and such key legislation as the Rehabilitation Act of 1973 and the Americans with Disabilities Act (ADA) of 1990.

TenBroek's passion for disability rights sprang from his personal experience of discrimination. He was born in 1911 in a log cabin on the prairies of Alberta, Canada. Blinded as a child in an accident with a bow and arrow, tenBroek enrolled at the California School for the

Blind in Berkeley when he was fourteen. There he studied under Dr. Newel Perry, a gifted blind mathematician with an unshakeable belief that his students could compete on equal terms with their sighted peers. Perry knew firsthand about the prejudice his students were likely to encounter. Despite his proven ability, the school for the blind was the only academic institution that had been willing to offer him a job.

TenBroek encountered similar barriers when he sought employment. After he earned a degree in history and a law degree from the University of California–Berkeley, he applied for teaching positions at some five hundred colleges and universities. Hiring committees were impressed by his credentials, but they refused to consider him when they learned that he was blind.

Unable to find work, tenBroek went on to pursue further studies. He earned a postlaw degree at Harvard and a doctorate in law at UC Berkeley. Finally he secured a part-time tutoring position at the University of Chicago. In 1942 he returned to UC Berkeley as an instructor, and later chair, of the Department of Speech.

Despite his personal success, tenBroek never forgot that most blind people in the United States were far less fortunate. Few were employed; most struggled to survive on meager public assistance grants. Their lives were controlled by a network of agencies for the blind run by sighted professionals. Blind people were encouraged to be passive and obedient, grateful for charity.

In 1940 tenBroek organized a meeting of blind delegates from seven states to discuss the problems faced by blind Americans. That meeting, held in Wilkes-Barre, Pennsylvania, is regarded as the founding convention of the National Federation of the Blind (NFB), an organization of blind people speaking for themselves. Under tenBroek's presidency (1940–61 and 1965–68), the NFB won blind people the right to compete for civil service jobs and challenged the practice of paying subminimum wages to disabled workers in sheltered workshops.

TenBroek firmly believed that blindness need not impede an individual from achieving success in his or her chosen field of endeavor. The real problems of blindness, he concluded, were the misconceptions of the sighted public. Through his work with the NFB he attempted to instill blind people with confidence in themselves and a sense of their power to bring about change. Isabelle Grant absorbed his message with all her being. It became a core part of who she was, a conviction that shaped the rest of her life.

•   •   •

Inspired by Dr. tenBroek and her other friends in the Federation, Isabelle Grant felt ready and able to resume teaching. A California statute stated that no blind or partially sighted person should be denied the right to teach solely on the basis of blindness. However, an ordinance in Los Angeles County stated that a classroom teacher must have a visual acuity of at least twenty-seventy. The Los Angeles County school board informed Isabelle that, due to her blindness, she was no longer competent to teach. Her duties as girls' vice principal at Belvidere Junior High School would be terminated, and she was advised to apply for permanent disability compensation.

State and national leaders in the National Federation of the Blind gave Isabelle their vigorous support. Fellow teachers rallied around her as well. On January 26, 1949, two days before her termination was to take effect, sixty-three Belvidere teachers submitted a signed petition on Isabelle's behalf to Assistant Superintendent Dr. Alexander J. Stoddard. "The Belvidere Junior High School faculty has just learned that Dr. Isabelle Grant may not return as girls' vice principal to our school," the letter begins. "The faculty, while fully aware of Dr. Grant's physical condition, unanimously asks that she be returned to Belvidere." The letter cites "Dr. Grant's outstanding contribution to the school and community through her sympathetic understanding of problems involved in our school and [her] deep affection for the Mexican American" and her "rare ability to solve the teacher/pupil/ parent problems to the satisfaction of all concerned." It concludes, "Belvidere Junior High School and the entire Los Angeles City School System would suffer a severe loss should her services be denied. However, our faculty would be very much pleased if Dr. Grant were to receive a promotion, which her ability warrants.... Our schools have placed special emphasis on rehabilitation at home and abroad. Could there be a more practical application than to rehabilitate one whose twenty years of undeniably superior work have proved her unrivaled in success?"[8]

On February 1, 1949, Dr. Grant was reinstated as a teacher in the Los Angeles school system. She did not, however, resume her position as girls' vice principal—and she certainly did not receive the promotion that her colleagues suggested. Due to her blindness, the school authorities deemed her unfit to work with sighted students. Instead, they assigned her to teach blind children, although she had no experience in the field of special education. Furthermore, not trusting her to be alone with her pupils, the school insisted that she have a sighted teacher's aide in her classroom at all times. In April 1955, she wrote to Dr. tenBroek, "The decision is that I am to be transferred to the Belmont High School; that I am to continue working with the severely retarded pupils, of whom there will be either four or at most five. A room is to be set up for me with a partition dividing it in two, and a sighted teacher is to be placed in the other half of the room. That's the story. I think that I must have turned white, for the thought passed through my mind of the blind teacher in a glass cage, with a sighted teacher looking on and after her. It is the most ridiculous situation imaginable—ludicrous, insulting to the individual, and degrading. It is medievalism outstripped!"[9]

Isabelle endured years of humiliating treatment at the hands of Los Angeles school officials. She was shifted from one school to another. The brightest students were transferred out of her class and sent to different schools. She was sabotaged from attending teachers' conferences. Yet she refused to give up. With the help of the National Federation of the Blind, she fought to keep her job and to be treated with respect.

Wherever she went, her fellow teachers recognized Isabelle's extraordinary gifts. In May 1956, Gjertrud Smith, principal of Belmont High School, wrote to one of her superiors, "May I say again how grateful we are to have Dr. Grant at Belmont. She is dearly loved and highly respected by everyone. It is a great pity that she is given only the slow learners to work with. She is so brilliant and such a superb teacher that she could make tremendous progress with blind students with normal and above ability."[10]

In the summer of 1957, Isabelle Grant undertook her first trip abroad since the loss of her sight. She attended an international convention on the education of blind children held in Oslo, Norway. According to Hazel tenBroek, she "came home imbued with the crusader's zeal to spread the benefits of training and organizing."[11] To Isabelle Grant, organizing meant building organizations of the blind that would fight discrimination and enable blind people to reach their full potential. She wanted to carry the philosophy and strategies of Jacobus tenBroek and the National Federation of the Blind to the nations of the world.

•   •   •

Isabelle Grant was eligible to take a sabbatical leave during the 1959/60 school year, two years before she was scheduled to retire. She decided to use the time to learn what she could about the lives of blind people overseas, focusing especially on the education of blind children. She was most interested in the conditions for blind people in the many nations emerging from colonial rule. With few clear plans about where she would go or what she would do when she got there, she embarked upon the journey that forms the basis for *Crooked Paths Made Straight*. As she explains in her brief foreword, "I am not a politician, a historian, a theologian, a diplomat, or a VIP."[12] She was a dedicated teacher with a lifelong commitment to learning, and she approached her endeavor with an eagerness to observe and absorb. She carried her typewriter, her Braillewriter, her bundle of documents, and her assorted luggage, and of course Oscar, her long white cane. She also carried her conviction about the abilities of blind children and the opportunities that should be open to them—the same opportunities, she believed, that should be open to all children the world over.

Sometimes Isabelle was appalled by the conditions she found. She talked with blind people who had spent their lives as beggars in the streets, who had given up any hope of developing their abilities and living with dignity. She learned that only a tiny fraction of all blind children received any form of schooling; those who did attend schools for the blind gained little that would prepare them to make their way in the world. Yet nearly everywhere she went, she was electrified by the excitement of newly forged nations leaping into the modern age. From Lebanon to Pakistan to the Philippines, she met the enthusiasm of teachers, social workers, and doctors who were eager to do battle with the entrenched foes of hunger, ignorance, and poverty. She also met young blind women and men with the courage to imagine a brighter future. They looked to her for encouragement and direction, and she offered it in abundance.

More than half a century has passed since Isabelle Grant made her journey of investigation. Many of the lands she grew to love have been wracked by war, derailing the progress she hoped for and expected. Yet even from this distance, even with our knowledge of what the years have brought, Isabelle Grant's optimism is infectious. She believed in the human capacity for learning and growth, and she was certain that the human spirit has the power to prevail against overwhelming odds. She tells a story of dreams deferred that do not shrivel but spring to life again and again.

NOTES

1. Isabelle Grant's Memory Book, June 1962, Jacobus tenBroek Library, National Federation of the Blind, Baltimore, MD.
2. Questionnaire for Irving Hall of Fame: Retirement Keepsake Packet, B-1, F4 Correspondence, 1962, Jacobus tenBroek Library.
3. *Crooked Paths Made Straight,* Postscript.
4. *Crooked Paths Made Straight,* Chapter 24.
5. Isabelle Grant Journal Entry, Jacobus tenBroek Library.
6. Hazel tenBroek, "Isabelle L. D. Grant: The Early Years," *Braille Monitor* (December 1977): 396.
7. Ibid.
8. Letter from Belvidere Jr. High Faculty Club to Mrs. Elizabeth Sands and Dr. Alexander J. Stoddard, January 26, 1949. Carton 1, File 6, Jacobus tenBroek Library.
9. Letter to Dr. Jacobus tenBroek from Isabelle Grant, April 1955, Carton 1, File 6, Jacobus tenBroek Library.
10. Letter from Gjertrud Smith to unnamed recipient, May 1956, Carton 1, File 5, Jacobus tenBroek Library.
11. Hazel tenBroek, "Isabelle L. D. Grant: The Early Years," *Braille Monitor* (December 1977): 400.
12. *Crooked Paths,* Author's Foreword.

AUTHOR'S FOREWORD

I am not a politician, a historian, a theologian, a diplomat, or a VIP. I am a schoolteacher, and I love people—all people, regardless of color. I would not see the difference, anyway; rich or poor, I would not see that, either. There is no color line or deposit line in kindness, only a sharing.

Then there are the children. I have served children for nigh forty years. The last year was as challenging as the first, and the little Hindu girl was as precious as my own child.

Sighted reader, come and journey with me, and see things my way for a change. And, blind reader, pick up your knapsack, and come visit with your fellow blind. You will find some of them less fortunate than you are, so share with them your know-how, your talent, and your substance.

And, blind readers in far-off countries, will you accept our friendship? We are a friendly people and kind at heart, though a bit awkward and ignorant of the ways of others. Will you pull your weight with the rest of us blind folks throughout the world so that the blind will no longer be captive but free men and women? Then all of us, blind and sighted alike the world over, may brothers be, for all that!

PART I
THE JOURNEY BEGINS

CHAPTER I
IMPEDIMENTA AND PICKPOCKETS

I almost heard their eyebrows arch, the silence was so great. A blind woman going around the world? What would she see? Nothing!

I was asking for a year's sabbatical leave from my school duties. Did I plan to go alone?

"Of course! Well—not exactly; I'll have Oscar with me." Oscar is my white cane. My students christened him to placate me when Oscars were being awarded to their favorite movie stars. So Oscar he was, and Oscar he has remained.

"And where do you plan to go?"

"Oh, to see the Acropolis, the Taj Mahal, the Angkor Wat, the Blue Mountains of Australia, the Maori huts of New Zealand, and perhaps a visit to the Fiji Islanders if my money holds out."

So on a hot summer day in July 1959, I sallied forth from California, laden with enough impedimenta for one of Caesar's soldiers on the march through Gaul. My suitcase balanced the scales at forty-four pounds. Besides a sheaf of tickets, a thick passport, health records, and a fat book of traveler's checks, I carried a heavy camelhair coat and a velour hat.

"Granny, this typewriter is heavy!" said my six-year-old grandson, who had come to escort me to the plane. The typewriter, a late, light, portable model, was to accompany me as personal luggage. It would be suspended from my left arm—if there was space left for it. If not, I did not know where it was going to go. All I knew was that it could not go along with my suitcase, for that would mean ten pounds excess weight.

I had had fifteen immunization shots pumped into my arms—smallpox, polio, cholera, typhus, typhoid, yellow fever. I was feeling the effects, but I was all right. I had the key to my apartment in my pocket. If I had to, I could return home in a hurry.

Was it the shots that made my temperature seem to rise? Was it the heat of that summer day? Or did I have a premonition of the maze of crooked paths ahead of me, paths that I could not yet imagine?

I was not afraid of travel. Those around me voiced ideas about what a blind person should and should not do, but their concerns never affected me. Sighted people seem always to think they know more about blindness than blind people do! I had been blind for twelve years, after eight operations for acute glaucoma. I had continued to live an active life, and by the time I set off on my journey, I felt as though I had been blind from the beginning. Blindness was natural to me; it was part of who I was. I had the memory of color, form, and size, but somehow those memories were of a piece with my experience of blindness. Even people blind from birth have concepts of color and form.

The girl in the passport office had the right slant on my situation. "Can you sign your name?" she asked.

"Yes."

"Well, sign it here." Then, when I turned from the counter to reach the door, everything arranged and paid for, she said, "Watch out for the step up." I duly caught it with my cane. "The door is straight ahead. To your right is Fifth Street, to your left Sixth. Happy vacation to you! Good-bye!"

My cousins in New York were not quite so understanding. "Going alone? India? What if a cobra jumps out at you?"

"It would be a trifle late to do anything then!"

"What if some pickpocket takes your purse, with your passport and all your money?"

"That would be more probable than the cobra jumping out at me. But I'm a match for any pickpocket."

"Well, you couldn't see him."

That was true—*but just let him try*, I thought.

Airports are easy to manage. A passenger service assistant showed me to the passport office, to the ticket office, the customs counter, and the money exchange. After a long flight, I finally ended up in a limousine bound for the city of London. As I was on a very limited budget, I chose to board in moderately priced hostels, YWCAs, and second-class hotels. Some of them I had booked rather indefinitely, for, with fifty-two weeks to spare, I was in no hurry. I had time to make arrangements as I desired. When I found the first YWCA full, I taxied to the one recommended as a substitute and encamped for a week or ten days. Time did not matter.

"Oh, to be in England!" said Robert Browning, and here I was, in Tottenham Court Road, as English as it could be. For breakfast there was tea, oatmeal, and pink sausages. There was a bath for which you had to arrange in advance, and there was a pay telephone that you had to crank. There were enormous pennies that filled my purse with nothing and taxis that confused me by driving on the wrong side of the street, with the driver sitting on my right. I was supremely happy, getting where I wanted to go, meeting the people I wanted to meet.

"And what are you going to do in these countries?" asked an executive of the Royal National Institute for the Blind (RNIB).

"I don't know. How could I make a blueprint of plans, sitting in Los Angeles?" I explained that I wanted to stay for a while and meet the people in each country I visited. I wanted to talk with them about their education, for I was a schoolteacher. I was particularly interested in the education of blind children, for I taught blind children. I had found very little reading material about the education of blind children in the countries I planned to visit, or about their blind people in general, except that they were beggars. I had consumed travelogues, advertisements, and histories, yet I still knew very little.

My answer surprised the RNIB executive. He said that Americans are usually hustling to go places and do things. They always have plans and projects and are always in a businesslike hurry. I just wanted to go and see things—my way.

In the sharp, cold air, a walk down Buckingham Palace Road was bracing, crisp, and dignified. The rain drove me into the subway for shelter. I stood around with the crowd, waiting until the shower had passed. The wind blew my hat off. I turned to run after it in all directions, for I had no idea where it had gone. My guide put it into my hand, hatpin and all. In the confusion, I broke my eye-drop bottle, and I had no intention of undoing that tightly packed suitcase to hunt for another.

I knew the name and strength of the medication, but the pharmacist, or "chemist," said I had better see a doctor to get a new prescription. So I had my introduction to socialized medicine. I was directed to a clinic and the services of a thoroughly efficient and courteous physician. I received a prescription and instruction to go to a special chemist shop for the medication.

Before long, I set off on the next leg of my journey. I took a taxi from the hostel to the bus station and caught the bus to the airport. Soon I was in the air again, on my way to Paris.

I had visited Paris many times, beginning at the age of sixteen, and the noise and confusion were exciting and familiar. The taxi drivers at Orly Airport shouted everyone out of their way and got into everyone else's way themselves. My driver was particularly vocal. He ignored the possibility that I might understand the blasphemy that came from his mouth in volleys as he tried to outshout his competitors in the race for nowhere. His volatile mood showed little sign of easing, even as the airport traffic thinned out. With my twenty-one words of French, I humbly begged his pardon and told him that we were going to the Rue de Constantinople.

After that we began to talk. As I leaned over the front seat, he gave me a lively rundown of the streets, buildings, and bridges on our way. I did not let the conversation flag; I was always ready to pose another question. Even if the drive took longer than I had anticipated, his account of the sights was as good as any conducted tour, interspersed with commentary on French politics, social welfare, and economics.

"This is not the Paris of thirty years ago," he explained. Paris was now poor; people had no money to spend, not even to keep the city clean. There were fewer flower boxes in the windows now. There had been too many changes in the French government. When I asked him about the condition of the blind, he told me that blind children went to special schools. Blinded soldiers were working; he knew some of them. Then came his friendly assurance that he would not leave me until I was safely established in my *pension*.

As we sped along our route, I took in the exciting smells of Paris. Fried herring seemed to be on the menu for *dejeuner* that morning. The aroma of dishes cooked in oil blended with the fragrance of that delicious coffee that only the French can brew. Proust might have identified and classified many more aromas. Nowhere can you smell these smells but in Paris. Just as exciting were the sounds of the cars, trucks, and buses on the cobblestones and the trolleys on the rails. I heard the loquacious vivacity of two French matrons at the street corner as the taxi came to the boulevard stop.

When we finally reached the pension, the driver insisted on carrying my typewriter and my newly acquired portable Braillewriter. He even wanted to take charge of my cane, an offer I declined with a brief but firm explanation. "Oh, no," he protested, "you do not need your cane for the steps. I will hold your arm." He also asked the concierge the price of my room, repeating it to me so there would be no doubt. At last I bade him au revoir with a thousand thanks.

Inside the pension, I was completely at home, or *comme chez moi*. The concierge presented me with the enormous *clefs de sureté*—safety keys—that I have seen nowhere except in France. Exploring my room, I found the well-remembered long bolster under the already high pillows, the tall wooden shutters outside the windows, the satin-lined door of the armoire, the superfluous bidet—and no soap anywhere.

Up from the street floated the garrulous chatter of the neighborhood women. The men were more subdued, and the women always had the last word. Voilá!

The pension served only my breakfast, so I was directed to the corner café. There I enjoyed the services of the host and hostess, who explained the menu and expressed their surprise that I ate dinner without wine. Our conversation ran the gamut from family matters to all the blind people in the neighborhood.

The Metro was just around the corner from the pension. I memorized the trains I would have to take and set out on my first trip. Someone laid a kindly hand on my elbow, and I was escorted to the trains down below and through the turnstiles. To ensure my safe transit, I asked my fellow passengers for directions, then sat back to enjoy the thrill of speed as the train raced through the tunnel. I was unencumbered except for my cane and my pocketbook, and I felt a glorious sense of freedom.

When I emerged from the station, I gadded around to see what I could see: the new UNESCO building, the headquarters of the World Council for the Welfare of the Blind, as well as Montmartre and the other landmarks I had seen many times before. I no longer could see the gargoyles of Notre Dame fiendishly sticking out their tongues, though they still saw me. But they were accustomed to change; those placid devils had watched the tumbrils of the revolution go by and never blinked under the Reign of Terror. They had listened to the "Carmagnole" and the "Ave Maria" from the cathedral below. *Autres temps, autres moeurs*! Other times, other customs. What did blindness and the individual mean compared to the history under their gaze! Very little indeed.

I took a conducted tour on a rubberneck and listened to the oft-told tales and wisecracks of the professional guides. We reached the steps of the Hôtel des Invalides. "Beware of pickpockets!" our guide cautioned in English, to make sure we understood.

I was seated beside an American tourist, a very charming retired schoolteacher from Texas. She was alone, as was I, and we soon made friends.

"How should I guide you?" she asked as we descended from the bus. I told her that I would take her left arm, and we could make good time, for tour guides don't wait for stragglers. In my left hand, I held my cane, and my pocketbook hung at the elbow of my left arm.

An unusually large crowd had gathered on the sward by the steps, for a ceremony in commemoration of the Battle of Okinawa was in progress. We were temporarily stopped on the steps, for the crowd blocked the entrance to the mausoleum. I stood balanced on the edge of a step, my right arm immobilized by my companion's arm and my left hand likewise immobilized with my cane. Suddenly I received a quick blow on my chest from a loud, rude, cigarette-smoking young man with a loud, rude, cigarette-smoking girl in tow.

"*Monsieur, s'il vous plait!*" I said indignantly. The pair disappeared. As we climbed the steps, I withdrew my arm from that of my friend. I put my hand to my pocketbook and found it open! I reached inside. My hand went down, down. My heart went down, too. My wallet was gone!

I closed my pocketbook, tucked it up under my arm, and struggled not to cry. I had been robbed! I hadn't had a spare hand to guard my pocketbook. The thief had seen that my hands were occupied. Flushed, furious, and fuming, all in silence, I wanted to throw the thief over the Tomb of Napoleon or banish him to Saint Helena.

I am sure we went through many rooms, heard more history, mounted and descended more stairs, but I do not know what I heard. I remembered my boast about pickpockets back in New York. This one had gotten the better of me! He took an unfair advantage, the rat! How I hated Paris!

It was a relief to take my seat on the bus again. My friend remarked on how much history lies buried in the stately Invalides. Quietly I checked over the documents in my pocketbook—passport, ticket, special letters, traveler's checks. Everything was there except the purse. Ha, I thought, what a fool that fellow was. He could have taken so much, and he took so little! My purse contained between five and six dollars in franc bills and some addresses in the billfold. Perhaps the depth of the pocketbook had saved the rest of the contents. Perhaps.

Ladies, do not carry a bag that opens from the top. Mine had a simple push-over button. It was an invitation to a thug. Buy a pocketbook with a flap over the top, a zipper that locks, a padlock and key, nothing less!

I longed to get even with the thug who had robbed me, but even more important, I had to settle with myself after such a disaster. They had fooled me once. I had lost five dollars so that they would not fool me again. They never did. Really it was cheap insurance, but I was not to know that until long afterward. I can still feel that poke in the chest!

CHAPTER 2
COUPVRAI

July 1959

The noonday sun beat down on the quiet countryside, lulling it into silence save for the chirp of the cicada under the trees and the soft lowing of a cow in the distance. The smell of the potato field penetrated the motionless air, and the narrow road reflected the stillness of the heat.

On a hot summer morning, I left Paris by the small suburban train from the Gare du Nord, heading for the village of Coupvrai. The wooden seats were crowded with happy children leaving the dusty heat of the city. Paris kindly shipped its children away for the summer, far from the madding crowd of tourists that all but took over the city at this season of the year.

The train took me as far as the village of Esbly, where I dropped into a café. Over a plate that overflowed with sliced tomatoes, I chatted with the concierge, his wife, and the village gossip who had come by for her usual morning aperitif.

"Have you ever been to Coupvrai?" I asked.

"No."

"Do you know how far Coupvrai is from here?"

She did not. Did she know anything about Louis Braille? Louis Braille was only a name to her.

"What do the people do around here?"

"They go fishing on the Marne, and they catch lots of fish!"

At the suggestion of the café owner, I hired the village automobile to take me the two kilometers from Esbly to Coupvrai. Not even the driver had ever visited Louis Braille's birthplace. He was interested, however; we would find out everything when we arrived at Coupvrai.

As the driver did not know the house, we went to the mayor, for M. le Maire would surely be able to tell us. M. le Maire pointed out the house, but no, he did not have the key. If we would go to the little house along the road and ask for Mlle. Le Brun, she would know all about Louis Braille.

The village woke at the purr of the car's engine and the sound of our voices. Children's shouts and the barking of dogs announced that strangers had arrived. With three hundred inhabitants living in their tiny garden-bedecked houses, Coupvrai was not much larger than it had been in the days of the Braille family, 160 years ago.

Mlle. Le Brun had the key to the house, and she certainly knew all about Louis Braille. We followed her along the country road that Louis had walked so often to the schoolhouse, which was that same *mairie*, or town hall. He had walked this road to the village church at Saint Pierre, counting his steps and tapping with the wooden cane his father had made for him.

The road led us to the Braille family's little house, nestled on the side of a hill. Here Louis had lived as a boy with his father and mother, two sisters, and a brother. Louis was the youngest of the four Braille children. On the ground floor was the workshop where M. Braille carried on his business as a saddler and harness maker. Inside the *atelier*, the original workbenches showed traces of the father's craft. On the wall hung saddles and blinders for horses as well as the saddle maker's tools, one of which caused the accident that blinded three-year-old Louis. The child let slip a knife from his fingers when his father was standing on the bench hanging up a saddle. There on the wall, too, were the pieces of wood with the alphabet traced in nail heads. The thoughtful M. Braille and the village priest devised this method to teach Louis touch reading, a predecessor to the reading method to which the boy later gave his name.

As we climbed to the living quarters on the main floor, I imagined M. Braille, distraught, climbing these narrow, winding stairs with his

CHAPTER 3

ROME AND GREECE, THE
ANCIENT AND THE MODERN

"If you look right below us, you might see Mont Blanc," announced the pilot of our Boeing 707. Mont Blanc was gone in an instant. The jet flew so fast that no passenger, blind or sighted, caught more than a glimpse.

I do not understand speed. As a sighted person, I used to see speed when I sat in a railway carriage, watching the palings and posts flash by. Now when I walk from fore to aft of the plane I know that I have gone more than fifty miles. Yet my foot is steady and safe, as if it were planted on terra firma. I have no sensation of forward motion, only the ordinary vibration of the motors. Perhaps this perplexity is as close as I can come to the theory of relativity, and to me it is just as incomprehensible.

I like jets. They take you fast where you have to go. This plane took me so fast that I had scarcely finished my second cup of coffee when we landed in Rome.

By this time, airport details had become routine for me. I was well used to pulling out my passport, validating my tickets, and exchanging currency from one country to another. Still, there were always a few surprises. When the customs official opened my suitcase, out popped a flattened roll of toilet paper with a cake of soap tucked inside. The customs officer may have blushed. I did not. Nonchalantly I stuffed the paper and soap firmly down the side of the suitcase. I have learned that these commodities are hard to come by anywhere outside the UK and the United States. Trivial they may be, but they are essential nonetheless, and I have learned to attend to trivia when I travel. One little razor blade can relieve the misery of a corn that would stop me in my tracks. Clerks never seem to have a pen handy when I need to sign a document, so I always carry one with me. I see to it that I get it back.

A limousine brought me to the busy air-conditioned station in the heart of the city. From there I took a taxi to the Domus Pacis, my pension in the outskirts. The driver found the street but insisted that the Domus Pacis did not exist. Should he go to the police station? he asked.

"No," I told him. "Drive from end to end of the street, and you will find it."

He seemed a bit timid about having a blind woman as a fare, especially one who was a stranger to the city and apparently had provided him with a wrong address. His fears were allayed when, behind the shrubbery and a wide gate, we found the secluded dormitories of the pension. I am sure the driver was much relieved as he brought my bags to the office. "Arrivederci," he shouted, and off he went.

•   •   •

I had arranged to attend the quinquennial meeting of the World Council for the Welfare of the Blind, which was being held in the headquarters of the World Health Organization (WHO). The meeting drew an interesting and interested crowd, but two observations crept deeply into my consciousness. First, I had expected more blind persons to be present. This was a delegate meeting with representatives from nearly fifty nations. For the most part, the blind delegates came from the United Kingdom, the United States, and Western Europe. In the main, the other nations were represented by sighted persons. I was greatly affected by this observation. Why were so few blind persons at the meeting? Could not blind persons from Asia and Africa speak for the blind of their countries? There were an estimated ten million blind persons in the world; why were not more of them speaking up? Four-fifths of that estimated population lived in rural areas, but that need not preclude their leaders from attending a world conference to discuss, compare, and counsel. *But did they have leaders?* I wondered. That was the pivotal question, and as yet it was one that I could not answer.

My second disturbing observation was that many sighted persons were speaking *for* the blind—not on their behalf but in their place. Based on their personal opinions, they explained what the blind should do and what would be best for them. Were the blind people of other countries incapable of thinking for themselves? Were they in such a helpless condition that they had to accept the decisions of others, remaining captive to sighted leaders? Were the blind underprivileged, second- or third-class citizens?

I believe that self-acceptance, independence, and action, underwritten by equality of opportunity, are the birthright of all blind people, just as they are for the sighted. For every blind person, education and training are essential for achieving these goals. In the new, self-determining nations of the world, the army of blind persons is an enormous source of untapped potential. Education and training, I thought, would free these blind millions from their captivity, free them to serve their countries. Such a reversal of old cultural patterns would call for imagination, hard work, and much more. In truth, due to my own limited background, I knew almost nothing of what was needed. But as I sat at the council meeting, turning the dial of my earphones in order not to lose a nuance of meaning from the foreign-language interpretation, the question of the place of blind persons in this modern age took shape in my mind. I would try to find out why blind people were static and silent. I would seek to understand what was holding them back. Was it fear? Hunger? Were they for some reason defeated before they began? I had no answers.

This was not my first visit to Rome, but this time, as a guest of the conference, I saw more of the attractions than ever before. I went to the beach where the mouth of the Tiber used to be. I walked through excavations of the Roman seaport, with their mute evidence of worldwide trade when Rome was in its glory and the forum was its heartbeat. In the enormous amphitheater of Caligula, I attended a full-cast production of *Aïda*, complete with horses and elephants. I sipped coffee flavored with brandy in the chilly air of a perfect evening.

The overtones of music in the Vatican and the Sistine Chapel were subdued and beautiful. I thrilled to the nearness of the grand masters as my hands explored the marble of *La Pietá*, cold to the touch. Climbing the steps of the coliseum over the rocks, I visited the altars along the Via Sacra. Then I was off to the Villa d'Este with its cool cypresses and its symphony of birds, the inspiration for so much of Franz Liszt's music. Rome lived and breathed in its classic grandeur. It laughed, sang, and danced with the romance of its fountains, its music, and its people.

Members and guests of the conference were invited to an audience with His Holiness, Pope John XXIII, in residence at his summer home, a fair distance from the city in Castel Gandolfo. The castle stood high on a hill overlooking broad plains below. We climbed the narrow, cobbled incline, skirted by fruit and candy stalls that nestled on the side of the hill, bathed in the Italian sun. Our guides described the deep blue lakes in the distance, reflecting the pure, cloudless sky. People stopped in wonder as we passed.

The steep road led us over a rampart with heavy portcullis gates. Inside the castle we found a maze of covered porches and entrances, arriving at last at the pope's chambers. In the audience room, we sat on low, narrow, backless benches. The guides told us that the guards, resplendent in red and black stripes, graced the dais as the pope took his place at the table, in the simplicity of his pure white robes. He offered a brief greeting in English and in French and then read his speech in Italian. It was a moving experience to be in his presence, to listen to his interpretation of work with and for the blind in the world—reverent, dignified, solemn, simple.

Afterward, some moved forward to kiss the pope's ring and have their rosaries blessed. Others remained to enjoy a brief moment of quiet, suffused with the prayer, "Keep your hearts and minds in the knowledge and love of God."

•　　•　　•

The next day, I was on my way again, this time with my compass set to the east. Greece was my next destination. From this point on, I would be on unfamiliar territory until I reached home again.

When I spoke to acquaintances of my plans, I was told I would meet with "a forest of frustrations." I did indeed, but the forest was by no means impenetrable. I felt an urge to meet people, to see them at work. I wanted to listen to them as they talked about themselves. I wanted to hear what they might say about me and about my country. I hoped to visit their homes, to meet their children, and to observe their schools for blind and sighted pupils.

I felt restless as I left the Domus Pacis, restless with that sense of peace that comes to me as I remember the lines from Goethe, *"Wer immer strebend sich bemüht, Den können wir erlösen"* ("Whoever strives with all his might, that man we can redeem").

I arrived in Athens at midnight. To my dismay, I had had to pay for my typewriter as excess luggage, though I had to admire the efficiency of the clerk who said that typewriters, even small ones, were not part of the hand luggage that was permitted. After the routine of customs and money exchange, I sat on the airport bus, ready to take off for the city. For the first time, I felt a trifle weary, with that touch of homesickness that overtakes you as the liner leaves the dock and casts out to sea. Suddenly a male voice at my side asked if I was Isabelle Grant.

In that unfamiliar place, amid the hubbub of voices speaking in a language I did not understand, I had never expected to hear my own name. But the stranger asked his question again. He explained that he and a blind friend had come to the airport to welcome me. Sure enough, Mini was there to greet me and invite me to her home. A fellow worker with the blind had written to her from the conference, telling her of my visit to Athens.

This unexpected welcome was my introduction to Athenian hospitality. Mini and I, both of us blind, both of us teachers, were friends from the moment we met. I could not speak Greek, but Mini spoke English.

Mini's house was in Kallithea, a suburb of Athens. She owned her home, did her own housekeeping as I did (though she did a better job than I), and taught at the local school for the blind. She was even putting a beautiful young niece through college. After a brief exchange on the causes of our blindness, that topic was put to rest. From that point on, we were two teachers, sharing our thoughts on family and friendship and of course talking shop. I am ever grateful to Mini for inviting me into her home.

The sounds of the morning woke me at dawn. The fruit-and-vegetable vendor rattled his wheelbarrow over the pavement, and the local dogs competed with him as he shouted his wares. Excited children joined the chorus. I was up in time to meet the fishmonger, who appeared at the door, his tub on his head. The tub was full of fresh fish cooled on ice blocks. Mini bought some and threw them into the kitchen sink. In a twinkling, she had them cleaned and salted, ready for the frying pan. I had never read about that in the work of the great philosophers, but here was life as it had been lived for centuries in Athens, a busy pulse that is scarcely known to most visitors.

Mini's work with blind children was a joy to her. She moved around the classroom with an eagerness that bespoke her complete dedication. Aside from reading, writing, and arithmetic, her specialty was handcraft. Her dexterity was unusual, and she passed on her talent to her pupils.

Though the day was hot and dusty, the evening on the beach at Poseidon was refreshingly cool. Buses poured out wave upon wave of merrymakers, and Mini and I were among them. It was no special holiday, just a family evening at the beach. Old and young were there, blind and sighted, all of us eating and making merry.

The water of the bay splashed and ebbed along the sand. The noises of the *tabernas* mingled with the talk from outdoor cafés. Music filled the air, and the swish of the sea underwrote the whole medley. The pungent odors of fried fish and burnt grease added to the gusto of the crowds.

Could this be the Athens of Socrates, Plato, and Aristotle? Gulls swooped close to my feet with their gurgling cries of *culla culla!* Were these the birds that inspired Aristophanes to write his satire? Were these people the Greeks whose great minds established the concept of the rule of law as the way of life, growth, and liberty? Were these the

Greeks of the *Aeneid* legends of my high school days? I remembered the phrase *"Timeo Danaos et dona ferentes"* ("I fear the Greeks even bearing gifts"). Did the Great Three ever leave the peripatetic school with their disciples and wander by the Poseidon Beach?

The next day, I set out to explore the city's treasures. As I ascended the steep Acropolis on the outskirts, I felt I was walking on holy ground. Twenty-five hundred years of history were embodied in the tumbled ruins. I touched the stones of pillars borne to the mountain on the backs of slaves and carved by their hands. With a sighted friend, Mini and I crawled over irregular broken marbles, feeling their patterns. We examined pieces of friezes, boulders of solid marble, jagged-edged cornices, and chunks of the bases, shafts, and capitals of fallen columns. I noted the grooved shafts of Dorics, Ionics, and Corinthians, all chiseled into the hard marble. I explored the broken columns of the dainty Erechtheum, a temple on the north side of the Acropolis, completed in 406 BC. I counted the flutes and fillets around the shafts of its columns and traced the exquisitely ornate designs around the Corinthians, searching for outlines of the acanthus leaves on the broken pieces.

The Parthenon came to life, high on the fortress. As I leaned against the noble grandeur that towered above me, I felt tiny yet sublime. We sat on a slab as people watched the afternoon sun sink between the pillars. The spirit of Athena was present—defender, patron, and goddess—hovering over this glorious assemblage of the past, down to the present and for all time to come. The Athenians are proud of their past and their present. They carry the spirit of Athens to the uttermost parts of the world.

Descending the hill brought us back to reality. The glorious past faded into the turmoil of the present. We would go back in other days, but the experience of that first day could never be forgotten. No, Mini and I did not see it, but we were very close to it nonetheless, she as an Athenian, I as a foreigner.

CHAPTER 4
INSIDE THE PYRAMIDS

U nfamiliar places fascinate me, but as I sat on a pleasure boat on the Bosporus, I found myself wondering just how I see those places without eyesight. In my mind, I lined up all of the things I actually was missing. Shop windows headed the list. When I could see, I spent many happy hours window-shopping. Now I could do little more than judge the wares of the shop by the smell and by touching the articles displayed on the outside. I had no inhibitions about handling them—cloth, baskets, pans, animals, anything! Produce shops and bakeries are easy to detect, and likewise saloons. But I acknowledged that I lost something of the uniqueness of Broadway or Piccadilly, the charms of the Rue de Rivoli or Prince's Street. I wanted to know the shops of Istanbul, of Beirut, of Jerusalem, of Cairo, each with its distinct flavor and style.

So, hiring a guide or enlisting the help of a student or a fellow traveler, I found my way into the bazaars of the Middle East. I handled, asked, and listened. Wherever I went, people were friendly, no matter what language they spoke. They used whatever words they had learned in my language. One shopkeeper described her costume to me— oriental pantaloons, upturned slippers, and a little bolero-like jacket. Another told me about her sari[1] and invited me to feel the fine texture of the fabric.

To a large extent, I could make up for vision with touch when it came to the wares in the markets, but facial expressions I missed woefully. In a strange, new city, I missed watching people's faces.

What would I not have given to see the face of the little Muslim boy who grabbed onto my skirt to balance himself as he and I slipped on our carpet shoes before we entered the Blue Mosque, or the face of the little girl at the bus corner who grabbed my cane and jumped around me, laughing and tugging! She probably thought it was a new kind of toy. Her mother intervened, but I did my best to ward her off and let the child play.

On the other hand, it was better that I did not see the face of the restaurant waiter when I told him to take away the plate he had brought me. I had ordered a simple fish dinner; he had brought me a large and expensive platter of meat. His voice told me the expression on his face. That sufficed.

Skylines, too, I missed. What could be more Byzantine than the outline of Istanbul with its domes, cupolas, minarets, and towers traced against the blue of a summer day, with the deeper blue of the Bosporus pointing east to the Sea of Marmara and west to the Aegean? I missed that as I listened to the chant, at first faint, then loud, calling the faithful to worship. The minarets came to life in the lull of the late afternoon. The hush of the evening fell over the city, interrupted only by the movement of thousands of boats on the water and the popping of their shrill sirens.

Istanbul was neither oriental nor occidental; it was a medley of both, a city built on two sides of an arm of water, different and yet one. It was a medley of religions, too. The Christian Saint Sophia's Cathedral now serves as a museum, though its mosaics and the gold and silver of its walls are covered over with unseemly plaster. The cathedral has had many occupants since Emperor Justinian built its cisterns, pillars, and domes fourteen centuries ago.

I enjoyed Istanbul, crossroads of the Middle East, but there were so many tourists I found it hard to get close to its people. I heard too much English and met too many bargain hunters. The romance of the Old City and the thoroughfare of the New City charged me to a frivolous pitch.

•   •   •

"And what do you think of us Americans?" I asked the proprietor of my boarding house in Beirut.

"We would like you more if we could see your money going into the right places," he said. "Look at all the beautiful buildings you are putting up for us, and look at the condition of our roads, the education of our children! Why not build houses for our people who don't have any?"

In this fast-growing metropolis, with its busy streets, its ultramodern hotels, its esplanades, and its delectable Mediterranean climate, I sensed unrest. A government had just been ousted, and a new regime, purportedly favoring the people, had come to power. Instability was mixed with fear. People warned me to take no risks. I felt unsteady in this ancient biblical city that rose from the Levant to the cedars of Lebanon atop the surrounding hills.

"Are there many blind people in this city?" I asked.

"Oh, yes, many—too many," a Lebanese guest told me. "If you want to know about work for the blind, you must see Mrs. Mahoud."

Mrs. Mahoud lived on the outskirts of the city. However, I learned, her husband had held a high position in the last government, and he was now out of power. It would be dangerous for me to visit her, but she was the only person who knew about the blind of Beirut.

Despite the warnings, it was not difficult for me to arrange an interview with Mrs. Mahoud. Her husband and her secretary greeted me warmly. My taxi driver was allowed to wait for me in the carport. In a brief hour, I formed a picture of the unhappy situation of the city's blind population. Workshops were poorly equipped at best, and a few of them had to be closed for lack of money. More trained personnel were needed. There were no leaders among the blind themselves. They depended on the patronage of philanthropically inclined officials. Custodial care was their only prospect.

The outlook would have been desolate but for the attitude of the young principal of the school for the blind. In spite of the desperate problems she faced, she tried to encourage her blind pupils. She was excited to tell me that one of her girls had been placed in a job at the local biscuit factory packing biscuits. This was a long, long step up from a sheltered workshop for the blind.

The principal was interested in my travels. Why did I not stop right there and spend some time with the blind children of Beirut? She told me a story that all but changed my plans.

One day, she said, she and her husband were driving through an outlying village when she saw a mother with two blind children, leading one with each hand. She approached the mother and told her about her work. Would the mother allow her children to attend the school?

"Oh, no," said the mother. "I would not send my blind children away from home. They are my children, and I am here to look after them."

The principal asked if the mother would allow her children to go to the village school if the necessary instruction and materials were provided. "Of course," the mother said. "They would be like my other children then."

The problem was clear, the principal told me, and the solution was plain, but the means were lacking. It looked as if the blind people of Lebanon would continue to depend on the largesse of the benevolent philanthropist, and most of the children would remain in their villages.

To me, Beirut was a challenging city, its people bent on progress. With my guide, I visited the university, where I spoke with students and faculty members. I visited the friends and relatives of guests at the boardinghouse. Every second one of them seemed to have a blind relative. The conversations never lagged; I wanted to know, and they wanted to tell me. I felt welcome and accepted. But for my fellow blind in Lebanon, from the little I learned about their lot, I ask only for consideration, opportunity, and a chance to develop self-respect.

•   •   •

Mount Cairo at night is a fairy paradise. We sat eating ice cream in the balmy, magic stillness of the top of the Citadel, with the hum and spectacle of the city far below. We were a jolly party of seven, two of us blind. I was the only foreigner in our group, enjoying the scintillating conversation of two professors, their families, and friends. They were all very familiar with the UK and the United States. They read our newspapers and periodicals. They knew our literature, and they understood our social welfare philosophy. It was a rare treat to see ourselves as others see us and to try to interpret where our policies and practices were not clear.

The United Arab Republic (UAR) is moving forward.[2] The people have complete confidence in their country and its government. They are working with it and for it. Higher education is for all who can use it—blind and sighted alike. The cultural inheritance of the country, its folklore, its history, its civilization as the foundation of its present stability, are the subjects of its university offerings.

My new friends were proud to show me the mosque of Mohammed Ali with its exquisite silver candelabras, which I was privileged to touch. The mosque and the tomb are revered as images of national dignity. They are symbols of nationality, faith, and self-determination, for now the people feel their nation has a soul that it can count as its own.

Until I met my Egyptian friends, I had some rough sledding, although my adventures were somewhat amusing. I made my way by bus from the airport to the company office in the city. I did not choose to go to the elegant Sheppard's or to the Hotel Continental, for my budget did not allow me such luxury. I chose the Magnolia, a modest hotel off Cairo's main thoroughfare, and recommended by the accommodating clerk at the desk. Fortunately, French was spoken as well as some English. I was comfortably housed and assured a warm reception by the proprietor and his staff.

I told the hotel proprietor that I wanted to locate a friend, and I gave his name. His name was a word that meant "light" in Arabic. Eventually I located my friend and found that he had been swamped by telephone calls and inquiries. To my unmitigated embarrassment, I discovered that a story had appeared in the newspaper in Arabic with the headline, "Blind Lady Looks for Light."

It was good to meet my friend again and to accompany him to a seven-acre site on the banks of the Nile, where a massive program for training blind persons was in progress, supported in part by the government. There are hundreds of thousands of blind people in the country, and their needs are tremendous, but this program is a small start. Blind persons from the villages train in agriculture, horticulture, small business, basket making, weaving, sandal making, woodwork, furniture making, and bookbinding. A blind man or woman was working in every possible job and teaching skills to other blind persons. Two blind girls from Baghdad were learning switchboard operation. I did not know their language, but they greeted me in English.

Ironically, I made a wonderful connection through the publication of that embarrassing article. A stranger telephoned and introduced himself. "I read the article in the newspaper," he told me. "I have a daughter who is blind also. She is in school abroad at the moment. But if you would not mind, seeing you are a stranger here, I would be glad to have my other daughter show you around the city in our car."

His daughter, the gracious and charming Zena, came to my room and took me shopping before we went to her home to meet her family. The courtesy and kindness of this family moved me deeply. I did not feel that I was a stranger in their home; they made me welcome. I accepted their help and hospitality with gratitude.

One afternoon, Zena and I were guests at a baby celebration. The Arabic pronunciation might be written in Roman script as SBOA, a festive occasion on the seventh day after the child's birth. Several families were present, and the children had the happiest time of all. We formed a procession with the grandmother in the lead, carrying the baby. We went from room to room, singing as we marched past tables laden with sweetmeats, cakes, and delicacies. Finally the procession stopped, and the grandmother chanted a hymn of great beauty in its translation, a prayer for God's guidance and love for the little one. I joined in showering congratulations on the father and mother. My prayers went with theirs, though I spoke in a different language and knew a different ritual. All of us addressed the same God.

After these deeply human and personal experiences, it was hard for me to come down to the level of the ordinary tourist. Still, I had to visit the pyramids and the Sphinx. Instead of taking a general tour, I preferred to hire a guide from the hotel. Prices were all government controlled, so taxi fares and guide fees were nominal.

On the appointed day, my guide appeared, dressed in his Bedouin cloak, turban, multicolored sash, and crook, all of which he described to me in great detail. He was a fascinating man. He told me all about his grandchildren. I concluded that he had estimated my age and assumed that I would be interested, as I probably had grandchildren, too. He was right; I listened with interest to the story of his family. My guide's English was very good, as he had served for some time with the British army.

When we reached the pyramids, my guide wanted to describe them to me, but I wished to see them for myself. I proceeded to scale the steps up the side of the first edifice, with my guide warning me anxiously not to get out of line. He was more afraid than I was, for he could look down and see the drop. I couldn't. My safety measure was to crawl on all fours. It was not hard to do, though it was hard on my nylons. But we got up and inside the tombs. We climbed steep, narrow paths, slipping into the empty tombs to get the feel of them.

As I climbed the pyramid, I heard camels neighing, and I could not resist the temptation to get a photo of "Granny riding a camel" for my grandchildren. My guide quite understood.

Later I persuaded my Bedouin escort to accompany me along the byways beyond the usual tourist haunts. Reluctantly, he took me down side streets, describing in simple fashion conditions that he himself did not like to see. When we passed a shop where meat was displayed on open trays, he commented, "More flies than meat."

I asked him about the beggars who tugged at my elbow. "Many," he said. "Too many." I asked him to tell me about the blind children who begged on the street. "Too many flies on their eyes," he said. "Eyes very bad."

This was probably his way of describing trachoma, a disease that causes much of the blindness in Egypt, along with malnutrition, lack of sanitation, and countless other known and unknown factors. This Cairo is indeed the city of extremes, poverty and affluence, health and disease, hunger and plenty. This is the capital city of the Arab Republic, the hub of a vast empire, progressive and progressing.

NOTES

1. The sari is a traditional garment worn by Indian women, consisting of a long strip of unstitched fabric. The sari is draped around the body in various styles, depending on the region, the occasion, and the age of the wearer. Everyday saris are simple, while festive saris may be decorated with embroidery and tiny mirrors.
2. Formed in 1958, the United Arab Republic (UAR) consisted of a union between Egypt and Syria. Syria withdrew from the union in 1961, but Egypt used the name United Arab Republic for the next ten years.

CHAPTER 5
UP THE VIA DOLOROSA

As the plane zoomed down into Jerusalem, an old hymn played through my head: "Jerusalem the golden, with milk and honey blessed." In my mind, an angelic halo encircled any reference to Jerusalem. The holy city was the threshold of heaven, the sanctum sanctorum on earth. Sermons and movies reinforced that idea. In no way was I ready for the reality of Jerusalem today.

Jerusalem was as Christian as it was Muslim, as Jewish as it was Christian. It was more Roman Catholic than it was Protestant. Once I swept away my fuzzy ideas of a Christian paradise on earth, I felt more at peace.

Eventually I secured a guide from a local travel agency. Together we climbed the narrow, steep incline of the Via Dolorosa, "in the steps of the Master." I imagined the cross being borne up the hill, the Master's pain and suffering, the wiping of his forehead, and the helping hand of Simon the Cyrene as ordered by the Roman centurion. The glory of the risen Christ is for the moment overshadowed by the sharing of His grief and pain as we follow in the crowd.

The crowd brought me back from my painful reverie. Children tugged at my skirt, asking for alms. Old men and women, beggars all, stopped our progress up the hill. Once in a while, the stench was relieved by the fragrance of sesame oil. We stepped aside to let the donkey carts go by. They were laden with anything and everything—firewood, clothes, vegetables, even live animals.

My guide tried to push the little children away, but I objected. "Is this throng of people always here?" I asked.

"Oh, yes," my guide explained. "They are refugees, living in encampments or in the fields. Begging is their way of living."

Jerusalem was a divided city, and we were in East Jerusalem, the side occupied by Jordan.[1] No Man's Land lay between the two Jerusalems.

As I stood on the spot marked as the place where Jesus was condemned to die, I thought about the mass of hungry humanity I had just encountered. What had we, as Christians, been doing over the past nineteen hundred and thirty years? Was this all we had to show for our Christian efforts? One could only weep and ask again for the miracle of the loaves and fishes, so that these little children would not have to beg.

I entered the area designated as the Garden of Gethsemane. The two sepulchers did not perplex me. Who could vouchsafe the authenticity of either one of them? Nineteen hundred years of crusades, wars, soil erosion, winds, and weather would change the face of any land. The spirit and meaning of the sepulcher was what mattered. The crypt of the nativity was avowedly the exact spot where Mary gave birth to the baby Jesus, but the straw-laden manger was more meaningful as a symbol than in its proclaimed authenticity. I knew that in these parts the Master preached, healed, and taught. This was indeed the Holy Land.

As I walked along the road between Jerusalem and Bethlehem, I knew I was in the land of Moab, where Naomi and Ruth were wont to cut and bind their sheaves. The freshness of the breeze brought back the eternal freshness of their story. But the halt, the lame, and the blind still huddled along the roadside, begging. The donkeys trudged along the road with their carts as they had in centuries past. I asked myself what Jesus would do about the hundreds and thousands of His people displaced, hungry, and sick? He would know their needs and help them! We could do the same.

I stayed in a quaint little boarding house beyond the city walls. The proprietor was kindly and genial, and his few words of English were all we needed to get along. Yes, they had running water, he assured me.

He showed me a square metal basin filled with water that was none too fresh. On the side was a tiny spigot, and the water ran into a bucket underneath the basin. The plumbing in the bathroom, too, constituted a noble effort that failed.

Breakfast was served in my room, and the maid sat by me while I ate. When I indicated that I had finished, she ate the second egg and the second slice of bread herself and even finished the tea.

Whatever else may have been lacking, chickens, dogs, and cats there were in abundance. The delightful farmyard symphony started early and ended late. The wind singing through the pines, the hush of the evening, the scent of the woods were just as they had been nineteen hundred years ago! This was the Holy Land.

It was good to sit in the cool of the evening and talk with my new Jordanian friends in Ramallah. They were interested in work for the blind, for one of them was blind himself. Hundreds of blind children lived in the camps, they told me, but there were no schools for them. Besides, refugee parents would not let their blind children leave their homes, however poor they might be. They suggested that if there were fewer missionary schools, the government might assume the responsibility for the education of these children. As long as the foreign missionaries came in, the government was not going to interfere. Most parents did not want to send their blind children to the missionary schools. The parents were Muslims, and the schools might want to turn their children into Christians.

My friends told me about some of the blind children they knew. One little girl in the missionary school had been found by the side of the road. She did not know of the existence of undergarments, for one garment was all she had ever worn. She had never eaten anything but bread, and she was afraid to eat the vegetables offered her when she entered the school for the blind. One mother could not let her blind child go to school because the family would lose the child's food ration.

My friends took me to meet three blind lads who trained at a missionary school and returned to the refugee camp in the Gaza Strip. Now they helped train their fellow blind to make brushes and brooms. With the little English they had learned, and with the combined efforts of all three of them, we exchanged questions and answers, friendship and happiness.

Girls are less likely to be sent to school than boys are. One unusually fine girl said she thought that women should not make baskets. She had heard that blind women could learn to knit with a machine, and she wanted to be taught that skill. She had heard that blind girls could be telephonists, too. A wholesome, normal girl she was, curious, creative, and intelligent. She would probably be trained to help other children in the school. The school sponsors, a group of British missionaries, were making plans to that end.

Two spots shone with a special radiance amid the desolation around them. One was a government-run school for blind boys. It was an oasis of happy, active, alert youngsters. The other was an Arab workshop for blind men where over twenty kinds of brooms were made, some with fancy handles, some of nylon. The men also made mats and simple household furniture. Many of these men were exiles. They had lost their homes and their property, every tool and household article they had once possessed. They had banded together in this broom factory, and now at least they were earning a living. I examined the articles they made and explained that in the United States we usually add a label that says, "Blind-Made Product." "Oh, no," they exclaimed. "We would never do that. If we put on such a label, people would not buy our brooms. Without the label, they think the brooms are made in the UK, so they buy them." We laughed over their business acumen. Through all their tribulations, they had retained their sense of humor.

Parting from the Jordanians was a sorry task. We had joked, shared family news, and broken bread together. I had heard the stories of their hardships following partition fourteen years ago. I had seen defeatism in many and courage in others. I recognized their justifiable bitterness. I also witnessed a new spirit of determination, especially among the young adults. But I felt that their own bootstraps were not enough. The children are hungry *now,* and the blind children are forgotten just because they are blind. They are born into the world with a needless strike against them. Yet these, too, are our children.

NOTE

1. From 1949 to 1967, East Jerusalem was controlled by Jordan. It came under Israeli rule following the 1967 Six-Day War.

PART 2
PAKISTAN IN KALEIDOSCOPE

PART 1

CHAPTER 6
HOW I LIVED

A blistering sun, torrid heat, and high humidity were my first impressions of Karachi as I deplaned on a late summer afternoon. An unfamiliar, dissonant language bombarded me. Karachi was to be my halfway point on my trip around the world. It did not feel at all prepossessing.

As I made my customary inspection of my room in the little hotel, I found myself thinking of the stables in Toledo, Spain, that Cervantes described in *Don Quixote*. In fact, my room had once been a stable, and one whole side of the bathroom annex was the old stable door, now bolted and barred, with a dressing chest and towel rail in front. The bath was a small tub with a wall faucet and a pan alongside. I learned later that one did not fill the tub with water but soaped as desired and poured water over one's body to rinse. But there was running water!

The door to my room had an enormous bolt, which I found difficult to slide, and a huge lock with a six-inch key. I could open both sides of the door by loosening two other enormous bolts, one top and one bottom. The walls of the room were covered with plaster; I thought at first that they might be made of clay. They were very thick, which made the room a trifle cooler than the outside. Hanging outside the door was a *chik*, a large coir screen, which I had to push aside whenever I left.[1] The windows were high up on the wall, and there was no glass, just plaster trellis with iron bars on the outside.

Like all of the other guest rooms, my room led onto the compound. The kitchen, office, dining room, servants' quarters, and guest rooms encircled a central courtyard. *Chokidars*, or watchmen, were on duty day and night to watch the two gates.

It did not take me long to get accustomed to my new surroundings. I found a place for my Braillewriter, another for my typewriter, and a receptacle for my paper, and I was in business. I felt perfectly safe in my strange, new surroundings.

The proprietor, Mr. Nazim, a stalwart from Pakistan's Northwest Frontier section, was a genial host. I was quickly at ease with his wife and family, as well as the office help. Our first conversation, however, took me by surprise.

"You are blind. You cannot see."

"That is true," I answered.

"Then you cannot go to the dining room. You might have an accident. I send your meals to you in room."

This was the first time on my journey that I had been forbidden to do what I wanted to do by reason of my blindness. I did not wish to quarrel with Mr. Nazim. I did not care to point out to him that I had come halfway around the world, getting along not so badly. As he was my host, I considered it the better part of discretion to accede to his instructions.

Three times a day, a servant, Sadig, brought in my tray, nicely covered with a serviette. Each time, the little fellow lifted my hand and laid it gently on the eating utensils, explaining, "*Kanta, churi, chumuch*" ("Fork, knife, spoon"). He would then place my hand on the teapot, saying, "*Chai, girm!*" ("Tea, hot!"). This rite took place three times per day for weeks on end. It never occurred to Sadig that I knew where to expect the utensils and that they would always be in the same place.

I had only one alternative, to turn the serving of my meals into daily Urdu lessons. Yet I encountered another problem. Sadig came from East Pakistan, where only Bengali is spoken. So our Urdu was confined to single words; I would have to learn to make sentences through some other medium.

I soon found another Urdu teacher and arranged to take regular classes, which I reached by rickshaw.[2] The rickshaw was high; I had to climb into it. After tearing every pair of nylons in my possession, I learned that I should go barelegged, as everyone else did. The driver manipulated his one-cylinder motor admirably. I do not remember ever going to my lesson without the rickshaw stalling. The driver would jump out, pick up formidable pieces of iron lodged under my feet, and give a few hard knocks to the machine. On we went.

Of course, there were occasions when the rickshaw did not go. I did not want to be late for my class, so I paid the fellow his fee and his tip as he hailed another rickshaw. I became as accustomed to emergency as to routine, but I almost always arrived where I wanted to go. Not many days and weeks had gone by before I felt perfectly at ease, thrilled with the new experiences, though not with my progress in Urdu.

Some of my rickshaw rides were positively rough, although the drivers were experts at swinging their machines around the potholes in the streets—and those potholes were really holes! Some rickshaw drivers took joy in their speed. They had no mercy on the fare. We rattled along, dipping into every pothole. At every dip, I bounced up to the canopy, and my head invariably bumped against the metal bar across the top. Hanging on grimly by the supporting bars at the side, my left arm immobilized with my cane, my pocketbook, and my Urdu books, I was like a ball bouncing inside an iron cage. Another pothole, and I hit the ceiling again. In desperation, I shouted above the din of the street, "*Ahista chelao, meherbani!*" ("Please drive slowly!"). Instantly the driver drew to the side of the street and launched into a long discourse in Urdu, not one word of which I understood.

When I thought he was near the end of the harangue, I said as if I had understood it all, "*Shukria, chelao*" ("Thank you, let's go"). I am sure the fellow was explaining that he could not help the bumps, as the roads were in bad condition. We resumed our race, but this time, though the speed did not slacken, he went around the potholes, thereby giving me an east-west jiggle to replace the north-south bounce. Eventually we got to my class, after a fashion.

Torrential rains came, lasting days and nights, with fearsome thunderclaps that seemed to shake the earth. The walls of my room were so thick that the rain hit at an angle and at first did not reach the inside. Then, all of a sudden, the wind rose and drove the squalls directly into the room. I rushed to pull the heavy cloth drape over the window. It was hard to pull, but when I gave it a brisk jerk I brought down a shower of insects. They lighted in my hair, on my shoulders, and along my arms. The folds of the curtain had been their hiding place. I threw off my dress, shook out my hair, and went under the faucet. No harm done! I think the crickets et al. were just as glad to be rid of me as I was of them!

Karachi is a difficult city to like. I loved the people, but I never warmed up to the city itself. Earlier in the century, Karachi was a coaling port for cargo ships, home to some four hundred thousand inhabitants. Now, since partition and the massive migration of refugees from India, the population has approached the two-million mark. Public amenities, however, have not grown with the city, and the antiquated sewage system caused some embarrassing moments. The water supply, moreover, was capricious. At night and in the morning, the faucets would turn, but no water emerged. Broken water mains were common, and my guide frequently helped me jump over unrepaired leaks in the road and along the footpaths. That was the fun of a walk along Elphinstone Street; I never knew what next to expect.

One day I leaned against a wall as I stood talking with a friend. "Watch out," she said, drawing me away gently, "the betel nut spittle is right up the wall. It is reddish brown."

Her warning excited my curiosity. I decided to try *pan,* or betel nut, too. To me it tasted like dried cork. Once one of my Pakistani friends remarked that she wished women would stop chewing betel nut; the pink saliva ran down the sides of their mouths and dripped over their beautiful saris. Chewing takes on its nationality. Betel in Pakistan and gum in the United States were an improvement over tobacco, if chewing had to be done!

I forgot the betel nut and the street refuse as the camel carts, donkey carts, and goat carts ambled along Elphinstone while the Cadillacs and Volkswagens shot madly by them. I could easily tell the difference between the carts, for the tinkle of the camel bell was quite different from that of the goat bell or the donkey bell. I could follow the bells just as the animals did themselves. The camel with its low-slung cart, the painted goats—my guide said they were dirty yellow and dirty pink—were fascinating to me.

The donkey carts were piled high with sacks, vegetables, and people, and the drivers whipped the poor animals mercilessly to goad them on. One day there was a complete holdup of traffic, and my guide and I inched our way into the middle of the crowd. There was loud talking and much merriment. A donkey cart had been piled so high that when the donkey gave a lurch forward, the center of balance was lost. The whole load tipped backward, throwing the three drivers onto the ground. The donkey had tipped over, too, and was struggling with his legs in midair. Nobody was in a hurry to see order restored; the drivers did not dare mount the cart again.

Wherever we went, I asked my friends and guides to describe the people we met. On occasion, after the necessary introduction, I would stop and get closer contact with their unusual dress. It was not surprising to find ten different kinds of *topi,* or turban, worn by the men. On the street, it was not unusual to meet broad-shouldered tribesmen from the hinterland or from the Pashtun country to the far north—tribesmen who still bartered brides and cattle, who sent their servants to the neighboring village to buy them a wife.[3]

I was supremely happy and amused—for my shoes were fortified with heels and toes. How people could wear sandals with open toes and heels, I could not understand! Amused? To the point of laughing outright as my guide picked up the red tip of my cane and pulled me after him, ride-a-cock-horse-wise. He probably thought the function of my cane was to pull me along. So I walked along serenely, dodging behind people but never losing the head of my cane—and my guide never lost the tip. It was a real art thus to speed along! I apologized profusely when I bumped a hubble-bubble smoker who burst into a torrent of words that I did not understand, or when I got myself too close to the snake charmer whose shrill pipe I had learned to spot on approach. As I look back, I should have found a bell or a whistle too!

The sounds around the hostel were no less demanding than the sounds on the streets. The raucous *caw-caw* of the hundreds of crows and the cold, piercing screech of hundreds of kites created a weird cacophony. A sparrow might try to work in a warble, only to be drowned out by the relentless chorus.

I missed music in Karachi. Considering the size of the population, radios were few. I missed voice music. The people did not sing as we do. I heard a woman humming as I passed by. My guide told me that she was the street cleaner, that she wore a sari of red cotton, and that she was sitting with her broom on the footpath. I wanted to greet her, but my guide moved along. She was only the street cleaner, after all …

In a nearby building that was under construction, several women were working, carrying hods on their heads. I felt I would be intruding to stop them in their duties. They were working hard in the heat. It was strenuous climbing steps to the top of the building with loads on their heads!

If the sounds of Karachi were easy to identify, the smells were not. Because Karachi is a wharf city, the smells were unpleasant and pungent, more so than anywhere else I have ever visited. I was very conscious of them; everyone is in Karachi. I missed pleasant smells to counter the stench of decaying fish, bilge water, and sewage. There were few flowers. A few impoverished chrysanthemums, asters, and thin-petaled roses occasionally—very occasionally—appeared. I was told that the soil had a high degree of salinity, so few flowers could grow without topsoil.

I learned that the acrid odor that hung around the hostel came from the fish oil used in the soap mixture, blended with the penetrating smell of burning asthmador powder. Many people in Karachi have asthma, which they relieve by smoking the powder. Two of the servants who came to my room coughed and wheezed from chest trouble. How they suffered! And there was so little one could do about it. But they went on with their work, stopping to talk with me if they had a few words of English or simply greeting me with, "Memsab." Very soon I was known to all of them, and I began to recognize them by their voices, their location, or their duties. They were highly amused at my fumbling attempts at Urdu, but they never hesitated to help me out with it. People told me I was learning "servant Urdu"—"Jungli Urdu," as they called it. It was a source of amusement for all of us; we all had fun as a result.

In the refugee quarters hung the breath-cutting odor of burning cow-dung cakes, used in the braziers for cooking. Once in a while the smell changed to the fumes of a kerosene stove. All of this was Karachi in its work-a-day life. To me it was all intensely interesting!

This was Karachi, and if you lived there, you accepted it. It took a visit from President Eisenhower to effect the semblance of a change.[4] The rumor went out that perfume was distilled into the air along the route the president would follow. I must say I did not smell any perfume, but at least the streets were cleaned. The buildings were washed, painted, and decorated.

Two of my Pakistani friends, who loved their city, were critical of its new facelift. "Oh, yes," one said, "Karachi got a new look, but it forgot to clean its fingernails." The back streets were still the same back streets, retaining their coating of dirt. My friends were intent on a good housecleaning. That is the spirit of the Pakistani.

I went to church every Sunday I could. There, for the brief duration of the service, I was among my American and British kinsmen. In church, everything was familiar; the order of the service, the hymns, the sermon, even the tea in the compound that replaced the familiar coffee hour.

On one occasion, I brought along the thirteen-year-old son of a Muslim friend who was broad-minded enough to allow the boy to come with me. The youth was awestruck by the singing and the music, though the organ could only wheeze out discords at best, and the crows and kites on the few trees outside screeched the preacher down. The boy was rapidly learning English. "Oh," he said as the collection plate approached, "now you have to pay."

From the mixture of the good and the bad, the pleasant and the unpleasant, the familiar and the strange, the dirty and the clean, I learned to know and understand the Karachi of my Pakistani friends. It was my Karachi, too, as long as I was there with them.

My favorite haunt in Karachi was the Bori Bazaar. The bazaar was a network of tiny alleys and streets, some cobbled, some dirt, all holed, irregular, dirty and noisy, crowded, smelly and hot. The dips in the streets, the loose rocks, and chunks of concrete made walking precarious. The path scarcely permitted a foothold in places, particularly when there was a double curb in the form of two steps up from the street level. I found myself gingerly balancing on the catwalk ledge, safe at least from the vegetable, animal, and mineral refuse of the street.

The shops ranged from holes-in-the-wall, corridors, and

passageways to tables, trays, and boxes. Pieces of wire scratched me or ripped my sleeve if I stretched over the boxes to handle the wares. If I hunted long enough, I could find anything in the Bori Bazaar: silver spoons, silver tea sets, silver trays, brass pots, candelabras, samovars, bells, bowls, and bangles. No bargaining was permitted. The government fixed prices to protect both seller and buyer.

One young vendor put a cardboard shoebox in front of me and told me to choose some charms. He would fix them to the teaspoons I had purchased. There were hundreds of these silver charms in the shoebox. I selected a miniature camel, the crescent and star, a bucket, a snake charmer, and a smoker. The young man wrapped the spoons in a corner of crumpled newspaper that hardly covered them. Paper was expensive and scarce. Then he surprised me by leaping over his stand to get change for me. He would be right back. Nobody was left to guard the stand, but nothing happened.

I could always get my bearings by finding the alleys with the spices, sweetmeats, and confections. The toy stalls were not far from there. I used to listen to the vendor explaining how they worked, winding them up and laughing as they did their tricks. One day I asked him where the toys were made. The question surprised him, and he searched for the mark. They were all made in Japan.

A young lad blocked my way. "Buttons, reels, elastic, black, white, Memsab," he hollered. Why was he not in school? This was his school; he was already making his living. If fewer than 20 percent of Karachi's children were in school, what chance had this poor boy?

The voices in the market were all men's voices; the noisy clatter was that of men and children. The women were silent behind their burkhas, their voices muffled beneath their hoods. One day I stumbled against a cordon of three or four women as I tried to hoist myself up to the top ledge to get a foothold. "Look out!" said my friend. "The lady in front of you is carrying a baby inside her burkha." This was unusual, for small children usually carry the smaller children.

Above the din of the vendors' voices, it was hard to unscramble the louder overtones—the brass-beater pounding his metal into shape; the table and chair maker hammering nails into roughly hewn wood; the row of shoemakers sitting along the ledge of the footpath, shouting to one another as they beat out leather soles. I heard the buzz of the *durzay*'s, or tailor's, sewing machine as he skillfully sewed European blouses and dresses for his foreign customers, making the accordion pleats around his toes; the *rat-tat-tat* of a cart coming over the cobblestones; and the swish of the street cleaner's broom too close to my feet.

A riot of odors competed with the riot of noise. I came to know the nauseating smell of boiled sugar and highly spiced coconut, the sour smell of soaking leather, the whiff of decaying fish and tidewater from the harbor at Kemari. I missed flowers, and I missed music. They were expensive luxuries.

The affluent visitor could emerge from the Bori Bazaar with a gold-embroidered sari, exquisite hand-tooled filigree silver jewelry, brass trays deftly beaten into lovely rose and leaf patterns, teakwood elephants, ivory carved smooth to the touch, a finely chiseled wood carving of a camel train, or a perfectly tailored cotton dress. The workmanship and the expenditure of eyesight were too high a price for the goods. The eyesight was not expendable, and the workmanship was not commensurate with the ten rupees (two dollars) remuneration for time, art, and effort.

Parks were few, and museums did not appeal. Most buildings were ordinary, lacking in history and romance. Yet there was always something for me to do in Karachi, someone to visit, some group to meet, some talk to give. The beach at Clifton was enjoyable, but even more I liked to stop by the roadside and, with the help of my guide, to speak with the crowds of children that sat along the edge of the footpath. The crowd doubled if I passed around a few biscuits or a few *anas*. There were so many children!

Some evenings I went to the beach to see the turtles come up the strand, dig holes, lay their eggs, and return to the water. I could get quite close to them, and I even stepped on the back of one of the largest ones. On another occasion, I went to the crocodile pool at Mungo Park. If there was any sound from the pool, it was drowned by the excited shouts of the children on the concrete wall where we sat and the chants of the droves of beggars, pleading for "Alms for Allah." It happened to be Thursday, Beggar Day.

I went to the movie to hear Rosalind Russell in *Auntie Mame.*

I listened to the youthful audience laugh at things that were not funny and miss the innuendoes and subtleties of the English with which they were unfamiliar. I sat with the children and the women in their burkhas in a separate section of the theater. The hilarity came from the men's section. I was amazed by the number of men who attended, with only a small part of the theater reserved for the women.

I thought about the sex-inciting movies that often were shown, the third-rate American cinema fare that we exported to Pakistan. The reaction to suggestive situations in the films was almost hysterical, while the clever witticisms went unobserved.

The tradition of *purdah* was explained to me as a way of elevating women. It raised the woman so high that she was not to be looked upon by anyone except her own husband and family. To me, the woman's withdrawal from the public seemed more an expression of man's superiority in possession. His possession was absolute, for not even the woman's footstep was to be heard by anyone outside the family circle. Yet my understanding grew out of ignorance. Purdah was a tradition with a long history and ratifications worthy of extensive study. It could not be written off by opinion. It was tied up with religion, social position, and pride.

Women in the villages did not hide themselves from the public view, for they had to work. The street-cleaning lady, the woman hod-carrier, the woman cement-carrier, and the beggar woman carrying the baby did not conceal their faces.

Originally practiced by the wives of rulers, purdah was actually a luxury, and the middle class copied the practice. Men, I felt, did not view it as a problem; they tended to continue the status quo. Furthermore, women would never be argued out of such a place of dignity. Some day, I believed, women themselves would give up purdah in exchange for open participation in community service. The beginning of change is evident already.

Mazim had already broken with tradition. "My country will never go forward until purdah ceases," she told me, "until women are free to work in the community, to take part in the education of the children instead of staying at home protected from the world. They do not know what is going on around them."

For the most part, Mazim maintained, Pakistani women are uneducated, for that is one way they are allegedly protected. Their only purpose in life is to bear children and more children. Infant mortality is high, and women do nothing about it.

Mazim planned to choose her own husband. She had shortened her hair to a neat braid, which she wore instead of the traditional heavy braids, some of them artificially lengthened, that reached below the waist. "Holy Writ," said Mazim, "does not advocate purdah. It tells women to help in society."

One day, Mrs. de Sosa, a Pakistani of Goan ancestry by her name, introduced me to a little Pakistani girl. "You never see her mother," she said. "She is always covered by her burkha. And," she added slyly, "what for are they covered up? Some of these women are so ugly no one would want to look at them anyway." Thus opinions varied.

Anna Anwar, a teacher, had made a survey as an assignment for one of her college courses. From the interviews she conducted, she estimated that 95 percent of the women who observed purdah did not favor the practice. They continued the tradition only because their husbands insisted upon it.

To satisfy my curiosity, I tried on a burkha. The long cloak-like jacket buttoned down the front. Instead of sleeves, it had slits through which the hands could emerge. The hood draped over my head, tied with a drawstring around my forehead, and hung down to my waist. Two long flaps covered my face. The lower flap had black gauze eye holes through which one with sight might look. The top flap covered the eyepieces for double protection from the inquiring male gaze. It felt very stuffy inside.

I then tried on another style of burkha, the kind that might be worn by a young girl. It was like an enormous tent. The top was large enough to cover my head, face, and neck, and the folds fell clear to the ground. I could only imagine this garment as a walking tent, for certainly it could not be beautiful. One Pakistani acquaintance, Mrs. Siddiqi, had a gray burkha, which I thought might be pretty, except for the headpiece with the flaps. Those flaps could not conceivably be attractive. They were not meant to be attractive but to envelop—and in that they succeeded.

As the Revolution Day parade passed me, I talked with a member of the one of the girls' bands. She described their uniforms of gaily colored boleros and shorts. The girls' legs and arms were bare, and they strode with athletic grace to the rhythm of their own march music. I could not help but think that this march was the death knell of the burkha. I don't think it will be long before the new look takes over.

•   •   •

I also pondered the topic of family planning. I argued that the *behra*, or servant, with the fifteen children could not possibly feed them on his earnings, far less educate them. But Mr. Khan had a different viewpoint. "If a vote were taken for family planning, it would lose," he told me. "Muslims and Catholics both are against it." The birth control question could not be settled by law.

Yet, Mr. Khan reflected, change might come about in other ways. If extended education, entertainment, and athletics were more available, sex would cease to be the only escape. "Compulsory education, better roads, radios for communication, sanitation—these things will make a difference," he explained, "but they are hard to come by."

In the meantime, he stated, certain religious traditions must be upheld. In every family, the eldest son assumed responsibility for the welfare of the father, mother, sisters, and any handicapped children. These were sacred traditions, inviolable and obligatory.

"Aren't these duties based on tradition rather than religion?" I asked. "Can't they grow and change with time?"

Mr. Khan had traveled widely in Europe and the United States, yet his mind was closed to all faiths, beliefs, and practices save his own.

My Muslim cab chauffeur thought quite differently. He had six children, and he found it hard to meet expenses. What effect would the pill have on his wife? he asked me. Would it reduce his masculinity? In all sincerity, he was asking for contraceptive help; he wanted to provide a better life for the children he had.

A social worker told me that she believed family planning was a vital means for alleviating the suffering and poverty she met in her work. Mothers came to her, asking for advice against conception. She said that contraception did not conflict with religion; it would be approved in the name of humanity. "A program of public education would help," she told me. "The people are illiterate. They cannot read newspapers or pamphlets, but they can listen to the radio and learn. A public address system could be set up in central areas of the cities, delivering information to the wife and mother."

Then there was the serious-minded believer who asked if these social workers wanted to make prostitutes of their womenfolk. There was the college professor, historian, and Islamic authority who knew that family planning would never be accepted by his countrymen and fellow believers. The pendulum swings to and fro, and the children keep on coming.

Walking through the refugee encampments, the "colonies," we would meet about half a dozen adults but literally dozens of children, the four-year-olds carrying the two-year-olds and the babies. One day, on our way to the beach, my friend remarked that she saw a row of ten five-year-olds carrying very young children. I suggested we stop and talk with them. That was the wrong method of approach! In a twinkling, we were surrounded by twice that number. Emboldened as they pressed around us, they all cried, *"Baksheesh!"*

•   •   •

I visited Anna's school one afternoon. At dismissal time, the girls, ranging from seventeen to twenty years of age, drew their starched burkhas over their heads, tightened their grip on the books and papers safely concealed inside the tents, and off we went to catch the bus. When the bus rumbled up to us, it was so crowded we could not climb aboard. People hung onto the outside door and stood on the steps. Another bus passed, and another, and we still waited. At last four of us managed to squeeze into the women's compartment alongside the driver. We breathed in the nauseating fumes from the motor and listened to the driver's wracking cough through the partition. All of these people were going home from work or school, another long day behind them.

I asked the girls what they were going to do when they finished school. They were all going to be career women, they told me. They were studying American books on psychology, social reforms, and education. They would not become teachers, for teaching did not pay enough for them to live on. They wanted to be journalists, sociologists, social workers, or psychologists.

"Not nurses?" I asked.

I had visited the medical center and talked with the matron. There was a serious shortage of nurses, she told me, and there were few trainees. Women who observe purdah cannot enter the men's wards, not even to attend the sick. Hospitals have to employ male nurses and attendants, but they are scarce, for the work is hard and the pay meager.

"Girls do not want to be nurses," the matron added, "for nursing has an inferior status. They want to be doctors, but they end up as neither. The very few who finish a medical course accept only women as patients."

The situation was discouraging, but I met a group of twenty girls of eighteen, all receiving nurse's training under the guidance of the Boston School of Nursing. Over supper I listened to their study troubles, their examination results, and their escapades. They were a wholesome, happy bunch of budding nurses, a group I could have met in any American dormitory. Although I did not speak their native language, they all spoke English.

The few girls I met who worked in offices were either Parsi or foreign. A girl of Muslim faith, in her observance of purdah, could not work in an open office with the general public. A young girl with a Muslim surname usually turned out to be a Christian.

In the beginning, Pakistan seemed so strange to me, so different, so far from home. Now, because of the people, I had come to love the country. Certainly it was not the food that had changed me! I was sick of boiled fish, rice and curry, curry and rice! It was not the beauty of the architecture; there was no beautiful architecture to see, and I couldn't have seen it in any case. It was not the comfort of the transportation, for my bones were shaken mercilessly every time I rode in a rickshaw. Nor was it the climate, with its soaring temperature and humidity. Yet I found something alluring, bewitching, lovable about Pakistan's people. Their variety, their frankness, their sincerity, their graciousness tied me to them. Perhaps it was because I was alone, and I needed their friendship. I don't think so, for I had a paid-up ticket in my pocket, and I was free to journey on. Was it because I was blind? But my blindness was never a primary consideration in any situation or conversation. I think it was the simple truth that they gave their love and demanded my respect. They were my friends, and national barriers had broken down.

NOTES

1. Coir is a tough, resilient fiber made from coconut husks. It is used for making numerous products, including fabric, handbags, filters, and netting to prevent soil erosion.
2. A rickshaw is a two-wheeled cart used to transport goods or passengers. Human-pulled rickshaws were outlawed in Pakistan in the late 1950s and replaced by bicycle rickshaws and motorized rickshaws.
3. The Pashtuns, or Pathans, are a group of approximately sixty tribes living in Afghanistan and northern Pakistan. Some still live as farmers or nomadic herders, but many have settled in urban areas. Pashtuns have achieved prominence as writers, sports figures, and political leaders.
4. In December 1959, US president Dwight D. Eisenhower visited Pakistan during a three-week goodwill tour of eleven nations. In Karachi, half the city's population turned out to greet the celebrated visitor. Eisenhower met with Pakistan's president, Muhammad Ayub Khan, viewed a display of outstanding horsemanship, and visited the tomb of Pakistan's founder, Muhammad Ali Jinnah.

CHAPTER 7
THE SCHOOLMA'AM SITS IN

With pointer in hand, the teacher lectured to fifty lads in a government school. The subject was geography. The language was Urdu. The boys sat on mats on the floor; some hunched over slates as they wrote. When the teacher stopped to speak to us, the visitors, not a sound was heard from the boys. Another class was in the throes of the Pythagorean theorem, and I heard the boys reciting in English.

In a government school for girls, ten-year-old pupils in saris were learning domestic science. The very progressive, American-trained principal saw to it that the home arts received the same emphasis as the academic subjects. To my delight, the girls entertained me with a program of singing and dance, an uncommon event in a Pakistani school. Most of the dances were Indian, with body action and graceful, sliding movements of the arm and hand. The girls played their own traditional accompaniment, and one of them explained each dance to me in words. I was moved by the pleasure they took in their own performance.

At the end of the show, the girls invited me to join them in some of the dance steps. Then two girls linked their arms through mine, and we visited the rest of the school, talking and laughing as we went. In their delightful company, I forgot the humidity and the torrid heat, the noise from the adjacent thoroughfare, the diesel fumes, and the penetrating stench of sewage.

I talked to countless educators on my travels, discussing the philosophy and practice of teaching. Nevertheless, I much preferred to visit the schools and see them for myself. I wanted to talk with the boys and girls, to discover what they thought about and what interested them most. On a visit to a school in Malir, just outside Karachi, the creaking floors, gritty chalk, and pockmarked chalkboards did not bother me. I was not troubled when I stepped over a plank into the curtained cubbyhole that served as the principal's office. In fact, such conditions stirred up childhood memories.

On the other hand, I was often pained by my inability to speak to the children in their language when they were so adept at speaking mine. My first greeting and introductory sentence in Urdu usually met with amusement and at times triggered peals of uncontrolled laughter. Fortunately, my faltering efforts cracked the image of the aloof American teacher. I built rapport with carefully selected, clearly enunciated words.

When I visited a school, I generally arrived with a party of guides and local ambassadors. I lost the party as quickly as I could, to find myself with half a dozen boys in the corner of a study room. They found me a chair, and within moments the group began to grow. I always carry my portable Stainsby Braillewriter over my shoulder.[1] A demonstration was called for, and samples of a Braille page went from hand to hand. I touched my watch face to check the time. I had stayed too long, but the boys had to see my Braille watch. They closed their eyes and felt it as I did. I produced another trick from my bag. I happened to have a package of self-threading needles and a tiny spool of thread with me. More fun!

All the time, as they marveled and asked questions, we talked. We talked about American boys and girls, American schools, their own school, their classes, their books. We talked about their future.

We were so engrossed that we didn't notice the pelting rain outside. An hour's downpour left our bus up to the hubcaps in water. A foot of water drowned the grass in front of the school. Some of the men and women in my party doffed their shoes and hose. With turned-up pants and uplifted skirts, they sloshed across fifty feet of lake from the patio to the bus. I prepared to wade across the stretch of water, too.

"Oh, no!" my new friends cried. Four boys appeared with a chair and hoisted me across the water like a princess on a litter. We all laughed so much they could scarcely hold the chair straight. With a whoop, they deposited me on the step of the bus, hale and hearty but rather wet.

One of the boys who carried me wheezed and coughed badly with asthma. Gladly I would have changed places with him and helped carry him instead, but that would have spoiled his fun. I latched on to his arm, and he showed me to a place on the bus. Then we said good-bye. Bless his heart!

•　　•　　•

At another school, 150 boys and girls packed into a single room, three children crowded onto benches made for two. Naturally it was unusual for them to have a blind schoolteacher from America as their guest. Blind people didn't teach in Pakistan, and blind people did not travel. When I turned to write on the chalkboard behind me, I was taken aback by a round of applause. In Pakistan, blind people could not write on chalkboards.

"Can you see what you have written?" the children asked me.

"No," I told them. "But I still can write." I explained that when I became blind I did not allow myself to forget anything I did as a sighted person.

"Then can a person who was born blind do the things you do?" they wanted to know.

"Yes," I said. "There are congenitally blind teachers teaching sighted children."

Our running exchange went on for two hours. Even when the class was over, the pupils crowded around the desk with more questions. I left the school in a flurry of handshakes and salaams and crossed the tiny patch of blacktop that served as the playground. It provided little more than standing room at recess time. Playing fields and swimming pools were not a sine qua non for school spirit, I realized. School spirit was present in rich measure in the hearts and minds of these young Pakistanis.

On yet another school visit, I observed a lesson with sixty little boys and girls. They chanted in unison after the teacher. There were not enough books to go around, but no one seemed concerned. Memorization took the place of reading.

Later I sat in on an oratory contest. Twenty boys recited poems, speeches, and quotations, displaying their fantastic memorization ability. I felt thrilled and humiliated as I listened to the Gettysburg Address, excerpts from *The Lady of the Lake*, and lines from *Hiawatha* in the Pakistani accent with the characteristic *v* sound instead of *w* and *R*s and *L*s interchanged. I thought of the pains these boys had taken to learn my language while I was still such a novice in theirs. These were children between the ages of six and sixteen!

During the election days, I heard the students deliver speeches on the principles of democracy that would have stood the test in any public speaking class in an American school. In deep reverence, I stood with three hundred boys and girls as they lustily sang their national anthem. Their enthusiastic singing drowned out the squeaks of the piano, its strings loosened by the heat and humidity. Young Pakistan is preparing itself for its responsibilities to come.

•   •   •

I arrived early at the training college where I was scheduled to give a talk. The students, about nineteen years of age on average, were watching an American documentary film. It showed a chemistry class in a US high school. The laboratory was equipped with everything a student or teacher could possibly desire. The film then portrayed the home of one of the students. The boy had a richly equipped laboratory in the basement of his own home.

When the projector stopped running, a strange silence hung over the audience. "Would you like to discuss the film?" I asked.

The students burst forth with a barrage of questions. Was that a typical American classroom? Did students in the United States really have all that equipment at their disposal? Who paid for it?

"Do all the boys in America have their own labs like the boy in the picture?"

"No," I said. "From my experience, I would say that this boy was unusually fortunate to afford such equipment. Either country would be likely to film the best situations available if the purpose was to stimulate and inspire toward self-development."

I felt the enormous relief of the students clustered around me. I more fully understood their reaction to the film after I visited their school laboratory. It had only a few test tubes, Bunsen burners, slide rules, and bottles, all locked in glass cupboards. Even the books in the classroom and the library were locked in cabinets for safekeeping.

Once the topic of chemistry studies was exhausted, we moved on to other things. The students asked me about the curriculum in the United States, the grading system, examinations, sports, fees, and student government.

"Are there Asian pupils in your school?" they wanted to know.

When I assured them that there were, they asked about Negroes. "Are there Negroes in your classes?" "Do they sit in the same rooms with the other students?" "Do they get free textbooks like the rest of the pupils?" "Do they play with the other children?"

"Since I'm blind, I don't know what color my pupils are," I said, prompting a ripple of laughter.

I felt exhilarated by the curiosity and imagination of these young people. Surely they are the teachers of tomorrow. The pity is that there are all too few of them.

These were some of the bright spots in the education picture of Pakistan. I met with many other happy situations in Lahore, Rawalpindi, and Peshawar, but the story in the villages was very different. Hundreds of thousands of children had no educational facilities whatsoever. The illiteracy rate over the country was quoted as from 80 to 85 percent. About seventy-five million of Pakistan's ninety million people can neither read nor write.

•　　•　　•

Illiteracy was not always so widespread in the Muslim world. The mosque used to be the seat of learning, and learning was given to all who came to the mosque. The emphasis was on the memorization of the Holy Quran at the hands of the imam, or religious and community leader. He himself was usually self-educated. His pay was in local produce, as the people desired to contribute of their bounty. If he received too much flour for his use, he sold or bartered the surplus. His wife helped teach the holy scripture to the girls.

The old *maktab*, or elementary school, had a definite program and purpose. It was a people's school, supported by the people themselves. The rich man's son and the poor man's son sat side by side, and the sighted sat with the blind, all learning together.

Then came the British.[2] They needed native help to run the lower levels of the government. Education was attuned to the practical needs of the governors, not to the needs of the people at large. The maktab declined. The imams, with their lack of money and their meager knowledge of class management, teaching methods, and school administration, were unable to build new schools. During the Raj, the English public school, with its deferential atmosphere, was transplanted to the Far East. It was a system as unsuited to the country as was a briefcase to a farm worker.

"How do you take your examinations?" I asked a group of boys at an English-style school.

"We cram. We get old papers and get the questions and memorize the answers."

Suddenly one of the boys ventured to ask me a question. "How do you say 'howdy' in American? What is meaning? How you use it?"

These young boys of sixteen or seventeen were intensely curious. They could not find the word "howdy" in their dictionaries. But their questions did not come until well on in my visit. The dignified atmosphere of an English grammar school pervaded the classroom. I knew it all too well, for I had grown up in that atmosphere myself. The students treated me with the same disciplined courtesy they gave their gowned master. Only when the questions started to fly did the atmosphere become more natural and exciting.

"No, our teachers don't wear gowns," I explained. "They dress the way I'm dressed today."

"Do American boys all have cars?" "Do they drive their cars to school?" "Do they play cricket?" "Do they play baseball at school?" "Dr. Mrs. Grant, did you really come from America all by yourself?" "Do all the blind people in America have jobs?" "Are there blind beggars in America too?" So great was the interest in turning the blind population into a contributing resource that a few of the boys dared to be late to their next class, staying behind to continue the discussion.

The boys in this school came from privileged families. Fees at the intermediate and higher levels averaged two hundred rupees per month, or about forty US dollars. It was a large sum even for a professional person to afford. The school curriculum was highly academic, and I felt that it was more traditional than the present-day English schools in the UK. I saw the system as an expensive import, precious but totally unsuited to the country's needs.

An enormous reservoir of youthful energy and intelligence lay pent up in the students I met. I wanted them to be less dominated by the textbook, to have more opportunity for self-expression. I, too, have been a teacher of Latin, but some years of Latin study could be exchanged for the study of the modern sciences, international affairs, and comparative civics.

Allegiance to the traditional British system is only to be expected, for British control is still comparatively recent. The English-trained instructor strives to follow the blueprint of British education. This adherence does not seem to be making for progress. One principal lamented, "Our schools are still too English, and their weak spot is in the field of secondary education."

I remarked on the tendency to conduct all the higher-level classes in English. Why weren't the students taught in Urdu?

"Most technical books are written in English," the principal pointed out. "English has to be used."

Couldn't English be studied as a second language? I wondered. Bengali, the language of Pakistan's East Wing, the old East Bengal, should also have a place in Pakistan's modern language study, as Urdu was studied in the West.[3]

The teachers at the upper-grade levels had more extensive training than the teachers in the elementary grades. As a result, elementary education was often inferior. So-called Montessori education is still much in evidence, but the philosophy of the modern kindergarten gradually is taking its place.

The United States has time and money to put into education. Many other countries have neither. We in the United States have developed a brand of education suited to our needs, but it cannot be transplanted. Through my many discussions with Pakistani teachers, I came to realize that some ideas and methods may be borrowed, but they have to be assimilated by the country that chooses to adopt them. For example, I took for granted the idea of compulsory education. In contrast, education in Pakistan and many other Asian nations is not guaranteed under the law. Compulsory education for children up to third grade may not be possible for another decade. In our country, education is a bulwark of our democratic principles. Where there has been no democratic tradition, however, there has been no need for comprehensive education. If a more far-reaching plan of education were mandated, where would the teachers be found? Young people have little incentive to enter the teaching profession. Training is inadequate, teachers' salaries are low, and social prestige barely hovers above that of the field worker. I met teachers who earned from 50 to 250 rupees per month—the equivalent of ten to fifty dollars. Many teachers have no training beyond a secondary-school degree. Schools are few in number, comparatively expensive, and, for the most part, staffed by purveyors of rigid British traditions.

Each year, through the Pakistani government or some foreign agency, a few young teachers study in the United States or the UK. Through this exposure to other ways, they see new possibilities for Pakistani education. They see that British education is no longer as it was during the Raj. Philosophical changes have taken place in Great Britain, particularly in the growth of intermediate education and technical schools. In the United States, they see that education is provided for all of the children of all of the people, with opportunity at the highest levels for those who qualify. It gave me joy to hear these teachers say, each in a different way, "That is what you have done, but this is what we can do."

Because of my lengthy stay in Pakistan, I met more teachers there than anywhere else on my journey. Throughout my visit, they impressed me greatly. "Yes, I get fifty rupees a month, and I live with my parents," said one teacher, Tahira. "But I love to teach." Mrs. Tangwi said she felt her pupils were her own children. When she noticed that a child was struggling in class due to eye trouble, she took her to the local clinic and procured an eye examination and glasses. The girl's father, a carpenter, could not afford to pay for either. Miss Anwahr saw to it that the children in her school participated in the CARE milk program, and she added a chocolate flavoring to make the dried milk mixture more appetizing to the little ones. Miss Kawaja, a school principal, met with her teachers in small groups to study articles on education, talk with some visiting educator, or learn about child psychology.

"Since partition, the village school is reviving," said a visiting teacher from the city of Quetta. "The villagers tend it by their own efforts. They try to provide at least two or three years of schooling for every child. Higher learning is still out of their reach, but it could be possible with government help." She told me that the children are beginning to learn their multiplication tables, their Urdu letters, and the Holy Quran.

•   •   •

Today, hundreds of thousands and Pakistani children drift without purpose. Encouragement, some financial help, and a little direction are the ingredients to bring them into the classroom for four or five hours a day. Education will stir up their enormous reservoir of mental energy and channel it toward the goal of better living for the individual and for the nation. It can be done, for it is being done. The groundwork is laid in the pages of the Commission Report, a comprehensive, forward-looking interpretation of a national program of education. It is a report worthy of the highest commendation.

The overall picture of education appeared to me limited but hopeful. Yet the program of education of blind children was totally inadequate and all but void of hope. It is a fair assumption that 50 percent of the world's children are at present receiving some basic education. To place the education of the world's blind children at 1 percent would be a high estimate. I visited schools for the blind that were nothing but charitable institutions. The executive boards considered blind children uneducable. They geared their programs to handwork, such as basketry and chair caning, to the exclusion of academic teaching. Many of the teachers had no training at all and merely served as caretakers. Corruption in some of the schools was obvious. The charity box hung at the door. The children received the largesse of any do-gooder who might supply lollipops or a trip to the beach. I met educators who believed that blind children were incapable of learning or moving around by themselves without the assistance of guides. I met educators who had never heard of Braille, though Braille codes exist for both Urdu and Bengali. Most of these educators believed that blind children should be segregated from society and kept in charitable institutions throughout their lives. I reflected that I might have become a beggar under such conditions. Still, I like to think I would have wanted to venture forth and see the world.

With the aid of interpreters, I talked with many blind beggars. The older ones were not interested in education for themselves, but every beggar I met said that blind children should have an opportunity for education equal to that of sighted children. "We have brains, too," said a blind beggar on the train from Malir to Karachi. Clearly he had brains, but he was not interested in learning a trade. He made a good living at his own profession of begging.

No nation thrives with mendicancy in its population. Blind persons should not be relegated to the ranks of second-class citizenship. They should be trained for self-development and self-realization.

The blueprint for a new era was approved at a meeting sponsored by the government. Under this plan, opportunities for basic and higher education would not be denied to individuals because of blindness. Colleges could not deny entrance to otherwise qualified blind applicants. More schools for the blind would be made available. A fantastic number of new schools would be required to educate thousands of blind children.

Schools for the blind are expensive to operate. The child must leave home, and his support becomes the responsibility of the agency that runs the school. Special schools for the blind certainly are needed, but other options are called for to reduce costs.

Itinerant programs and integrated classes offer a possibility, and some young Pakistani teachers see the way ahead. First, new teachers of blind children must be trained. Guidance and training must be provided for teachers in the general classroom to help them include blind children in their programs.

From letters and studies, I estimated that 150 blind children were enrolled in schools throughout the country. I was told that there are 150 thousand blind children between the ages of six and eighteen in Pakistan. However, no one can be certain of these figures. No census of blind children has ever been taken, and no statistics on blindness have been kept. Social welfare records give no clue. Careful guesswork is the only source of information.

The government still seems dubious about a program of education for the country's blind children. Furthermore, supervisors and staff at some of the existing rehabilitation centers see their blind clients merely as charges whose presence guarantees them a lifetime occupation. Some individuals, however, are starting to recognize that blind people can be educated and trained to make their living, to become contributing members of society.

At present, the government leans on voluntary agencies to assume the financial responsibility of training programs and education. Many educators and officials are eager to take blind children off the streets and place them in schools. "It would be better for a blind child to sit in a classroom listening than to be tied to a bedpost at home," said Shokat, a local merchant.

Whether by evolution or revolution, the idea of mandatory education lies deep in the hearts of the Pakistanis. The lack of universal public education is a sore point when they discuss their country's position among the nations of the world. They are bent on attaining the goal of free schools for all children.

As I talked with young blind men in Lahore, Rawalpindi, Karachi, and Dacca, I was aware of their determination to participate in the building of a nation that they now called their own. One day I sat with four of them on the verandah of the modest hostel where I was staying. "Spell out what you think is needed," I said.

"First," they told me, "we would ask that blind children be included in any program of general education. Recruitment and training of teachers would be part of the goal. The second proviso would be that the government assume as complete responsibility for the educational program and the financial outlay as possible. Private volunteer agencies were not trained for the work, and they are too prone to corruption and the intrigues of vested interests. Lastly, as the families are poor, the children need scholarships, materials, equipment, and books."

Their answers were wonderful, but they did not explain how it was all to be achieved.

Before my departure from Pakistan, I made sure to visit one of the American schools set up for the children of diplomats and businessmen. These schools made a conscientious effort to match the academic content that the pupils would have received at home. Employing the Calvert Correspondence Method,[4] they provided a glorified mail-order education. Universities in the United States sent textbooks, lessons, tests, and a teacher's manual. The pupils worked through the textbooks, and the teacher followed her manual of directions. Examination papers were sent back to the United States to be graded. As one teacher put it, "I don't need to know the foreign language I'm teaching. I just follow the manual and keep ahead of the class." Teachers were scarce, so wives of the embassy personnel were enlisted for the task, regardless of their training. The pupils were shortchanged in a genuine effort to keep them from falling behind their classmates at home.

Other foreign children were allowed to attend the American schools, but local children were strictly excluded. I felt that the very spirit of American education had been lost. To me, there was a taint of colonialism about the situation, and I knew that the Pakistanis did not like it.

The American children could have learned far more by sharing their school life with Pakistani boys and girls, learning how the Pakistanis live, telling them about our country and absorbing the Urdu language along the way. What did it matter if the standard content of the English literature class was omitted? The gains from a true Pakistani immersion would have been immeasurable, a step closer to international understanding.

My own learning in Pakistan never ceased. Just as I thought I had mastered some Urdu turn of phrase, I was reminded of how little I knew. As I awaited a rickshaw on the steps of my boarding house one day, a Pakistani man inquired in his halting English about the white cane I carried. *"Mein unda,"* I said proudly, meaning "I am blind."

"Chickens?" he asked, puzzled.

Apparently the way I pronounced the Urdu words meant, "I have eggs." After months in Pakistan, I still could not tell the difference between *unda*, meaning "eggs," and *undha,* meaning "blind"!

In my long experience as a teacher, I have observed many, many classrooms. No observations were ever so revealing to me as those I made during my sojourn in Pakistan. I had nothing to give my fellow teachers, and they had everything to share with me—a new nation, the new challenge of democratic principles, a new reason for living. Education would be the straight path to a new era.

NOTES

1. Introduced in the UK in 1903 and improved in 1933, the Stainsby-Wayne Braillewriter had a folding wooden base and a moveable carriage with six keys for forming the Braille characters. With some models, it was possible for Braille to be written on both sides of the page. As most of Dr. Grant's surviving Braille notes are written on both sides of the paper, this is probably the type of Stainsby Braillewriter that she used.
2. The rule of the British Crown was established in most of today's India and Pakistan in 1858. The period of British rule, known as the Raj, continued until 1947.
3. Bengali is the language of today's Bangladesh (formerly East Pakistan) and is also spoken in the Indian state of West Bengal.
4. The Calvert Correspondence School was established in Baltimore, Maryland, in 1897. The program was frequently used in schools for the children of diplomats or corporate officials stationed overseas.

CHAPTER 8
HOW I ADJUSTED TO A DIFFERENT WAY

I could not take my bath. There was no water pressure. I pulled the chain of the toilet twenty-five times, and still it would not flush. I waited an hour for a rickshaw. I was sick and tired of fish and rice.

My friend Mrs. Faruqi listened as I wailed. After I exhausted myself with my peeves, she said quietly, "This is the best we have!"

Her words brought me to my senses. I was a visitor, and they offered their hospitality in full measure. I received the best of everything.

An old Pakistani waiter also helped me understand. "Why?" I asked laughingly, when he brought me an egg the size of a walnut. "Why don't you feed your chickens and get bigger eggs?"

"Yes," he answered softly, "but we have to feed our people first." In that moment, I realized that I had to put aside my American expectations and regard life from the Pakistani vantage point. It took a lot of time, patience, and frustration before I began to put myself in Pakistani shoes.

Frustration filled my first two months in Pakistan. Whenever I needed information or an official signature, I faced a jungle of bureaucracy. People broke appointments without warning. No one would make a decision; someone else at a higher level always had to be consulted. The person who promised to come at four o'clock might arrive at seven—the time I had set aside for another appointment. Now I, too, would be late—but in Pakistan, the concept of lateness did not seem to exist.

Sometimes I concluded that Pakistanis did not know their own streets. But how could they? Who could find an address, surrounded by acres of huts dropped anywhere, made of anything, covered with gunnysacking when they were covered at all? Even when we found the right street, the numbering was erratic. I was convinced that each address was the house owner's lucky number or perhaps his birthday.

One day I sat talking with Mrs. Ansari, a social worker who had studied at an American university. Suddenly I realized that her experience in the United States mirrored mine in Pakistan. She told me that her first two months in my country were devastating. She could not handle the freedom of college life. All of the classes were coeducational. Women threw themselves into discussions as if they were men. They dressed as they desired, some even wearing men's clothes. Libraries were open to everyone; any student could get whatever book he or she wanted.

Students were expected to do their own housekeeping. Telephones, electric irons, and washing machines all operated flawlessly. Streetcars and buses all ran—and they ran on time. The pace of life dismayed her. "I sat for hours, trying to think it through," she told me. "How was I going to get hold of myself in this confusion?"

The campus was so large that she had trouble finding her way from place to place. Her next class always seemed to be miles away. "People frowned on you," she said, "if you arrived late to a party."

I thought of one of my own recent experiences in Pakistan. I had been invited to a party and had waited for promised transport that never arrived. Finally I called my host, only to learn that the party was off.

I began to understand Mrs. Ansari's dilemma in the United States and mine here. Both of us felt a great temptation to give up and leave. Mrs. Ansari did not give up, and neither did I. The crooked paths could be straightened somehow, I knew.

For my own peace of mind, I decided, I would try to forget about the things that were not being done according to my standards. I would focus instead on what was being done—even though the former outnumbered the latter ten to one. I sat down at my Braillewriter and composed a list that I called "Ten Great Expectations."

1. When promises are made, they will be fulfilled. I would try to

ignore promises, for I did not understand what caused them to be unfulfilled.

2. Appointments are going to be kept. Mazim promised to come for me to go to the Girl Scout meeting on Saturday morning. Mazim's mother became ill. Her first concern was for her mother. I was well; no sickness was coming over me. If she did not keep our appointment, she had justification. That I had to see.

3. Appointments will be kept at the hour arranged. An appointment was made to be kept, I thought—but if streetcars and buses never run on schedule, if sometimes, without warning, they do not run at all, if there is no rickshaw within hailing distance and you have to walk, how can you keep an appointment? I was arguing against my own convictions, but I was coming to know there was another way to look at things besides my own.

4. There will be more action and fewer words. If I had all the radios people said they would bring me, I would have had one in each corner of my room. Everyone talked about my need to have a radio, and I made the mistake of taking all those words seriously. I waited and waited for action to follow the words. I should simply have gone to a shop and asked if I could rent a radio during my stay.

5. There will be fewer sickness alibis to deal with. Sickness is very prevalent in Pakistan, but it is not so prevalent that it can excuse every mere forgetfulness. I could not count the times when sickness was given as the reason for a broken engagement. I would have preferred people to tell me the truth. Sickness, I thought, is too serious to be used as an alibi. I found myself treating rather lightly the sickness excuses, and I did not become too concerned about them.

6. There will be respect for the allocation of my time. In Pakistan, I was not master of my own time. When I scheduled an interview with Bashir for eight to ten in the morning, and Bashir arrived at ten all prepared to sit for two hours, my time was his. If I had to go out at ten thirty, I simply asked Bashir to accompany me. He was very happy to do so; he thought nothing about it. I expected my time to be my own, but it need not always be so.

7. Their standards of cleanliness will match my own. I won't expect other people to clean house as I do; mine may not be a good way

after all. If the servant beats the dust on the table or on the stair rail instead of wiping it away, I have to learn that all my remonstrances, demonstrations, and explanations are good for the moment only. Next day, the dust will again be beaten and stirred up to fall again. The servant pointed out how smooth and clean the table was with the beating. What did it matter if I knew the dust was up in the air and would fall again in due time? As the crumbs were beaten off the table instead of brushed, why should I remonstrate? But I did, when they fell in my tea! That was his way. Was my way any better?

8. They will not proffer false directions to save face. Directions were given by landmarks, not by street address. I had to learn that if I wanted to get to a certain office, it was "opposite the Karm House," or "by the old Exhibition," or "by the Victoria Theater," or it was "above the Kawaja Auto Shop." If I was told to go "past the grocery store on Love Lane," that was considered ample address.

9. The whole array of shopkeepers will not assist me in every purchase. If I wanted to buy writing paper in the shop, I did not think I required four clerks to help me select the cheapest brand, but they did.

10. They will have mercy on my nylons. When I held out my hand for a lift—or a heave—into a rickshaw, no hand reached out to meet mine. I had to withdraw my hand and climb in as best I could, tearing my nylons to shreds, snagging my dress, scratching my shins and elbows. Many men did not want to touch the hand of a woman or to touch her in any way. Should I expect a deep cultural practice to give way so easily? I knew it would—in time.

So I got the petty frustrations once and for all out of my system. They had their way; I had mine. As long as I was in their country, I would seek out those differences. I was determined they would be frustrations no more, or at least they would be disregarded. Mrs. Ansari had done just that in my country, and now there was no greater proponent of my country than she was. I knew that if I could take care of the little frustrations, I could take care of the bigger ones, too, or at least understand them better. That was my resolve.

•   •   •

I was visiting one day with Mr. and Mrs. Siddiqi. Mr. Siddiqi owned several trawling ships. He was one of the younger-generation Pakistanis, those who see the potential in their country and do something about it. Mr. Siddiqi had made several visits to fishing centers in the United Kingdom and the United States to study the science of sardine trawling and shrimp fishing. His latest venture was to can the fish he received from his fleet. The shrimp were dried, ground, and exported in large containers to Burma and other eastern countries. I felt Mr. Siddiqi's growing excitement as he told the story of the development of his project. I was excited, too. He had purchased purse seine nets and would start to manufacture more.

Mrs. Siddiqi served tea and imported biscuits—a rare delicacy. As the afternoon progressed, Mr. Siddiqi's first wife came to visit with the children. The situation was normal and natural. Our talk went from fishing to the children, then to the blind persons of the country, then to America. Everyone took some part in the conversation. How embarrassing it must be, I thought, for the two wives! But again this was my idea of the situation, not theirs. Mr. Siddiqi explained the situation as part of his religion. It did not call for an explanation, but he described it as freely as he discussed the purchase of his trawling fleet.

I admired Mr. Siddiqi; he was one of Pakistan's progressive young builders. His wives were charming, courteous, self-effacing, and gentle. Here, I was the exception to the rule; it was my culture that was strange.

One day, a young man named Waqr called on me. He had heard me speak at one of the colleges, and he had a pen pal in the United States. With all the enthusiasm of his nineteen years, he explained that he wanted to be a public administrator. He was a shipyard worker. In Waqr, I saw the dream of the vast majority of young Pakistanis—the dream of becoming a public official. A public official with a briefcase was the acme of prestige, of dignity and position. I suspected that this quest for government officialdom was a hangover from the days of the British Raj. Under the British, the then Indians were recruited into government service as secretaries, clerks, and semiofficials. "Secretary" was the most coveted title.

I asked Waqr if he would consider a trade. Would he like to be a plumber? Plumbers were badly needed in his country.

"Oh, no!" he replied. "A plumber has no dignity."

"What about a schoolteacher?"

"No," he said, "teaching is one of the poorest-paid jobs in my country. It has no dignity either."

"What about a shipyard worker?" I ventured to ask.

"That, too, has no dignity. That is why I want to leave it." He wanted to be of the most service possible to this new country of his, and the only worthy way was to be a government secretary.

"But couldn't you serve your country better in the shipyard than in an office?" I asked. "You could learn to build better ships, carry more merchandise."

Waqr was one of the men, I thought, who had the energy and imagination necessary for service. I did not understand that ideals and goals had not yet matured, for the culture had not yet emerged from its traditions. The image of success came from the tradition of the past. I could not convince Waqr of the need for shipyard workers in his country. But I had no doubt but that, given time, he would learn it for himself.

Could I ever divorce myself from my own traditions and background and see the Pakistani point of view? Did I always have to compare what I saw in Pakistan with what I knew from my own culture? I was put to the test many times. I criticized, passed judgment, and condemned, all based on my standards.

• • •

I stood on the edge of the Polo Grounds. It was Revolution Day, October 27, and the streets were lined with people. My guide described the procession as it went by. There were trains of camels, elaborately colored trappings draped around their necks and over their backs. Elephants passed by us with their howdahs on top and their draperies with gold fringe dipping almost to the ground. Bicycles by the hundreds followed, decorated with paper streamers, which the crowd caught up as they passed.

At intervals during the parade, we heard all of six bagpipe bands. My pulse quickened as they struck up "The Bonnets of Bonnie Dundee" and "The Road to the Isles," and my curiosity was aroused when they played "Auld Lang Syne." This was neither the time nor the place for that old masterpiece. *What were the Scottish Highlanders doing in this parade?* I wondered.

My guide was so enthralled with the parade that he almost omitted to tell me that the pipers were Pakistanis—big, tall men, he said, from the Northwest Frontier. I listened more intently. Did I recognize a slight difference in the downbeat of "The Campbells Are Comin'"? I had to satisfy my curiosity. What were they wearing? Glengarry caps with streamers down the back, my guide explained, and gaily colored boleros, broad sashes, long, purple, silk bloomers, and shoes with turned-up toes. I was mystified. I found it hard to visualize this transfiguration of Scottish Highlanders, who to me could wear the kilt, the sporran, the white spats, and the rest of the costume but nothing else.

The flower queen followed in her float. She wore her sari, and there were flowers in her hair. She rode on a flower-decked dais—all the flowers made of paper. There are few real flowers in Karachi.

Clowns and roustabouts performed their antics, to the tremendous joy of my guide, and so to me. Girls' bands followed in the rear. The girls wore uniforms of tunics and short pants, and a majorette carried a baton. Could these girls ever hide under a burkha after such an experience and such training?

Here was a parade that was just as Pakistani as an American parade is American. Here was the Pakistani Revolution Day celebration, as much a national holiday as the Fourth of July was to me. Yet there were differences—camels, elephants, and purple-pantalooned pipers playing Scottish tunes that were not Scottish at all to the Pakistani crowds. I enjoyed it thoroughly, entering into the spirit of the celebration with my friends.

I spent the afternoon of Revolution Day with about a hundred Pakistanis. We were dinner guests aboard a cruiser of the Pakistani navy, lying offshore at Kemari. The ladies and children were served in a separate dining room from the men. During the dinner, the women removed their burkhas and hung them over the backs of the chairs. The dinner over, they donned their burkhas again and accompanied the children to the decks, where games, shows, and contests were in progress.

In Pakistan, every new person, every new situation interested me. The people of Pakistan were my people, too. Their skin color might have been different; I would not know, for I did not see it. Their language was wholly different to me; they spoke mine, and I was ashamed that I could greet them only falteringly in theirs.

• • •

One day my friend Anna said to me, "You know, I cannot realize that you are blind. I can't believe that you cannot see me."

"That is right," I said. "I cannot see you, but I can hear the smile in your voice."

"Have you an ashtray? May I smoke?" Anna asked.

"Yes, the ashtray is here under the lower shelf of the table."

Anna began to laugh. "You see," she said, "you know everything. I could have seen that for myself, but I just forgot and asked you."

"No, Anna, I don't know everything," I told her. "I want to know more about your country."

By her name, I knew that Anna was a Christian. She had been born in Delhi, but at partition she left her family to come to Karachi during the general exodus. I don't know if Anna herself was very clear as to why she came. She had the chance of a position as teacher in a girls' college, and she took it. Her mother and sisters remained in Delhi. To come to Pakistan, they would have to forfeit all that they had—the family house, their small interests, everything except their personal belongings.

Anna's training was good; she had completed her BA in psychology and was teaching psychology now. She had a positive attitude, and she loved her adopted country. She loved its newness and its challenges.

"What we need," Anna would say, "is wise direction until we know where we are going. At this point, we need strong leadership, and I don't mind if you call it a dictatorship. We need a strong hand to pull us out of the mess we have just come through. Aimless fanaticism won't get us anywhere. Communism is not the answer. And be it Islam or Christianity, we must keep our religion."

I asked if she could talk this way in the classroom. "Of course I can. We are a free people, and we are going to remain so."

Anna had other ideas, too. "If only our people had a fraction of the energy and know-how that President Ayub had! Our young people will work with you as long as you are working with them. But left alone, they lack initiative."

I asked if that could not be said of any people. There are always more hangers-on than leaders.

That idea did not satisfy Anna. This drive after civil-service employment, she thought, was the bane of the nation. It perpetuated the old British regime, and in its obedience to authority, it stifled individual initiative. "In this respect, we are now more British than Britain itself," she said. "That type of rigid discipline was mid-Victorian. Our people have much originality and imagination, if they know how to release it."

Pointing out to Anna that her nation is still a teenager did not help. She had studied history. She reminded me about the Greek invasion of this part of the world, of the period when Alexander the Great extended his conquest far beyond the limits of India. Then came the Buddhists from the East.

"Just go to Tata or Mohinjadara," she mused, "and you will see the background of my people."

Anna was deeply patriotic. The subcontinent was her country. To my question about Kashmir, she said simply, "It is Muslim, and if a plebiscite were taken, it would come to Pakistan."

"Our stock," said Anna, "is Indo-European. The Aryan invasion took place three to four hundred years before Christ. Our known civilization dates from that time."

I am sure that the girls in Anna Anwar's class were as hypnotized as I was by the magnetism of her voice, her sincerity, and her dedication. With the telling of her story, she waxed ever more enthusiastic. "We need land reform," she urged. "We need to limit the ownership of vast pieces of land, encourage the small farmer, and regulate taxes."

Her voice softened as she spoke of the naked poverty among her people, the poverty that created beggars, robbers, and murderers. It left the man lying in the middle of the street, asleep, injured, or dead. It allowed scarcely a handful of corn or rice for each mouth.

The picture was as grim and ugly as Anna said it was. Yet I saw the work of the Health and Social Welfare Department, the UNICEF office, and the medical missionaries. They were out in the field administering to the sick and poverty-stricken. Therein lay the welcome gleam of hope.

Anna and I had many talks together. We took rickshaw rides to the bazaars. We bought saris together, and Anna showed me how to wear one. She said she could put her sari on in one minute. I always seemed to get tangled up in my six yards of fabric. I had to unwind and start all over again, with yardage spread all along the floor. I would never have been on time for school if I had to teach wearing such a garment.

Anna gave me the pattern of a *choli*, the little jacket worn under the sari. She thought it was sheer magic when I threaded my self-threading needle and started to sew up the seams. She wanted me to meet her girls, so she divided them into groups, and we had two delightful parties. The girls did the talking and asked lots of questions. Obviously Anna had described our conversations, and they were verifying everything she had told them. They were from seventeen to twenty in age—full of fun and curiosity and as giggly and happy as our own American girls. They loved their Mrs. Anwar.

•   •   •

Two terms confronted me at every turn. They were "intrigue" and "social order." The two were interrelated; the social order was such that you could not avoid the intrigue. I wondered if those terms were employed deliberately in my presence, with the idea that, since I was blind, I would have to exert special care not to be ensnared. Because intrigue had been rampant during the preceding regime, I wondered if perhaps it was an unnecessary extension of the difficult times undergone during the Iskander Mirza administration.[1] There was a black market in nearly everything—in dollars, passports, traveler's checks, and, in this Muslim country, even in liquor. There was intrigue in the giving of jobs—Punjabis received jobs while others had to stand by, Bengalis against West Pakistanis. There were regional cliques in office, and it was impossible to break down the barriers.

Somehow or other, it all seemed very familiar to me. One can look for intrigue anywhere and find it—according to your point of view. But Begum Baig, a social worker who loved her people, sought reasons for what appeared as intrigue on the surface. Since the release of the British strong hand, Pakistanis feared to assume responsibility for their own welfare. They were afraid to tackle problems they had not known before, to claim their own rights. They were afraid, and they had no education to dispel their fears. They could neither read nor write. They had never had to think for themselves. The idea of the Basic Democracies was new to them.[2] They felt safer under a military leader who would protect them, even from one another.

Begum Baig explained what happened before the Basic Democracies election. Of 112 candidates running for office, 100 withdrew before the election took place. "They could have been bought off," she said, "but it is more likely they felt too inadequate to run. Education alone could remove fear," she concluded thoughtfully. "It can be done."

But what about the woman who left on a holiday and returned to find her house emptied of furniture? What about my own experience of taking fifteen pieces of mail to the post office, having them weighed for airmail, and finding that not one of the pieces was ever delivered? My fifty-rupee bill may have been too great a temptation; worth about ten dollars, it was two weeks' wages to the clerk at the stamp window. Dishonest? It depends on how you look at it. If there were hungry children at home, if appropriating the bill meant two handfuls of rice and an extra banana for everyone, then I am not sorry. I only regret the labor I expended. Next time, I decided, I would see that my letters were franked before I left the window.

Books are few in Pakistan. They are locked up in bookcases because they are so precious. A stolen book is missed. The solution is to have more books. There simply aren't enough of them to go around.

The stamp of dishonesty must be seen from both sides. An English friend employed a *durzay*, or tailor, with his sewing machine to sew curtains for her. The man arrived, set up his sewing machine on the floor, worked for two days, was paid, and disappeared, leaving the curtains unfinished. But he also left his machine. He returned in ten days and resumed his sewing.

Mr. Alcott lost his suitcase. Oh, it had been stolen! It turned up two weeks later, after having been transported by air all over the country. The luggage tag was lost, preventing identification, but Mr. Alcott's letter of inquiry helped to identify it. Mr. Turnbull's passport was swiped out of his inside coat pocket in a crowd. It turned up later, though his traveler's checks never did.

Let me see—am I talking about America or Pakistan? I have not forgotten how the not-so-smart pickpocket grabbed my purse in Paris and left my valuables. I cannot think that I condone it. Yet I was brought up in the Judaic Code of the Ten Commandments. What about these people who weren't? All of this cry, "Beware of pickpockets in the Far East!" had its amusing side for me.

• • •

I was moving from one room to another on the second floor, for rain had flooded the floor and soaked the bed and bedding. The servant was to transfer my clothes from the closet, and there was still much water on the floor. He reported that the job was done, and I duly paid him. We were both satisfied. Next day, I thought that my dresses were missing and asked what had happened. "Lady," he said, "we not steal your dresses. We do not want your dresses."

I discovered that the closet in my new room had two sections, each with a separate door—and there were the dresses I had missed. I was ashamed, for I thought I had offended the young man. He accepted my apology.

About two months later, I had another unfortunate, if not amusing, experience with the same young man. I had a large box of soap flakes. I used them very sparingly, for I had brought the box from home. The soap flakes disappeared. I searched everywhere to no avail—under the bath, under the basin, under the bed, on the window. The box was not to be found.

A week went by, and I had to do something, for soap flakes were hard to come by in a country where soap is very expensive. I took my courage in hand and asked if the servant had seen the box. "Lady," he said, "we do not steal soap. Here is your soap on window."

Up at the ceiling of the bathroom alcove was a tiny window. The soap was on the ledge.

"It's a good thing you are not blind," I said in Urdu. He got the point. We both laughed.

In my attempts to understand how the people lived, I found that I was all too ready to make snap judgments. I passed judgment from my own limited experience in situations that were altogether different. I found it hard to search for the extenuating circumstances in every case.

Kafur was a prepossessing lad of twenty-three. He was well kempt, wearing slacks, a white shirt, tie, and shoes instead of sandals. He was applying for a job in an office. He said he was the sole support of three sisters, that they all lived together in one room in a refugee hut. Prior to coming to Karachi, he had been a teacher. His English was very good. He said he had taught history and science. He said he had been taught in a Christian missionary school. He had no evidence in the form of credentials, but that was not unusual; moreover, credentials are not always necessary for teaching. He indicated, too, that his father was Muslim; as he and his sisters were Christians, they had to leave the home—not an unusual occurrence.

I accompanied some friends to investigate. The hut was one of the concrete constructions leading onto a compound. There was only one room, with one window. Two benches ran along the wall, and there was room for two cot beds, or *charpals*. The cots were covered with rags, which, by the smell, were anything but clean. Two tin trunks stood close by me. I sat in a broken-down chair by the edge of one cot. Some men's clothing hung on a nail at the back of the bed.

Two young men were sitting on the benches, obviously living there, too. They were silent. There was not the smallest piece of evidence that any sisters lived there. When asked about this, Kafur explained that his sisters had gone to the hospital because one of them had a sty on her eye.

There was no table, and there were no cooking utensils. Kafur said they ate out of their hands. Sometimes they went down the street to the man who cooked rice on a brazier. His brazier was set up on the footpath, as there was no sidewalk.

Kafur's story was obviously a fabrication, yet he stuck to it. He offered to bring the girls to us when they returned from the hospital. Probably he could have brought any girls, selecting three who did not understand English.

The compound was filthy, sticky underfoot with decayed garbage. There were no latrines or toilets. My friend kept pulling and pushing me, helping me to avoid the refuse underfoot. In the scorching heat, the stench was overpowering. Never deviating from his story, Kafur accompanied us to the car. He helped me in with the utmost courtesy and good manners.

How should we piece the story together? Probably the three young men took turns sleeping on the two charpals; the third would sleep on the bench. Were they all beggars when necessary? Was young Kafur nothing but an imposter, a professional mooch? Did he use his intelligence to this end? Was this his only way to survive? He was a personable fellow, Kafur, and he would have had no problem receiving used clothing from anyone he approached. Was he really a Christian, or did he use this device to appeal to Westerners?

Did Kafur really want to work? Was he immoral, amoral, or just a scoundrel? According to our standards, he seemed to be all three—but was he?

Our standards are based on an assumption of physical decency, freedom from hunger, the possibility of work, and a moral code. Was Kafur trying out his story on us to see how far he could go with it, or how much he could get out of us?

As a school counselor, I asked myself where I would start with a boy like Kafur. Could I ever get his point of view, step into his shoes? I felt sure that if his environment were changed, if he were held to a job and had the advice and counsel of a friend, Kafur could become a worthy citizen of his country. Or is this just the school ma'am speaking?

I was very much moved by Kafur's way of living. I felt no bitterness toward the boy; I was simply nonplussed. How long would Kafur go on in his way, in his dirty hut, in the dirty compound?

Intrigue, social order, dishonesty? Ignorance, poverty, and disease! What would they not do to anyone? Add to these three the differences in standards of education, culture, and morals. I still had far to go before understanding, and still further to go before I could condemn.

•　　　•　　　•

In the United States, I often felt that people avoided me because I was blind. I found the opposite to be true in Pakistan. I felt that people went out of their way to talk with me. I heard hellos, salaams, and memsabs from all sides. I learned that "okay" was meant as an attempt to greet me in my own language. There were always people around me at the dining table. The German waiter who had been in Karachi for eight years and was always on the point of returning to Switzerland but never did, the young cleaner from Mumbai who had been married at the age of twelve and had never lived with his wife, the fellow with the fifteen children—I recognized their voices.

Mr. Ziauddin introduced himself. He said he was a businessman and a Communist. This introduction caught me off guard. Was he joking? He reiterated his pride in being a Communist, and after gaining my composure, I became highly curious. I wanted him to continue.

His English was excellent. He came from the manufacturing center of Lyallpur. He knew that Communism was the hope of the world. He knew that the democracy of the United Kingdom and the United States was dead. It was, he knew, a complete failure in both countries. "The Americans and the British should take all of their money and get out of Pakistan immediately," he told me.

With a pseudo-concern, I commented that if that happened, chaos would result. "Yes," he said. "That would be the opportunity for the Communists to step in and take over."

He informed me that he was rich, that he earned five thousand rupees (one thousand dollars) a month.

"Well," I said, "in any man's country, a thousand dollars a month is a good salary." Would he expect to retain that money should his country turn to Communism?

He did not answer. He continued with his tirade that Pakistan will take money from the UK and the US as long as it is handed to them but had no respect for either country.

"So," I asked, "how do you account for the enthusiasm showered on President Eisenhower just last week?"

He had no answer for that question, either. I felt he was not listening to me but to himself. "The poor people will all benefit under Communism," he continued. "They will all get eighty rupees [sixteen dollars] a month."

"Oh," I said in surprise. "Eighty rupees will not keep a family in rice and *chapatis* for a month. It won't send the children to school." I ventured a little farther afield. "Are you Muslim?" I inquired.

"Of course," he said. "The essence of Communism is in Islam. In Islam, as in Communism, all men are equal," he argued.

"Then, would you still give the laborer eighty rupees and keep your five thousand rupees to yourself under Communism?"

He was disgusted with me. I asked the wrong questions. "Democracy is dead," he said, and rose abruptly.

I had not realized that we had an audience in the little dining room. Everyone was enjoying the fun. I did not see the passing show, and I was too intent on listening to my zealot to hear anything unusual.

I made a noble effort to make Braille notes on "My Impressions." I never had any impressions; the people I met were just people. I could have met them in any other country, in my own country. They were different in that each person is different. We had interests in common. Their questions came as fast as mine. They lived their way, and I found that I could live their way, too.

There was also a mutual trust. They did not look on me with suspicion, nor I on them. Yet I was a stranger in their country. I wondered if I, in my country, would have had the same degree of acceptance of a stranger as they had of me.

Was my way of living perhaps too comfortable, too affluent, such that I could not accept the stranger as warmly as I was accepted? I cannot say. I know I shortchange the blueprint of human relations—the Golden Rule.

NOTES

1. A Muslim leader of Bengali origin, Iskander Mirza (1898–1969) served as Pakistan's first president from 1956 to 1958. When Pakistan was swept by civil unrest, Mirza imposed martial law. He was driven from office and spent the rest of his life in exile.
2. The Basic Democracies program was instituted by Mohammad Ayub Khan (1907–1974), who served as Pakistan's president from 1958 to 1969. In an effort to control corruption among government officials and the police, Ayub Khan created local governments that were meant to respond to the will of the people.

CHAPTER 9
WHAT I THINK THEY BELIEVE

I never attended service in a mosque. Being a woman, I would not have been permitted in the main sanctuary; only men and boys kneel there. There is a gallery where women may assemble, but not being a Muslim, I could not go there.

Islam is paramount to the life of the Pakistanis. Their country took its birth from and owes its existence to Islam, as a religion different from Hinduism, from Buddhism, from Christianity. Muhammad Ali Jinnah and the Muslim League achieved their goal, partition from Hindu India.[1]

I listened to the lectures of Bishop Naz, who was born a Hindu and converted to Christianity. The bishop's devotion, dedication, and service testified to the Christian way of life he had adopted. I was greatly surprised to hear a talk of this nature in a Muslim country. Without exception, the audience was made up of Protestant Christians. My inquiries brought out the estimate that Pakistan's population was 4 percent Christian, including Protestants and Roman Catholics. There was also a very small percentage of Hindus and Buddhists, but there seemed to be no official figures.

I observed that many people I met in boarding houses, hotels, and banks bore Spanish or Portuguese names, though none of them spoke Spanish or Portuguese. They were Roman Catholics, I was told. They had immigrated from Mumbai and Goa, Portuguese territories on the west coast of India. As Christians, they could be trusted to handle money. I heard this statement often enough to realize that it was an accepted belief.

Nonetheless, Christians were feared and persecuted in Pakistan. A boy told me he ran away from a small private school because the principal was trying to make him become a Christian. A woman was killed mysteriously shortly after she professed Christianity. I heard many such stories. It appeared to me that there was fanaticism on both sides.

Had anyone asked me about the Christian doctrine, I would not have hesitated to tell them to read the New and Old Testaments. But no one ever encouraged me to read the Quran. Muslims do not read the Quran as Christians read the Bible. The Quran is written in Arabic, and it is memorized in the original language, whether or not it is understood. The magic of its sound, the beauty of its rhythm, the divinity of its words are sufficient reason for its total acceptance.

When I asked Muslims to tell me about their scripture, they seemed reluctant to discuss it. Often I heard prayers chanted before meetings, and I asked what was being said. No one seemed to know. On one occasion, I inquired at a teachers' meeting if we were praying for the welfare of the children or for guidance in our work. The answer was in the negative. The chanting was beautiful; the clear cadence of the rhythm was harmonious, lovely. We always stood as prayers were chanted. But I felt a vacuum, even as I admired the voice of the chanter and the ability to memorize at such length.

In Islam there is one god. Allah is His name; Mohammed is His prophet; Imam is the teacher, who from the Quran teaches brotherhood and the equality of men. Abraham, Isaac, Jacob, and Jesus all are prophets, but Mohammed is the Chosen One. The idea of the Christ and the crucifixion—the essence of the Christian doctrine—is not accepted in Islam. The Holy Writ is regarded as a miracle from the mouth of an illiterate man. Muslims do not analyze or criticize their holy book; they do not read it; they memorize from the teacher. God is all-powerful. He epitomizes love but not the love that is conveyed in the concept of "Love one another." God is not the god of the individual. His love is not love for the individual. Therefore, the Christian belief that "God so loved the world that He gave His only begotten Son, that whosoever believeth in Him should have everlasting life" is not acceptable to the Muslim. In other words, the Muslim denies this purpose in God and the promise of everlasting life through the crucifixion. The sonship of Christ is denied. The whole idea of an anthropomorphic God, essential in Judaism and Christianity, is not accepted, and the concept of "our Father" is refuted.

Over time, I gathered bits and pieces of information, much of it from conversations with Catholic Pakistanis and a little from lectures at local Protestant services and meetings. With my Muslim acquaintances, however, I felt that raising the subject of Islam showed discourtesy and bad taste. I certainly did not wish to offend. I missed the freedom of discussion and analysis and the open expression of opinion to which I was accustomed. Here again, my way was not the accepted way. I believe I was open-minded enough to know that it was not a matter of competition between two religions. Respect had to supersede curiosity. After all, I had no right to question another's beliefs.

I might have gathered valuable information from books and articles, but here I was at a further disadvantage. It was hard for me to find people who could read to me, and my time with these readers was very limited. I could get little or no satisfaction from the few chapters and scraps that were read to me. Perhaps Islam was so deeply engraved on the national character, so divinely inspired, as to be inwardly cherished, a feeling not to be committed to words.

One day I was touring a fine private college on the outskirts of Karachi with a group of visitors from the UK and the United States. The principal of the school was unusually dedicated, a scholar in every sense of the word. In his overview of the program, he mentioned that classes were given on character building and on the Holy Quran. When he invited questions, I asked why these two classes were separate. "Are they not one and the same?" I inquired, puzzled. "Does not one build character through the precept, teaching, and code of morality of the Quran?"

"No," the answer came, "they are two entirely different subjects. The class on the Holy Quran is for the memorization of the Holy Writ; the class on character building is discussion of behavior, of team spirit, of fair play, of character, of esprit de corps." I suppose I have been imbued with the Sunday-school method of Bible reading and its application, and I was eager to learn that there might be a different way of moral and spiritual instruction.

I could not stand by my policy of noninterference one day as I talked with a Muslim friend about the blind people of the country. My friend explained that, as the blind man was an individual, his needs were not the concern of his fellow Muslims. Islam concerns itself only with the community. Giving alms for the blind man's sustenance was expected, but the philosophy that ascribes dignity to the individual, even to a blind man, seemed to be absent. To the question, "Am I my brother's keeper?" the answer was "No."

The concept disturbed and baffled me. I tried as discreetly as I could to get other impressions. In the student, the teacher, and the businessman, I found a different point of view, one that savored of Western culture. The dignity of the individual did count, and the blind man had certain rights and privileges as a person. I believe this new generation is beginning to think for itself, to feel the inevitable impact of foreign culture and concepts. I am sure that this change, subtle though it is at the moment, is the outcome of reading, of discussions, of meeting with the West and Western ways. But with only 20 percent of the population literate, it will take time to affect any change.

When my attempts to understand the theology behind Islam failed, I returned to my Catholic Pakistani friend to talk about religion and the implications of beliefs on the social order. Josephine, a social worker, ascribed many of her country's ills to illiteracy and religion. Certain types of behavior were attributable to the dominant religious concept that the individual was actually not responsible for his behavior. The family was paramount, and its concerns did not extend into the larger social community. To this restricted community concern, Josephine also attributed the lack of self-discipline, taking the form of an unwillingness to assume responsibility, even on the job. There was always a higher-up official responsible for making decisions.

According to Josephine, religion has influenced dress, the enveloping of women in the burkha. It has shaped the attitude toward women as secondary members of society. Mendicancy is another expression, for almsgiving to the poor is a religious duty; raising the dignity of the beggar as a man would not be understood.

I was grateful for Josephine's viewpoint as we walked through the park on a Sunday afternoon. Children played and ran around on the grass, a commodity far too uncommon in Karachi. Josephine loved her country too much to desire anything less than the best for it. Her criticism was a challenge to herself to continue the noble work to which she had dedicated her life. Her parents were Christians, and she had been brought up in their faith. "We will never understand Islam," she said, "but we of other faiths can respect it, as we trust they will respect our religion."

Josephine corrected me when I referred to Islam as Mohammed-anism. The word Mohammedanism placed the stress on Mohammed. God, not Mohammed, is the center of Islam, the perfect peace of God. With that respect that Josephine inspired in me, I read *The Meaning of the Glorious Quran* by Mohammed Marmaduke Pickthall, published by the New American Library in 1953.[2] The Quran was translated by an Englishman who was a Muslim. But the Quran is not translatable. No language would fit the glorious Quran except its own. The hypnotic charm of the Arabic cannot be reproduced. I lost the charm of the revelation, even its significance, for in translation, the Holy Writ becomes a code. Feed and clothe the poor, it says, and speak kindly to them. To the male, it allocates the equivalent of the portion of two females. To the parents goes one-sixth of the income of the eldest son. There are no images, no pictures, for Allah is supreme. There is no intermediary, no Christ. To keep his accountability to Allah, one must turn to him five times daily, to ask for His guidance. Mohammed is not deified as Christians deify Jesus. Mohammed is dead, but Allah lives, is eternal. When Ramadan came, I marveled at the obedience, supplication, devotion, prostration, and fasting, day after day, without even a drop of water.

With all due respect, I give to my Pakistani friends their rights to their beliefs, and they reciprocate with me. As we work together, play together, and even pray together to the One God of all creation, let us hope that we come closer to the realization of absolute Truth, the universal brotherhood. From minaret and steeple comes the call to prayer. The code of Judaism and the code of Christianity both came before Islam. There seems to be nothing in one that is not in the others to some degree, though perhaps changed by culture, time, locality, and history. Out of the many faiths will come one Truth; the lives of all of us continue in its quest.

NOTES

1. Muhammad Ali Jinnah (1876–1948) is revered as the founder of Pakistan. He led the All-India Muslim League from 1913 until Pakistan became independent in 1947. His birthday, December 25, is celebrated in Pakistan as a national holiday. Pakistan broke away from India during the War of Partition to become a Muslim nation.

2. Muhammad Marmaduke Pickthall (1875–1936) was a British Islamic scholar. He spent much of his life in the Middle East and converted to Islam in 1914. Later he settled in India, where he worked closely with Mahatma Gandhi. In 1927, he published a series of lectures called *The Cultural Side of Islam*, and his translation of the Holy Quran was published in 1930.

CHAPTER 10
I LEARN TO BE SERVED

I was never sure of the word *behra*. Spelling it did not help, for, as is usually the case with Urdu, each person spelled it in a unique way. (Urdu is written phonetically from right to left on the page.) I was told to spell the word however I liked. I could choose between *bera*, *berra*, *beyra*, or *behra*.

The origin of the word, I found, was the British *bearer*. Since the days of the Raj, the servant was the purveyor, the bearer of food, of messages, of clothes. A behra had a job; he had lodging somewhere in the home or compound of his master. The position of behra was a coveted one, for it connoted security and prestige. Class among the behras is inevitable. The lucrative job of cook-behra paid one hundred rupees a month, or twenty of our dollars, while the lowest in the order, the sweeper, usually receives about thirty rupees, or six dollars a month. The cook-behra would not stoop to clean up the floor of the kitchen after his cooking; that was the work of the sweeper. The *mahli*, or gardener, did not pick up the twigs after clipping the hedge; the sweeper had to do that.

A Pakistani friend of mine who had lived in the United States thought he would try to change the pattern. After he had assisted the mahli with the pruning, he started to pick up the clippings. The mahli did likewise. The next day, however, the mahli was back to his old pattern. He actually hired the sweeper, paying twenty rupees for his services out of his own salary of eighty. Such is the price of prestige.

Some Americans who employed several cook-behras and sweepers in their quarters thought up an ingenious plan. One day a week they would do the cooking and ask the cook-behras to sit down at table and be served. The plan worked while it lasted, but on their own, the behras reverted to pattern.

•   •   •

In the boardinghouses and hostels where I lived, I came in contact with many behras. Whenever I found one who spoke English, I entered into conversation with him—all of them were men. Those who knew some English usually had worked for British masters in British homes. A few had attended missionary schools, but most were illiterate. The behras were tireless in their service and greetings. They always had something to tell me in their way and in their language.

The behras were not at all hesitant to talk about their work, their families or their pay. The average salary was thirty-five rupees, or seven dollars, a month. On this amount, the fellow would support his parents, his wife, and five to fifteen children.

"Do your children go to school?" I would ask.

"No, we have no money to send them to school."

"Would you like them to go?"

"Oh yes," the behra would say, "but food comes first." He took home some food from the hostel, and that helped.

"Wouldn't you earn more if you were a street cleaner or a plumber or a taxi driver?"

"No, behras are good positions; I like being a behra."

The sweeper who came to my room was wracked by a deep cough. His voice was low and husky. He had had the cough a long time, and asthma, too. He was a kindly old gentleman—old at thirty-five.

My sweeper had never had an examination for tuberculosis, but it is estimated that about 65 percent of the people in his stratum of society are tubercular. And he was cleaning my room! I should have been doing the work, and he should have been drinking milk! But milk wasn't the answer. Few of the cows were ever tested for tuberculosis, so the circle went on.

Shila, a Pakistani social worker, described the disfigurements caused by smallpox. Half of all Pakistanis had had the disease, and in some cases the scarring was quite severe. What these people have suffered—pain, hunger, chronic disease! The average life expectancy is forty-six years. These are the parents of the children. What chance do the children have?

As the behras slid along the corridors with their bare feet, it was difficult for me to hear them. They soon realized that I could not see them coming, and it was not unusual for me to hear out of the air alongside me the greeting "Memsab" or a rough but genuine "Good day," even at night. These behras in their lowly station, living on starvation pay, were courteous, kindly, and thoughtful.

•   •   •

One day, after my ground-floor room had been flooded with rain, a behra assisted me to move to the upper floor. It was necessary to walk around the outside of the building. The behra took me by the elbow to show me the way. It led over a cement alleyway, with a step in the most unexpected place. We were hurrying because of the rain, when all of a sudden I stumbled over the step, which I had trusted him to warn me about. I sprawled on the cement. That was the only time during my entire year of travels that I had a bad fall. My knuckles, my arm, and my elbow were bleeding. I called for *panni* (water), and the behra took me to the faucet. In the excitement, I found myself with my arm and hand in the running water—water so polluted I had vowed never to use it unless I made sure it was boiled first. My concern about the water on my open wounds was much greater than my worry over the wounds themselves. Furthermore, I was much more disturbed about the behra than I was about myself; I knew he felt responsible for the mishap, and he was terribly sorry.

I procured a box of Band-Aids from my suitcase. Before long, with the behra's help, I looked more like a veteran of Waterloo than a visitor. After that incident, the behra and I were friends. We often laughed over the twelve Band-Aids he plastered so carefully over my arm.

That same evening, I sat in the lobby waiting for a telephone call when I heard the behra say, "*Gi, Gi,* old lady waiting here in lobby." For that I never forgave him! I don't think he understood me when I told him it was an insult to call a woman an old lady. The episode deflated my ego.

One day an amusing incident in the dining room sent behras and visitors into fits of laughter. One behra wanted to be of special assistance to me. As I was leaving the room, he lifted my cane. Facing me and walking backward, he led me toward the door, telling me meanwhile to watch out for the little tables and chairs. The poor fellow was telling me, "Now, left, Memsab," when he meant right, and vice versa, until the two of us were doing a veritable cakewalk down the passageway between the tables. I struggled to smile politely. The other behras and the visitors could hardly contain themselves, until one behra shouted, "Leave Memsab, herself better alone." The overly officious behra beat a hasty retreat, and order was restored. These young folks had a real sense of humor—with all of their seven dollars a month.

The little *shokra*, or houseboy, who guarded the door could hail a rickshaw from the street on an instant's notice. I would hear his bare feet scoot down the steps, and back he came with his man. This seventeen-year-old shokra was the sole support of his parents and four brothers and sisters. His father was "old," probably about forty, and could not work. As the shokra was the oldest son, he had to assume responsibility for the family.

I met and made friends with the wife of a British official stationed on a cruiser at Karachi. Like me, Mrs. Parker was interested in the ordinary people without whom the country could not run. Her cook-behra was called "Misri"; to our ears it was "Misery." He was an excellent cook. He went out on his bicycle every morning to shop at the Express Market before the flies got to the meat and vegetables. One day someone collided with Misery and buckled the front wheel of his bicycle. Luckily he had only a few cuts and bruises, but his bicycle was in pieces. He had no insurance; that would have cost money. The bicycle could not be repaired, and there was no way to claim damages against the culprit who ran into him. Walking was out of the question because of distance.

As I talked with Misery and realized his plight, I thought of how many bicycles could have been bought for the price of the American tractor that lay discarded in the outskirts of Karachi. As I was informed, people did not have the know-how to repair it, and it had corroded with the intense heat and humidity. Not being an engineer, I could not verify the authenticity of this information. I only wished that some foreign aid money could seep down to the poor people who worked so hard to make a living and were thwarted in the attempt by so little.

Misery borrowed a bicycle temporarily until he could buy a secondhand one for himself. I admired him deeply. One day he was invited to bring his wife and family to the house. A charming, little person in her sari and four children with little, shining faces came to enjoy the party of Rich Tea Biscuits and Cadbury's chocolate in the dining room. They were spotlessly clean, dressed for the occasion, and happy to be honored. We were happy, too.

•   •   •

Behras love to carry around little plastic pockets with their *chitti*. Their chitti are letters of recommendation from previous employers. It used to be easy to sell chitti, so sometimes a photograph is attached, but that is a luxury. At least one can identify previous employers and get further information about a job applicant. One can check the dates and verify gaps that might be due to imprisonment, the cause of which might further reflect upon the character of the applicant. The behra question can be a very discomfiting one, particularly when the employer finds it necessary to leave the house frequently.

The behras were in the main illiterate; some of them spoke English, but few could read the language. They presented their chitti with pride, though they had no idea what was written upon their cherished papers. On one chit, proudly guarded by its owner, the following credential was written: "Mohammad very lazy, a very good cook, but doubtful with children." Another read, "Aslan does not take corrections well; otherwise, all right." Still another, "Somewhat listless, but honest." A chit that read "good with children" was much sought after. One employer was forthright in her appraisal: "Not worth a crumpet." The country of her origin was obvious.

My friend was leaving the boardinghouse and asked to have her suitcase brought down to the taxi. When she opened the door of her room, she was confronted by ten behras standing in line on the landing, each with a hand outstretched. Five rupees to each would have been ten dollars. Five rupees would have been a welcome windfall to add to their seven-dollar-a-month paycheck. It isn't right that families should have to exist on that pittance! Services, menial and at the same time necessary, call for more consideration. More vital still, human dignity demands more recognition. These, too, are our people.

Cook-behras, room-behras, sweepers, mahlis (garden hands), *ayas* (children's nurses), *chokidars* (watchmen), shokras (house boys), durzays (tailors), *dobhis* (washermen), chauffeurs, messengers—these are but a few of the servants who live at the very brink of poverty. There is no scarcity of manpower, but the power is abused. What could a little training in home mechanics, light engineering, road mending, building, agriculture, horticulture, poultry raising, or fruit farming do for this vast army of young men! Is it only an occidental idea to put tools into the hands of young men and train them to handle them? I think not. The young manhood of Pakistan seeks guidance from those who have pioneered and won. Given food, training, and tools, the working men of Pakistan have the potential to be productive and creative.

My friend Rachida, a teacher, thought it was a blessing that her small salary could not provide her with behras. She preferred to do her own housework, cooking, and laundry. "Between behras and government clerks, our young men have inherited a legacy of false standards," she commented. "Our country needs the fruits of their labors."

One day, Rachida and I sauntered through the Bori Bazaar, pausing to talk with the durzay who was deftly pleating a skirt for her. He folded perfectly symmetrical pleats, holding the material in place between his big toe and his second toe, and pulling it taut with his hands.

"I would like to see every boy learn a trade at school," Rachida told me. "It can be done, and it must be done, if we are to take our place among the free nations of the world."

Thousands of young men made a living for themselves and their families driving little bicycle rickshaws. These bicycle *wallas* were my friends, too. Taxi fares mounted up, and I depended on the bicycle rickshaws for my transportation. The walla pedaled his way over the long, hot, dusty streets while my guide, Mr. Salman, and I sat in the little seat behind. To listen to the wheezing of the walla as he puffed along the road was a source of deep anxiety to me. Mr. Salman said that many of these men had respiratory illnesses; some were tubercular, and others had heart trouble.

I suggested to Mr. Salman that we take a motor rickshaw. "And leave the bicycle walla and his family to starve?" he said. It was a comfort to know that in due time bicycle rickshaws would be taken off the streets, replaced by motor scooters and motor rickshaws. How hard the wallas worked, and how little they received for their efforts! Yet how courteous and kind they were in their long-suffering.

· · ·

Wherever I went, I was deeply suspicious of the water. I had heard stories of Pakistani students dipping their jugs into a scum-covered pond; they skimmed off the scum in their cups and drank the water down. Buffaloes frolicked in the ponds in the morning before they were taken out to work. The *dohbis* washed the family linen in the same dirty pools; children played and swam until the pools dried up, for they were only filled with stagnant rainwater.

Perhaps these young people had acquired a high degree of immunity that helped them withstand disease. Or perhaps the water accounted for the short lifespan. Typhus, typhoid, cholera, and malaria could not be avoided.

Yet when I spoke with a physician, the father of two of my Pakistani friends, I heard another side. Dr. Contractor—that was his Parsi name—said that we Americans and British are too fussy. "You take shots for everything," he argued, "and you have more diseases than we have." He said that Pakistani mothers gave their babies unboiled water right from birth.

"Doesn't that explain the infant mortality rate?" I asked. "It's tremendously high."

"No, it does not," he insisted. "The water helps immunize the babies." The same, he said, applied to milk. He ordered cow's milk for babies, despite the fact that the cows might have tuberculosis.

I still eschewed all milk and milk products, and preferring tea to water. I felt I could trust the tea; I knew that the water had been boiled.

I will always be grateful to the behras for their care in seeing that I received bottled water, though they must have considered me something of a crank for being so particular. There were times when tea would not quench my thirst; only water would do. There were times, too, when I did not have the leftover cup of tea with which I usually cleaned my teeth.

On one occasion, in spite of all my precautions, I became sick with bacillary dysentery. The room-behra brought me an enormous bucket, about two feet in diameter, with water covering the bottom. There I lay, sick unto death I was certain, with my head half on the pillow and half hanging over the bucket, for the dysentery was complicated with nausea and vomiting.

"Memsab, my people all ill like you," the behra told me calmly, quietly, stoically. "Just wait, Memsab, you get better. Just wait."

He was right. It took three and one-half weeks before I was able to straighten up my back. It took the skill of Dr. Mohammed Ali, his assurance and his understanding, together with his bottles of streptomycin tablets, kaolin, and doses of enterovioform.

"How did I get this dread disease, Doctor?" I asked when I began to think that maybe I wouldn't die yet. "I have controlled everything I eat; no milk, no butter, no ice cream, only boiled water."

"But," said Dr. Mohammad Ali, "you did not control our flies."

During my illness, the behra became my receptionist. Many, many friends came to see me. Friends from the Saint Andrew's Scottish Presbyterian Church brought arrowroot pudding. They brought a tidbit of Bournville chocolate that might or might not have come from the British naval ship in the harbor. They brought a bottle of Rose's lime juice, even better, that somehow found its way from Australia.

My Pakistani friends poured in, too. They kept the behra busy opening the door from the outside, for I could not get up. They brought their home-brewed remedy for dysentery, a kind of gelatin made from roots and herbs. And some of them brought flowers—a rare luxury!—daisies, asters, and even two tiny roses in tissue paper.

Asad, an engineering student who had a pen pal in California, dropped by and was very sorry to find me sick. His grandmother had died, he said. They had just buried her, wrapping her in a sheet, no casket. They perfumed the body, and lowering it into the grave the very day she died. Somehow or other, I was on the mend from then on.

Never was I so jubilant as on the first Sunday morning when I returned to church! Never did the squeaky, wheezy organ in the little church sound so musical, so melodious! I had lost nearly twenty pounds. I was limp and listless. I could not stand while the hymns were sung. My cheeks were wet, but I was not crying. I was supremely happy but infernally weak. I had had my bout with Karachi Tummy—KT, as it was familiarly called. Now I was thoroughly Pakistani.

From then on, I was death on flies. I swatted them wholesale—mercilessly, murderously. I could not see them, but I heard their buzzing. The zoom of a mosquito sent me flaying the air. Perhaps I never was lucky enough to kill a single one, but I had the dubious satisfaction of declaring war on them.

Kindly and helpful, the behras, the dohbis—a whole retinue of little men—are the backbone of a great nation. Given a little education, more food, a few tools, and some medication, together with sanitation, the fate of a nation and its people can be changed. This is not asking very much.

CHAPTER 11
THESE ARE MY FELLOW BLIND

About two months after I arrived in Karachi, I visited the home of a well-to-do Pakistani ship owner, Mr. Habib. He had traveled widely, was well educated, and had served as an officer in the Pakistani navy. We talked about the social conditions of blind people in his country—a situation over which, it seemed to me, he was not much disturbed. By this time, it was dawning on me that his attitude was not unusual among Pakistan's wealthy class.

As Mrs. Habib served tea, Mr. Habib remarked, "You have no reason to be blind. I know a man who can cure you."

"How can you be so certain?" I asked.

"Well," he said, "you still have eyes. I know a man who can give you back your sight."

I tried to equate Mr. Habib's superior intelligence in business matters with his belief in the work of fakirs. "Will you come with me?" he asked.

"Surely," I said. "I shall be happy to go with you, under one condition."

"What is that?"

"That I be allowed to bring with me one little blind boy or blind girl whom I have found begging on the streets," I said. "The doctor should work his miracle on the child first." When Mr. Habib seemed to hesitate, I pointed out the child had his life in front of him while mine was pretty nearly over.

Mr. Habib changed the subject immediately. Though I was the

guest of the Habib family many times after that, the topic of a cure for blindness never came up again. Obviously Mr. Habib scarcely saw the blind people who were his own countrymen. Yet, in his kindness and generosity of spirit, he wanted to help me, the visitor to his land. He saw my blindness, but the blind people of Pakistan were taken for granted.

Not even the girls from the college could take in the fact that I was blind. "Our blind people do not talk like you do," they said. I thought it would have been more accurate to say that they did not talk with their blind people as they talked with me.

A blind woman in Malir, whom I visited with my social worker guide, also had ideas about a cure. She told me that in "Amrikki" they can take out a blind person's eye and put in the eye of a dead person. With the new eye, the blind person will see again. It did not occur to her until after she had spoken that I was from America and that I was still blind.

Concluding that she referred to corneal transplant surgery, my guide and I tried to explain. I told her there were many blind persons in America, nearly four hundred thousand of them as far as we knew. She was not impressed. For her, "Amrikki" was the land of all answers. It was an open bank where everyone was rich. Somehow she could not connect me with the land of her imagination.

The woman was about forty and had become blind due to glaucoma. She had migrated from India after partition. Her husband deserted her because she was blind, but she received help from members of her family.

The family lived in one of the new concrete huts, a place with two rooms and running water. There were rows and rows of these huts, some with little gardens in front. The community had no sidewalks, and the dirt streets were full of ruts gouged by the rain—a trifle hazardous for my walking. There were millions of flies, and they could bite. It was hot—no shade, no breeze. Still, the quarters were so much improved over the ramshackle huts I had visited that I could say they were comfortable.

The blind woman's hospitality was touching. I sat on the edge of the bed and drank a most welcome cup of tea. Her daughter had spread a cloth over the little folding table.

She had two sons, fifteen and seventeen years old. They were both bright, studious boys, very devoted to their mother. She asked me to get scholarships for them to study in the United States. I pointed out that their own country needed them and that Pakistan offered scholarships, too. "No," she said, "they must go to Amrikki." "Amrikki" was the panacea.

Sad and discouraged, this woman reached out for a bit of happiness. I suggested that she learn to read Braille. Then she could gather a few of the blind children from her village and teach them to read and write. I would introduce her to a teacher I knew at the local school. But the idea did not appeal to her. She never went outside.

Hoping to pique her interest, I told her about my visit to the new refugee section called Saudiabib. It was a gift from the people of Saudi Arabia to the refugees of Pakistan. I told her about the children in the colony who greeted my guide and me as we stepped off the bus. They led the way along the path, saying, "Good morning, Memsab." They probably had learned these words in school, and those who did not go to school quickly picked them up, learning a few more greetings en route.

She listened politely but showed no spark of interest. She had much to give; she had an education herself. Yet because she was blind, and a blind woman at that, life had absolutely nothing left for her. She would only live through the achievements of her sons.

My guide and I took the local bus to Malir, for me always a new experience. I was beginning to understand some Urdu, but I did not have enough of the language to follow a conversation, which frustrated me very much. I wanted to know what the blind beggars were saying when they boarded the bus. One blind man sold medicine for the eyes—"Make eyes better!"—while others boarding the same bus begged for alms. A boy was selling sweetmeats with a brand name. He told us they were made in Pakistan; we should support national products.

We returned to Karachi by train, taking a third-class compartment. A blind beggar came to the door of the long coach with its wooden benches on which we were sitting and chanted his request for alms; then he proceeded to walk the length of the coach. I asked my guide to have him come and sit down with us, so that I could speak with him. My guide gave him a tip and, I presume, told him that I was a blind American lady.

The beggar sat beside me on the bench, and we talked about his "work." He made a living at least, he told my guide in Urdu, and did not mind begging. He had been blind for fifteen years and might have been about thirty years of age.

I asked him if he wanted to learn to read and write Braille, as he had read and written when he had his eyesight. The topic seemed to make him uneasy. His uneasiness increased as I asked if he knew about the training and rehabilitation center in Karachi. The program was small but good, and he might even learn his own trade again.

In a flash, he flew from my side. I heard his quick footsteps running along the coach and down the steps to the outside, for the train had stopped. He did not want to hear anything about work!

Our conversation had attracted the attention of a number of Pakistani men in the compartment. (There were never any Pakistani women in open coaches like these; they rode in the women's compartment.) Some of the men spoke English, and the conversation that followed was very revealing and informative. The blind, they said, did not want to work, and the sighted were at fault for allowing things to go that way. The blind should have been given the opportunity to do what they could to get on their own feet. The conversation then turned to my ideas about the education of blind children. Several men spoke to the point that blind children should receive education like other children. Eventually the discussion slipped into Urdu and became unintelligible to me. My guide grew so excited about the necessity of education that he even forgot to interpret.

As we left the compartment, several of the young men shook my hand and wished me a happy stay in their country. This gesture surprised me. In my experience, Muslims usually do not shake hands with Christians—and certainly not with strange women. I wonder if I would have had the same courtesy and presence of mind in a similar situation at home. I wondered, too, why they did not just pass me by as another foreigner. They were just naturally kind.

I was eager to gather statistics about blindness in Pakistan, but my search was a frustrating experience. I had trouble using the telephone, for when I asked for a name to be spelled, I was told to spell it as I chose. When three or four names were given and I asked which was the surname, no one seemed to know. Would Mr. Mohammed Suba Khan be listed under M, S, or K? No, his name would be listed under the department of government or the firm or the social agency for which he worked.

I tried to find studies or theses in the university libraries. I located two very fine studies of mendicancy and social welfare at the University of the Punjab. Even in these, however, I found more opinion than information, more estimate than fact.

A ten-year general census had been taken, but there had been no census of blind persons. Officials explained that people would not admit to having blind persons in their families, so a census of the blind population was impossible. Were there social welfare files? Yes, but they did not cover all the blind. The estimate remained at four hundred thousand out of a population of ninety million. That estimate is considered conservative.

One-third of Pakistan's blind population consists of children from one year to fifteen years old. Half of the nation's blind people are between the ages of one and twenty. Malnutrition, cataract, smallpox, diabetes, conjunctivitis, measles, trachoma, glaucoma, and inadequate hygiene—the causes of blindness run the whole gamut of the ophthalmologist's index. In one case, a whole orphanage was affected with the scourge of pink eye before the alarm was sounded. The ophthalmologists traced it to one cause, the use of a common towel among the children. The school was treated en masse, and within a comparatively short time, only a few stubborn cases persisted. Such is the power of treatment, when it can be procured.

According to the nation's ophthalmologists—there are very few of them, considering the prevalence of eye problems—65 to 70 percent of the blindness in the subcontinent is preventable. Due to the improved control of social diseases, infantile blindness from ophthalmia neonatorum (the result of maternal syphilis) is now relatively uncommon. The spread of trachoma can be arrested through prolonged prophylactic treatment, for the virus has now been isolated.

Glare is reported to induce the growth of cataract, a condition whose severity might be reduced by the use of sunglasses. An eye bank has been established for corneal transplants.

I was privileged to meet some of the ophthalmologists from a local medical school and eye clinic. They were dedicated, brilliant young men, most of them trained in the UK or the United States. They knew their country's needs, and they were there to help all they could. One young doctor, who had just returned from the United States, had paid close attention to the programs of eye inspection in the American schools. He brought the idea to a meeting in Karachi, and I was there to witness the way it caught hold. The young doctor was excited; he saw the way to start, and he had with him a handful of principals and teachers who were close to the problem. Sadly, Pakistan did not have enough doctors to carry out such a program, and as yet not enough leaders see its necessity. Yet when someone pointed out the lack of nurses to do the vision screenings that would precede the examinations, Dr. Engineer had a quick response. "The teachers can do it themselves if we show them how." His common sense, practicality, and enthusiasm are the stuff of which the new Pakistan is being made.

These doctors were well aware of the barriers inherent in public attitudes toward blind people. They knew the local beliefs in the work of fakirs and holy men. They knew the religious precept of zakat, the Muslim's duty to help support the unfortunate. They knew the prevalent belief that in the next world the blind will receive their sight. Alms will always be given; if one doesn't give alms, one becomes blind himself in the next world.

These young doctors know, too, that they are fighting a winning battle against ignorance and superstition, and they know that it will take time. Some people say it cannot be done, but actually it is happening already—slowly and surely.

Again and again, people told me that the destitution of the "blinds," as they were called, was due to things that could never change, such as religious beliefs or the social order. It was refreshing to talk with Setna, a Parsi medical student who refused to accept the social order as immutable. He thought that drastic measures should be taken. By law, the blind should be removed from the streets and put into workhouses to weave baskets and cane chairs.

"If the blind heard they would be forced to work," he told me, "half of them would disappear overnight." He thought it was too easy to blame religion for the mendicancy of the blind. "Mohammed the Prophet did not wish to perpetuate mendicancy. He advocated that people provide for themselves by their own work and efforts. He taught that mendicancy was due to neglect—neglect and laziness over a long, long period of time. It's time for something to be done."

"Where would you start?" I asked.

"With workshops," he said. "But that would cost money that the government does not have, or at least cannot spare because of more urgent needs. We're trying to deal with famine, floods, disease all over the country."

I suggested beginning the remedy at another point—with the education of the children, and he agreed. Then he told me an old story. One day Moses saw that the fat sheep were grazing on the land with the juiciest grass, while the lean sheep painfully ferreted out a few stray blades from under the rocks.

Moses asked the farmer for the reason behind this arrangement. "God gave me fat sheep and lean sheep," the farmer said. "I keep the fat sheep fat and the lean sheep lean, as God gave them to me."

"No," said Moses, "you are wrong. God gave you the lean sheep to see what you could do with them."

"My people are doing what the farmer did," Setna concluded. "They are not facing the problems of the blind population."

Setna saw the possibilities. He believed that strides could be made in the prevention of blindness and in the education of blind children. He thought that, with some help, blind children could enter the already existing schools.

Was Setna ahead of his time? I wondered. Was this the spirit of starry-eyed patriotism reaching for the clouds?

I felt I received my answer sometime later. I met with a group of some 150 young people at a local college. At their request, I gave a short address on education in general and on my own work. The professor who was my host thanked me cordially for my efforts. "But perhaps," he added politely, "the speaker does not know that the blind have a very honorable place in our society. Many of them are *hafizes* who have memorized the Holy Quran and repeat it at the religious services."

The students did not share his defense of the status quo. Their attitude was not one of acceptance but of analysis. Were blind persons actually working in industry in my country? If there were blind farmers, teachers, Dictaphone operators, and telephonists, how did they do their work? How did they find their way to the workplace? Did blind girls work, too? Were there actually blind lawyers? How did they study for their law degrees? When I said that I counted among my friends a blind chemist and a blind physicist, both with their doctorate degrees, the question came, "Do you think that can be possible here?"

I felt as comfortable with these young people as I would have felt with students in my own classes. They sensed my informality as the discussion continued. One fellow asked how I got to the college that afternoon. I am sure his question was prompted by the professor's remark that blind pupils should always go to schools for the blind, for they need guides to lead them around. I answered that I came in a rickshaw.

"Did you come alone?"

"Yes."

"Did you have a guide on your trip?"

"No."

"How do you tell the time?"

I explained that I had an alarm clock and a wristwatch. My watch they had to see, so I passed it around.

A young woman spoke up and said she thought sighted students would be mean to blind pupils. I said that blind pupils could be mean, too. That brought an explosion of laughter and the realization that I was emphasizing the normality of blind persons.

As their interest grew, the students grew braver with their questions. Did I live alone? Yes. Another barrage of questions along that line. How did I keep my notes? How did I keep track of my money?

The afternoon was a happy one indeed. The applause was long and enthusiastic. As they passed by me on their way out, the students shook hands warmly and invited me to return.

Young Pakistan was on the move. Perhaps these students would think about their blind people from a different viewpoint. They would, I felt, not be satisfied with the status of their blind citizens.

One student made a telling remark as he shook my hand. "You have convinced everybody except the professor."

I told him I did not come to convince, I came to share. Inwardly, though, I felt a distinct kinship with the professor. I belonged to an old school of die-hards just as he did. In my country, my ancestors had fought for public education. In my way, I, too, was defensive and protective of the status quo. I sympathized with the professor, but I was hopeful about the attitudes of the younger set. In the name of human relations and conservation of human resources, I believed that the new generation of Pakistanis would give more consideration to their nation's blind youth.

•   •   •

One day I received a telephone call from Mr. Shakat, the new secretary of an agency for the welfare of the blind. He wanted to talk with me about his ideas for a new program for blind persons. He had been in his position but a few months, and he had had no training for the work. His inexperience was not surprising, for training in the education and rehabilitation of the blind is discouragingly meager in Pakistan.

Mr. Shakat's idea was to collect all the blind people and place them in a colony by themselves where they could make baskets and other marketable commodities. They would never be hungry, for they would be paid for their work. They would never be idle, for he would see that they always got more baskets to make. He planned to approach the government with his idea. Between the voluntary agency and the government, he hoped the colony could be established.

"More segregation?" I asked. "Wouldn't you like to bring the blind into your society instead of keeping them out?"

He seemed confused and puzzled by my question, so I went on, "Don't you think they have rights as individual men and women, rights to their own choice of a living?'

"No," he said, "they are blind." He explained that the blind people of his country were not like the blind people in mine. I simply did not understand the social order of his country, he insisted, and it was probably true. He had no answer, however, when I approached the question from the humanitarian point of view. Were people to be treated as inferior in his country, so recently committed to a program of basic democracies?

I asked Mr. Shakat if the blind people in his colony would run their own financial affairs. "No," he said. "I will be their manager. They would have every security in the world."

"But," I said, "would you like to be held captive in such a situation?"

"No," he said, "but I am not blind."

"I would not like it either," I said, "and I am blind." I noted how easily the blind could be exploited under such a plan, though I gave him credit for not desiring so base a goal himself.

"Blind persons do not know what freedom is, for they are blind," he said. When I pointed out that the beggar in the street was free, in that at least he was not condemned to captivity in a colony, he still thought his plan was a sound one.

Perhaps I did not understand his point of view. I found it difficult to break down my own prejudice and seek to understand his perspective.

Mr. Shakat was indeed a challenging visitor. He did not give blind people credit for being able to think for themselves. He wanted to think for me as he wanted to think for all of the blind people of his country. I felt that he automatically ascribed the illiteracy, hopelessness, and helplessness of the blind to their blindness. As he saw it, their blindness was immutable, and so was their poverty. I tried to listen to his point of view, but still I came back to the human factor. Didn't blind people have rights as people? Didn't they have the right to self-determination, just as he had himself?

He would not change. He had accepted the blind in their present state of inferiority as part of his culture. It would take the younger generation to see differently and to effect change. To my relief, however, he did not go any further with his brainstorm.

My search for other points of view brought me one evening before a group of men and women of a certain philosophical cult. Everyone spoke English. The chairman opened the meeting with a story and a speech. He said he used to watch a blind girl sitting on the street corner, begging. For some time she disappeared from her usual place. Then one day he was surprised to see her walking on the arm of a blind man, and she was carrying a baby. "What do you think?" he asked me. "Do you think that blind people have the right to get married and have children? Isn't it bad for society? They will only perpetuate blindness!"

"Was the man her husband?" I asked.

"Yes," he admitted. "He was."

"Well," I said, "the girl got what every girl wants, a husband and a baby."

At this point, the reserve of the group broke down. As the meeting proceeded, we had the most open and animated discussion I experienced in Pakistan. My copanelist believed that blind people could not make decisions for themselves because of their blindness; therefore, sighted people had to make decisions for them. I am sure he was perfectly sincere in his convictions. The discussion turned on the idea of educating blind people before they attained this state of "mental blindness." At what point the "mental blindness" developed, I never found out.

Then a very common type of discussion followed. Someone told the group of a blind man whom he knew who could tell the height, width, and length of a room almost to the inch after he had little more than stepped inside the door. The same blind man could run his hand over the pages of his business ledger and tell all the figures written on the page, along with the computation. His conclusion was interesting. "What is the use of providing education for blind persons? Because they are blind, they already know more than we can teach them." The lack of logic in this argument was all too obvious. The blind could not learn because they were blind, and for the same reason, they knew more than any sighted person could teach them.

The question was posed as to whether the blind could speak for themselves and make themselves heard in society. The answer was a decisive NO! They were not competent to speak for themselves. I suggested that if the opportunity were given for some of the blind to be trained as leaders, they might be able to help themselves and others.

What lay behind the attitudes of the panel member and Mr.

Shakat? Was it a fear that the blind might gain strength or become independent? Was it a fear that, if the blind should gain equal status, the sighted people whose positions depended on caring for them would feel insecure? Was there a fear that the volunteer agencies, supported by donations, might not be necessary if blind persons were able to earn a living? I could not substantiate any of these conjectures.

My big day came when I was a guest at a meeting of business and professional women. They did the talking! "We have allowed our blind, and all our handicapped, for that matter, to remain neglected," said the speaker. "We have failed to provide education to make them worthy members of our society, alongside the rest of us. It is not too late to start." In the new era, it is inevitable that women will play a decisive role in the progress of their country.

• • •

My difficulties in finding readers and locating reference materials limited the studies I could make, particularly in the area of blind history and welfare. I had to depend on unauthenticated information and opinions and the experiences of others. I must say, however, that what I gleaned came from many sources. Many people shared with me what they knew or believed.

I had conflicting impressions of the blind *hafiz,* both in history and in current society. I had been told that if all the copies of the Holy Quran were destroyed, the Holy Writ would never be lost. It had been memorized in the original Arabic by many hafizes. For the most part, hafizes were blind men. By tradition they had been attached to the mosques, receiving one to three meals a day. Their function was to repeat the Holy Word from the original Arabic. To me, such memory seemed phenomenal, particularly when I learned that much of what was repeated was not understood.

I had the good fortune to meet a very unusual blind man who, besides being a businessman, a government advisor, and a man of letters, was a hafiz. Mr. Ali had been blinded at the age of three. He came from a wealthy family and was sent to school, where he learned Persian, Arabic, and English. In college, his studies were in the field of literature. He did not know Braille. He had taken no notes during his school and college careers and had depended entirely on his memory of what was read to him. He believed there were very few blind hafizes left who had memorized the entire Quran. A few, he said, had memorized parts. However, in recent years, sighted persons had taken over the work of the hafizes in the mosques. It was thought that blind persons could not perform satisfactorily the duties imposed upon them and could not perform the holy rites or say prayers correctly.

We talked about the education of blind children. Other things being equal, he said, the school for the blind is not a place where blind children can test themselves. They must match themselves against the rest of society.

Mr. Ali was extremely busy with his business concerns and other duties. At the time of our interview, he happened to be visiting in Karachi, and I was very fortunate to have even a brief talk with him. He did not seem concerned about the blind in his country. Like so many others, he accepted the situation as it was. Beggars were part of the community's responsibility, and they would be kept alive by the sighted. He accepted the same paternalistic point of view as the rest of his kinsmen. To him, the blind as individuals did not exist. He could not conceive of standards that placed the blind on a basis of equality with the sighted, even though he himself was blind. The blind should remain wards of society.

The concept of individual rights was new to Pakistan, and it did not fit into the cultural milieu. Could the Christian concepts of human dignity and equality be found in the Holy Quran? Are we asked only to throw alms to the suffering sick man on the roadside between Jerusalem and Jericho, and thus consider our duty done? After talking with the younger generation—with those who have read widely and have seen the image of the West, I feel that another interpretation of Muslim Holy Writ is evolving. Perhaps it is nearer the original intent of the Great Prophet. Perhaps it will slowly evolve as the way of life improves for all and new freedoms come to all people.

The blind themselves will give impetus to a new evaluation of their status. Change will not come from the older blind but from the vanguard of those who have had some schooling, be it ever so little. They have caught the image of the blind in other countries, working their way through to equality. They will probably organize to speak for themselves to their own government, asking for permission, opportunity, and preparation to serve. Half of the blind population of Pakistan are beggars. Yet there is emerging a thin corps of young blind people, some seizing the opportunity so recently set down by the Department of Health and Social Welfare—blindness shall not deter a person otherwise duly qualified from entering a school or institution of higher learning. In this corps, too, are those in the scattered rehabilitation centers, making baskets and straw sandals, who are asking to enter open industry. There are the few who are asking for training in agriculture like that provided to blind people in other emerging nations. There is the newly blinded doctor who wishes to continue her work in the social welfare office, advising mothers about their health and that of their children. There is the new interest in admitting girls to the schools for the blind. Girls, too, need to be educated.

Of course many educators say they have problems enough teaching their sighted children; they cannot attend to blind children as well. Yet there are also educators who say they would like to put half a dozen blind children with a helper or advisor into their schools and give them the opportunity to work beside their sighted sisters and brothers. Alongside the educator who says that if the school opens its doors to four blind children on Friday, on Monday morning forty will want to get in—alongside him is the educator who says, "The only answer to the future of our country lies in its people, so we are going to educate them."

Impetus will come from the men of the service clubs—the Lions, the Rotarians—who have already initiated programs of education. It will come from the teachers and social workers who participated in my study groups and those led by others on the education of blind children. It will come when the volunteer agency forgoes the temptations of corruption and indifferent administration and seeks to work with the government toward the education of thousands of blind children and adults. It will come when society matrons, seeking more kudos and newspaper publicity than their rivals, will be replaced by trained social workers and teachers who understand social problems and have a love of humanity.

It will come as the inevitable outcome of the work of such great men as Sir Henry Holland and his two sons.[1] Working as medical missionaries, they established hospitals in the Quetta and Shakutpur hills. They had to provide space for the whole family of each patient, including the family's goats and donkeys. They even had to find room for the family's bedding and cooking stoves. Only with his accustomed food, family, and friends around him would the patient stay in the hospital long enough to get well.

Will it ever be known how many blind people were restored to sight with Sir Henry's help? When sight was irretrievably lost, how many received his guidance and education? The male nurse with whom I spoke was the Braille teacher at the hospital, outside of his hospital duties. The seeds of progress already planted are germinating, and progress is on the march.

· · ·

It was not hard to make a survey of educational facilities for blind youth, for there was little to discover. An aggregate of eleven schools reported a total enrollment of 153 pupils, some of them as old as thirty-five. The schools might more appropriately be called institutions, for academic education was scant. Basketry and chair caning played major roles in the curriculum. Custodial care was paramount, as in the old asylums.

I gave a six-week seminar on the education of blind children in one of the local schools. Forty-three teachers and social workers enrolled, and all forty-three received certificates at the completion of the course. I had never worked with such a dedicated group! It was a joy to meet them for two hours every afternoon. As often as not, our time together expanded from two hours into four.

The class was a jolly bunch. Together we laughed about our transportation problems, the narrow, uncomfortable benches that served as our seats, the chalk that would not write, the oppressive heat. We even laughed over the demands of an exacting teacher. The outcome was the publication of a booklet called *New Horizon: Education of Blind Children.*

When discussion became heated, the group members reverted to their native Urdu, and I was lost. Fortunately, they always came to my rescue with an interpretation. We even learned to write Urdu Braille.

•　　•　　•

The social worker who acted as my guide minced no words in his descriptions of the beggars we met. Their open sores and maimed bodies could not but elicit pity. They were hungry and suffering. The woman who came to us as we waited for the bus had no hands, only stumps.

Reports pointed out that there were many types of beggars—fakirs, barren women, the crippled, and the blind. Forty-three percent of the beggar population are destitute refugees, living in squalor. The problem is increasing as more refugees swell the numbers of the homeless and jobless.

There is no easy solution. Family planning? Public works programs? Foreign aid? Land reform and development? Or all of these and more? Is the solution to leave half the problem, the older half, alone and concentrate on the nation's youth? Some hope seems alive in the latter possibility, but time must be found to accomplish it.

When I learned of an encampment that was home to a colony of blind people, I was eager to visit. My guide was somewhat hesitant to accompany me, but finally he agreed. The cluster of huts lay at the bottom of a ravine, its sides gouged into deep ruts by the rains. Nothing could grow there, for there was almost no topsoil. The thin layer of soil that survived was too saline for plant growth. It was very hot, and there was no shade. A sour smell hung in the air.

The first hut we approached was the home of the group's leader. He greeted us cordially and offered us the hospitality of his hut. I sat on the edge of the bed, and my guide sat on the bench with Mr. Ahmad. He was a tall man of about fifty who had a severe bronchial cough. The hut was made of bamboo with sacking on the sides. Wooden beams held up the hut; my hand grasped one as I was entering.

Mr. Ahmad was interested in my work and happy to talk. With my Urdu-speaking guide as interpreter, we communicated easily. Mr. Ahmad told us that about forty people lived in the encampment. It was their practice to appear near the mosques, at the railway station, and on the streets every Thursday. By tradition, Thursday was Beggar Day, Friday was Prayer Day, and Sunday was a general holiday.

Through his begging, Mr. Ahmad made a good living for himself and his whole family. He had never gone to school, but he was clearly intelligent. He did not want to beg, he explained, but he could do nothing else.

"Would you wish blind children to make their living this way?" I asked.

He sprang to his feet. "Nahin!" he cried. Not at all. "You are a schoolteacher," he pointed out. "You must see that blind children get an education so they do not have to beg."

He broke into a passionate speech in Urdu. The gist of his speech, which I got from my guide, was that the government should see that blind children get an education.

No visitor came to Mr. Ahmad's house without being served tea. As we drank our tea, people began to gather in the little hut. Before long, there were five or six, all asking questions of me through my guide. After tea, they entertained me by singing a song in my honor.

As I rose to take my leave, I shook off a cloud of ants and other insects. They seemed to be disturbing me and nobody else. The ants were huge and persistent, particularly when they got trapped inside my shoes. After a while, one gets accustomed to the nuisance, and the discomfort was lost in my enjoyment at the villagers' reception.

My host asked me to write and tell him about America. He requested that I send my letters to the headmaster of the school on the highroads at the top of the ravine. The headmaster would read and translate them.

On Mr. Ahmad's invitation, I made several more visits to the beggar encampment. Each time we spoke, he urged me to work for the education of blind children. He was a most gracious host, a gentleman, and a beggar by profession.

I also visited a leper colony, where many blind persons lived.

My guide was a social worker who visited frequently and knew the people well. She especially wanted me to meet a young man who was interested in the education of his son. He had contracted leprosy and been isolated for treatment in the colony with four hundred other patients. He was responding to treatment, he explained, and hoped that in a year or two he would be free to leave.

Down a path between the closely built huts was the clinic, staffed by Sisters of Mercy. The sisters were aided by some of the patients whose condition was not infectious. The facilities were totally inadequate to meet the needs of the patients. Many of them had lost their feet and hands to the disease and were covered with painful sores.

For most members of the colony, begging was the only livelihood. Some dragged themselves to beg outside the mosques or along the streets. Others were carried to their begging places on chairs or litters.

In an attempt to provide opportunities for some of the patients, a little hut beside the dispensary served as a shop. One could buy betel, paan, cookies, and tea.[2] One man repaired sandals; another was the sweeper; another was a carpenter.

When a baby was born, it was separated from its parents and removed immediately from the colony. In this way there was little chance that the child would contract the disease.

The situation would have been overwhelming had I not attended a conference on leprosy, today known as Hansen's disease, given by physicians, nurses, and social workers. I learned that the outlook is not hopeless. Progress is being made in treatment. Prevention is a positive part of the program. The person with leprosy is a person in need, and it is society's responsibility to help him.

These visits were a revelation to me. They helped remove me far from the smugness, complacency, and well-being of my own society. These people were my fellow blind.

NOTES

1. Sir Henry Holland (1875–1965) worked for more than fifty years as a medical missionary in Quetta, Balochistan, in the mountainous country along the Pakistan-India border. He became an expert in performing cataract surgery, and some estimates claim that he restored sight to as many as one hundred thousand people.

2. Betel is the leaf of a vine that is cultivated in South Asia. The leaf is commonly chewed as a stimulant. To make betel quid, or paan, for chewing, the leaf is rolled to form a pouch and stuffed with lime, spices, and sometimes tobacco. A key ingredient in the mixture is areca nut (often called betel nut), the dried fruit of the areca palm.

CHAPTER 12
JUST PEOPLE

Had I expected the people of Pakistan to be different from me, just because they were born in another country, spoke a different language, and had a different complexion? In truth, I believe I had. I was the product of my own background. Self-concern was very much with me; my shell was so thick that I found it hard to put myself in the place of others. The Pakistanis were different because I made them different.

I began by feeling superior; looking back, I cannot explain why. As the weeks went by, as I came to talk, walk, play, laugh, eat, and work with many, many Pakistanis, I felt a change come over me. I began to feel myself one of them. They accepted me, even before I awakened to what was happening. If a measure of education is the ability to meet life—and people—at all points, they were better educated than I was. Their welcome was open, warm, kindly, and quiet. They told me how happy they were that I had come to their country. They invited me to visit their homes, and they came often to fetch me. They introduced me to all the family, young and old.

If we did not know one another's language, we expressed ourselves through our gestures. The little girl of three learned quickly to say "Hello, Anti," and the grandfather greet me with his gracious *"Salaam Aleikum."* The beggar and the executive met me with the same courtesy and hospitality. Their kindness pierced the shell of my ignorance and showed me a way to know myself better.

One evening after a meeting, Mr. Habib and his two daughters accompanied me to my room at the hostel. Inviting them in, I hastened to offer them each a seat. As there were only two chairs, I scurried into the bathroom to bring a folding stool.

"Oh," said Mr. Habib, "I must have light, even though you don't need any." I had omitted to snap on the light as we entered the room. We all laughed and turned the joke to the possibilities of my saving on the light bill. Later, the girls shrieked with laughter as I recounted the sad story of my trip to church dressed in all my Sunday elegance—hat, gloves, high-heeled shoes—and still wearing a kitchen apron. Their kindness never abated. I drank tea and ate salted biscuits ad infinitum in their company.

One night, Dr. Jafr, a woman physician, Maryan and Anna, two nurses, and I were the dinner guests of a couple named Mr. and Mrs. Siddiqi. Maryan was scheduled to leave in two months for the States, where she would take a nursing course. Her husband was in the navy. She would be gone one year.

Everyone at the gathering spoke fluent English with the exception of our hostess, Mrs. Siddiqi. She took part in the conversation with the three guests as interpreters. The talk never lagged. Maryan was eager to know what to expect in her new venture. Dr. Jafr knew both cultures, and she was forthright in her evaluation of each of them.

"Do not be surprised," she warned, "at the informality of the Americans. They mean well, and they are kind, but they can seem rude. Wear western sport clothes—blouses, skirts, and sweaters; you will be less of a showpiece, and you will learn more. Wear saris on occasion. Study hard and study consistently. The American student studies in spurts—when examinations come up."

She told Maryan not to take too much in the way of clothes. "Watch for the basement sales. Buy your winter coat, shoes, and wool dresses in the basement."

The institutions of basement shopping and the winter clearance sale were unknown to Maryan, as were department stores and bargain counters. I was impressed by Dr. Jafr's sensitivity to our mode of life. Maryan was accustomed to bazaars and streets of cramped, stuffy little shops.

Dr. Jafr turned to me. "You are eating your meat rice with a fork and spoon. We are using our fingers. We use only the left hand and the tips of the fingers. We have cloth napkins; you have paper napkins, but paper is expensive and scarce here."

I had surmised that they were not using table cutlery, for I had not heard the clink of silverware at any moment in the meal. I also surmised that there was no hand washing before dinner, for I did not notice any of the guests leave the room. Having touched the floor of the rickshaw and having hung onto the side bars en route to the party, I felt I could not eat with my hands. Then I realized that I was handling my bread with my fingers, so what was the difference? Dr. Jafr had a keen sense of public and personal hygiene, but she saw the extremes in both cultures. She let common sense be her guide.

Mrs. Siddiqi's two daughters assisted their mother in serving and listened to our lively exchanges. Though they understood English from their school studies, they remained silent. My efforts to draw them into the conversation were fruitless. The daughters attended high school and junior college respectively. They were bright, attractive girls, dressed in their *shalwar kameez*.[1]

We women ate in the kitchen, for the male section of the guest list was in the dining room. Mr. Siddiqi had two business guests, whom we met in the front porch for a brief conversation prior to the dinner. Then the party separated. Mr. Siddiqi's son served the male element, receiving the dishes in the kitchen from the hands of his mother. The males and females never got together during the evening. But as it was, the party was perfectly delightful.

•   •   •

I wanted to buy a hat! My all-purpose beige, velour felt hat was hot and heavy. My leather shoes were hot and heavy, too. Mr. and Mrs. Kahn accompanied me on a shopping tour. Mr. Kahn walked slightly ahead. I hooked my arm in Mrs. Kahn's—or as much of her arm as I could grasp through the obstruction of the burkha, which enclosed her from head to foot. Mrs. Kahn showed me the peepholes through which she could see where she was going.

Mr. Kahn was the shopping tour manager. For shoes, he thought we should go to one special shop. Sandals were to be the choice for a light shoe. Everybody wore sandals, and I could get them with soles of leather, jute, straw, or even crepe. To me, sandals are a headache! Stones work their way under the soles of my feet and throw me off balance. With no real protection, I step into water, dust, and dirt. I wanted shoes with toes, heels, and sides. Not one of those features was to be found. People did not wear that sort of shoe.

A happy thought struck the willing shop attendant. "Would she like tennis shoes?" he inquired of Mr. Kahn, who interpreted the question in English.

We settled for navy-blue tennis shoes, which I wore incessantly for the next six months. Eventually I had to jettison them to make room for my accumulating papers, notes, and reports.

The next problem was the hat. There were no hat shops. People did not wear hats. Saris and the burkha took the place of hats for the Pakistani ladies, and the foreigners all seemed to have brought their hats with them. I cannot go even to the mailbox without a hat, so I had to have one.

Mr. Kahn's quick eye spotted a possibility. He led the way to a Chinese stall where straw and bamboo coolie hats were made. He showed me a jute creation like a flattened-out Breton. It had a huge, flat crown and narrow brim. It would do nothing to keep my hair in place. It would not even stay on my head.

Then came a dazzling number that would have dwarfed the imagination of a Hedda Hopper. It was bright rose-pink with rose-pink strings, Mr. Kahn explained. The hat was engineered by taking two pieces of straw matting about twelve inches square and binding two sides together. The result was a bonnet with a pixie-like tip. The hat was certainly airy and light, though somewhat unstable and scratchy. It had no lining, of course, but it would serve my purpose nicely. The Kahns thought we had made a good selection.

I often wondered what I looked like, perched up in a rickshaw, in my washable blue nylon stroller dress and navy tennis shoes, carrying my spacious, black plastic handbag, my white cane, my ever-present Urdu books (enormous things, because they were in Braille), and topped by my rose-pink coolie creation. No one seemed to mind the heterogeneity of the outfit, so I didn't either.

The Kahns told me it was *comme il faut* to have afternoon tea at Shesan's on Victoria Road. My imagination went awry. I thought they were saying "Chezanne's," and I pictured an ultra Parisian oasis in the east. Shesan's was a delightful air-conditioned tea shop, as Pakistani as it could be, and I enjoyed the tea to the last drop. Clean though it seemed to be, I still refrained from ordering ice cream. A radio supplied the atmosphere, playing old-time jazz—old-time American jazz, no less!

At Shesan's, my Urdu-speaking friends taught me to order my own tea and biscuits. "*Meherbani, bugar chini, bugar duh!*" ("Without sugar and milk, please!") I learned to add, "*Putla chai*" ("Weak tea"), when the first cup of the brew bore too close a resemblance to bitter bark.

●   ●   ●

Over many cups of tea during my stay, I learned from the people who were Pakistan. I learned from them the meaning of the name of their country—the country of peace, fertility, and good. I learned of their pride in their new capital, Islamabad, seat of Islam, to the far north in the Potwar region beyond Rawalpindi. I listened to what they told me of their national problems—the need for family planning, the struggle for the basic democracies, the question of purdah. I realized the anxieties, frustrations, and aspirations of the people I met.

From time to time, I had to dispel the notion that all of the solutions to the world's ills could be found in the United States. They wanted all of the things we took for granted in my country—the abundance of food, medicine, schools, and books. How could they get them? Like them, I wanted to see less poverty throughout the land. Like them, I was particularly concerned with Pakistan's congested East Wing, where opportunities were fewer, the rains heavier, and the floods more devastating.

Maria, a social worker friend, put it squarely on the line when she said, "You people in the United States have no idea of the conditions here." She had done postgraduate social welfare training in the United States. She had returned to the poverty of the huts, the disease, hunger, lack of sanitation, and defeatism of her country. The information she culled from her American lectures and books was of little avail. She carried on with courage, dedication, and a love for her people. She acquired boxes of medicines through UNICEF and collected food packages from wherever she could. Her ceaseless quest for the things her families needed was of the utmost avail.

Maria is one of the people who make a nation great. She taught me how a nation is made. But as I saw it, there were far too few Marias and far too many Sahibs.

It took three men to deliver a parcel from the United States containing two pairs of nylon hose. Two officials came from the post office, and the third man was an official from the boardinghouse. The official from the boardinghouse had to identify me, even though I held out my passport for them to view. One post office official had to witness my signature, and the other had to supervise the procedure. I had to sign sheaves of papers. I could have been signing my own death warrant, for, with their meager English, they could not even read me the titles of the documents. I had to pay ten rupees customs duty, and that meant yet another sheaf of documents and signatures.

But alas! One document was missing! They would have to take the package back to the post office and return the following day, repeating the whole procedure, before I received my two pairs of stockings.

"Is all this precaution taken because I am blind?" I ventured.

"Oh, no," they assured me. "This is how it is done. This is official business." It required the services of three men.

Over time, I grew accustomed to this officialdom of secretaries and filing cabinets. These officials, too, were just people, but there were crowds of them, eternally checking and filing. I was never in a hurry, nor were they. But I could not help thinking that if a few women were in those administrative jobs, matters would be quickly expedited.

Like everybody else, I found myself buying carbon paper and onionskin. I located a mimeograph machine and made copies of letters. I began to enjoy it. There was nothing else to do.

On another occasion, a fellow of about eighteen, judging by his voice, came to deliver a chit from the travel agency. The day was unusually hot, humid, and smelly, and the young man asked in Urdu for *panni*, a drink of water. I invited him in and asked him to sit down.

On my way to get the water, I almost stumbled over the enormous briefcase he placed by the side of the chair.

"Why do you carry such a big briefcase?" I asked.

He spoke enough English to answer my question. "Important men carry briefcase," he said proudly. The size of his briefcase was a mark of distinction for any executive, and there was no doubt this young man took his work seriously.

"What work do you do?" I asked.

"Just carry chitti to people."

"Do you type in your office?"

"No."

"Can you write or read?"

"No."

"How did you know which paper to give me?"

He showed me the various empty pockets in his briefcase. He knew where he put each paper, and he was never wrong.

He told me he was very happy to greet me, for that was the Christian thing to do. He had attended a missionary school for a few months, and that had been the extent of his education. I thought of all the eighteen-year-olds I had taught over the past thirty years and the opportunities they had had.

Suddenly the young man announced, "I like to go to your bathroom. I want to piss." His directness threw me completely off balance. For thirty years, I had heard, "Please may I leave the room?"

He must have thought I did not understand him, for he repeated, "You know? I want to piss?"

"Of course," I said, regaining my composure. I showed him the door to the bathroom.

As he left, he told me not to tell his sahib that he had been in my room. I surmised that his instructions were to deliver the paper at the door.

I admired the young man's curiosity, his sincerity, and his straight-forward approach. He left carrying his formidable portmanteau, with the warmest exchange of *choda hafiz* and good-bye. It was not until after he left that I wondered if he knew that I could not see. We were both so engrossed in his business, official and personal, that my blindness never became a topic.

•　　　•　　　•

After five o'clock, there were few women on the streets. Sometimes I asked my guide to stop and count. Two women to fifty men was a common ratio. One evening I sat on the balcony of the embassy with a group of Pakistanis and Americans, awaiting the arrival of the parade in honor of President Eisenhower's historic visit. "Count the people on the opposite side of the street," I said. The consensus was five hundred. "Now count the women," I said. Altogether there were five.

As we worked our way through the slowly dispersing throng after the parade, I reflected that the male-dominated crowd would soon belong to history. Large crowds of boys and girls had been conducted from the schools to take their places in special areas along the streets. These girls, now exposed to public appearance, would never be satisfied to live behind windows and trellises or to go out wrapped in burkhas.

Among my Pakistani friends, I counted many lovely Parsi women. Mrs. Calcutawalla had a sewing party in her garden, a patch of stubby trees with no flowers at all. She asked me to speak to the group as the women carried on their work. They were sewing garments for the hospitals and undergarments for children. Parsi tradition and philosophy are akin to those of the Mormons. No Parsi can ever go hungry or be in want, for Parsi brothers will come to his aid. Mrs. Calcutawalla told me about her sewing circle and its many charitable activities.

Mrs. Calcutawalla was eager for me to meet Mrs. Setka, a member of the sewing group whose little girl was blind. The child remained at home, as there were no educational facilities for her. Mrs. Setka believed that a school for the blind was merely a charity home for waifs. Her family could take care of their own children, but how was a blind child to receive an education? "We do not know," said Mrs. Setka. "We just want to know what to do!"

Another group member, Mrs. Minwalla, introduced me to her little nephew and niece, who had just arrived from school. Their English was good, they were learning their multiplication tables, and they were also studying geography.

Mrs. Calcutawalla served tea to all of us. She was assisted by her *aya*, who came from Mumbai and looked after her children. The aya lived in the house with her husband and her nine children! No, the aya's children did not go to school, for there was no money to pay for their education.

My afternoon with the group became more interesting as the hours went by. Each of the women had her own charm, her own story, and her own graciousness. I believe I met all twenty of them individually.

About three weeks after the party, a package was delivered to my room. It contained a hand-sewn shoulder scarf with tiny discs of mica buttonhole-stitched around on the cloth and satin-stitched flowers, soft to the touch, in an all-over pattern. The colors were red and green. This was their way of saying thank you for talking over their problems with them. My efforts were indeed overpaid, for the joy of being with them and talking with them was ample return. I was in their debt.

In the main, Parsi women are socially emancipated compared with their Muslim sister-citizens. Their dress is distinctive; they do not wear the burkha. The sari is draped in a slightly different manner, with one end used as a scarf in situations when etiquette demands that the head be covered. All of my Parsi friends spoke English, indicating that they had attended English-speaking schools. I found, too, that they were active in social welfare groups, giving freely of their services. They are willing to work for the betterment of their social order and not only for the kudos attached. But there are all too few of them.

I also met many members of the All Pakistan Women's Association, a group dedicated to social betterment, with education high on its list of objectives. Among its other goals is the promotion of home industries and occupations for needy women. In the company of these women, I felt the exaltation of belonging to a new nation and having a part in building it up. Alert, active, competent, and understanding, the women of the association pushed forward against great odds. They could not help but win out.

Amazons they were not. Dressed in their delicate textured saris or their *shalwar kameez*, with a long scarf, or *dupatta*, around the shoulders, they appeared to me like a group of dainty Dresden china dolls. They were small of build, with tiny hands, and short of stature, so that few reached even to my medium height. When I linked arms with them, they seemed almost frail in comparison with my 115 pounds. These women generally did not observe purdah. They appeared at public meetings and on the street, in full view of men, without covering their faces.

I learned some of the etiquette of purdah from my friend Mrs. Siddiqi. One day I had tea with Mrs. Banot. Mrs. Siddiqi, who lived across the compound, was invited to join us. Mr. Siddiqi came to the tea, for Mr. Banot was also present, along with several other friends. Mrs. Siddiqi did not appear until Mr. Banot had left and we women were alone. Tea was over, but she was served when she appeared. There was no breach of etiquette in her late arrival. I wondered if she had seen Mr. Banot leave from her window.

On another occasion, Mrs. Siddiqi remained in the car outside rather than coming inside my room; another Pakistani woman and her husband were visiting me. Mr. Siddiqi came in alone, and she sat in the car outside. My first impulse was to go out and ask her to come in. It took me a little time to grasp the social rules of the situation. In her own home, one could scarcely meet a more gracious hostess or a more kindly soul than Mrs. Siddiqi. I tried to restrain myself from making a snap judgment about Pakistani attitudes toward women, for it was entirely new to me.

NOTE

1. The shalwar kameez is a traditional form of dress worn by men and women in Central Asia and the subcontinent. It is considered the national costume of Pakistan. The shalwar is a loose pair of trousers secured at the waist by a drawstring. The kameez is a long shirt with the sides split below the waist. The shalwar kameez can be simple and practical or highly ornate with elaborate embroidery.

Isabelle Grant conferring with blind students and
their principal in a sighted school regarding use of the
long white cane in Lahore, Pakistan, circa 1964.

Isabelle Grant greets a blind student at the Surabaya School
for the Blind in Surabaya, Indonesia, circa 1968.

Isabelle Grant poses in a group picture at the home of Mr. and Mrs. Soediarto in Semarang, Central Java, Indonesia, in May of 1968.

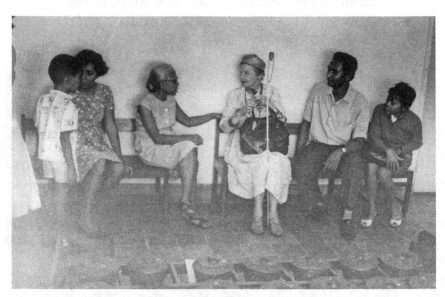

Isabelle Grant converses with Dr. Surti, Zaki Mubarak, and Miss Ariani Soekanwo in the music room at the Surabaya School for the Blind in Surabaya, Eastern Java, Indonesia, circa 1968. A set of gongs used in creating Javanese gamelan music is seen in the foreground.

Isabelle Grant sits with her grandchildren Alan,
Eric, and Lee on the couch in March of 1965.

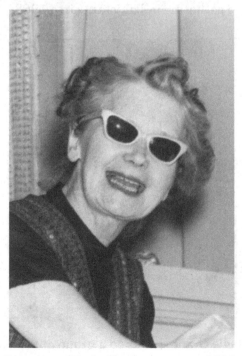

Portrait of Isabelle Grant, circa 1965.

Isabelle Grant stands at the podium to address
a gathering in Pakistan, circa 1968.

Isabelle Grant speaks to a group at a Rotary
Club meeting on April 12, 1968.

Isabelle Grant wraps packages of Braille books for shipment to blind people overseas, circa 1965. (Photo courtesy of Jack Davis, Los Angeles, CA)

Isabelle Grant walks with her trusty long white cane, Oscar, at an event in Pakistan, circa 1968.

Isabelle Grant is introduced to Liz Douglas's
pet monkey in Africa, March 1968.

CHAPTER 13
"TO SEE OORSELS AS ITHERS SEE US"

E very now and again, a teacher has to stand aside and look at herself. Is she really saying what she means to say? Are the students getting what she thinks they are getting, what she means them to understand? Are the pupils listening but not hearing? Are her attempts to make "desirable changes" in the pupils just wishful thinking on her part, and will the students go on thinking their own thoughts regardless?

Often I stopped to wonder whether I was conveying anything from my background and experience to my friends in this new country. With their preconceived ideas about my background and my culture, were they politely pretending to understand? The balance was in their favor; I understood them less well than they understood me. I felt that imbalance in their kindness, their acceptance of me, and their countless courtesies. I was hampered by my lack of knowledge of their language. They could speak to me in my tongue, but then they would turn and speak with their own people in their way. My inadequacy lay heavily upon me.

During the six-week course I taught on the education of blind children, a humorous incident demonstrated how easily misunderstandings can occur. Along with the teachers and social workers who enrolled in the course were five young blind men, employees of a sheltered workshop. I had been talking about the normality of blind persons, trying to choose simple words and to minimize my ever-present Scottish burr. The following day, when we resumed our discussions, I found an unsigned Braille note lying on my desk. "Dear Teacher," it read, "You said blind people have no sex sense. I am blind man. I have plenty sex."

I puzzled over the note all day. This young man's interpretation of what I had said ran completely counter to what I meant to say. Then, suddenly, I understood the confusion. I had said, "Blind persons have no sixth sense."

When our discussions grew animated, the students often reverted to their native Urdu, and I was lost. As the talk abated, one or two of the students would explain in English the diluted content of their argument. I was grateful for the explanation but jealous, too. I wanted to be with them in the heat of the discussion, at least as a competent listener.

What do we foreigners look like to the Pakistanis? Some believe that money grows on trees in "Amrikki," for they see Americans who turn a two-year foreign assignment into a two-year "Lost Weekend." They seem to have no other responsibilities than to attend dances, clubs, and gymkhanas, where imported liquor flows in reckless abundance. Some Pakistanis see our embassies and commissions as diplomatic enclaves, with their separate commissaries, schools, housing, and social life. They know that the women start their bridge parties by eight in the morning. Some Pakistanis tell us we are smug and complacent. We take our freedom and our comfortable way of life for granted. Some think we are empire builders who do not know how to build a nation, and they are not afraid to tell us so.

Some Pakistanis think we do not see the conditions under which they live—the rough wooden platform off the ground, its burlap walls supported by bamboo shafts—a dwelling place that cannot be a home. We are not aware of the barnyard stench that envelops their encampments at all times since there are no sewage facilities. How can the foreigner see these things from the shelter of his enclave? "Do you realize," a student asked me, "that the food they eat at the embassies—the fresh meats, turkeys, flour—are flown in from a place called Kansas?"

Miss Zamir and I had much in common, as both of us were teachers. Many an afternoon over a pot of tea we challenged each other with our personal interpretations of the ideologies of our separate countries. One day the topic was food. "You know, Doctor Mrs.," Miss Zamir said as she lit another cigarette, "your people burn their potatoes while our people go hungry." Her statement was a fact, and that fact was known to the starving people of her country.

On another occasion, a well-dressed foreign lady visited Miss Zamir's classroom and addressed the girls. After a brief discussion of "things abroad," she asked the girls if there was any way she could be of assistance to them. One of the girls glanced through the window at the waiting Cadillac and patient chauffeur. "You would not understand," she said kindly.

Even as we talked about these sad discrepancies, I never felt any bitterness or cynicism from the Pakistanis. For my part, I did not respond with bitterness over their stinging accusations. It was good to hear them, for understanding and acceptance are only possible with frankness. At times I even envied their positive outlook, their determination to raise their nation's standard of living, a goal to which they were dedicated, individually and collectively.

•   •   •

Foreigners do not understand the Pakistanis, and it is hard for the Pakistanis to know and understand foreigners. Some of the foreigners I met were very fearful. They had no experience with people other than their fellow Americans. Never before having left the security of their hometowns, they reestablished familiar patterns as closely as possible. Pulling their skirts out of the dirt, they barred themselves and their children behind the gates of their air-conditioned compounds. As Tom, an officer in the foreign service, remarked, "The American private here lives better than the Pakistani general."

Even under the most ideal conditions, however, life in Pakistan can be very frustrating for the foreign visitor. After repeated demonstrations to the contrary, the servant insists on whipping the dust into the air with his duster until the whole household starts on a sneezing rampage. The conscientious American airman shows the Pakistani servicemen a simple filing system to save time and effort in the workshop; he returns three weeks later to find the old order restored and everyone happy with the status quo. The American industrial arts teacher instructs a class of boys on more practical methods, while the Pakistani teacher, looking on, insists that the new methods cannot succeed. The foreign technician looks with dismay at a rusted piece of machinery, knowing that timely repair could have rescued it for use.

The foreigner thinks that time-saving and labor-saving are worthy goals. However, the worthiness of these goals is not so obvious to the Pakistani. The foreigner expects a worker to take pride in the finished product. For the Pakistani, it sometimes seems, simply building the toolbox or making the repair is sufficient. The foreigner leaves with a discouraged sigh or comments ruefully, "Maybe next time."

After my months in Pakistan, I began to find a middle ground. As people, foreigners and Pakistanis can view ourselves and one another frankly and find the places where mutual understanding lies. I talked endlessly about my country's democracy until I took the time to listen to my Pakistani friends. They told me of their happiness and satisfaction with their military regime. One friend, Begum Tasnim, told me that her country would now go ever forward. "We can cross the street in safety," she explained. "We can talk over our problems together. We can retain our personal property without having it pilfered and plundered. We can even listen to the candidates for government offices and vote according to our conscience." It was Mrs. Tasnim who reminded me, when I complained about my living quarters, that I had the best they had to offer.

I was a Christian, but Muslims, Parsis, and Hindus did not shun me. They lived their religion in the welcome they extended to me, a stranger in their country. I had nothing to offer, no pipelines to favors or gratuities. I was no VIP; in fact, I was at the other end of the social scale. But it turned out that we did have something in common. Like me, they were interested in the welfare of Pakistan's blind people. I shared with them an idea that blind children would and could respond to education, if given an opportunity. I shared my belief that mendicancy and defeatism need not be the lot of these children in today's world. They listened.

I found other areas of common interest as well. We cared about the education of all children, and we talked about that. I wanted to know about everything in their daily lives. Nothing was too insignificant, too familiar to share. I asked about the chapatis (flatbreads) they made and the curries they served with their rice. They showed me how to drape my sari and gave me bitter brews against dysentery. I shared my culinary tricks with them, too. Their arms, enshrouded as they were in their burkhas, guided me countless times as we shopped along Elphinstone Street or walked, barefoot and respectful, around the tomb of Mohammad Ali Jinnah. I shared with them the meat in the middle of the low table, all of us stretching to pick our portions from the common dish.

To not a few children my name was Anti, and Anti taught them to say "Hello!" That really was fun; the three-year-old sitting on my lap prattled along, taking time out from her Urdu soliloquies to say again, "Hello, Anti." The teacher, the social worker, the government official, the businessman, the Lion, the Rotarian, the navy man, the box-factory worker, the clerk, the servant, the taxi driver, the rickshaw walla, the camel walla, the beggar, the student, the telephone girl, the durzay, the *rialhi* watering his few sparse plants, the *chokidar* at the gate of the compound, the doctor, the dentist, the shopkeeper, the police officer—all of us had common cause together, just in living. And how many more friends could I have made had I been able to speak their language!

•　　•　　•

I quite understood, I believe, the plight of the evangelical missionary. He had come to save souls, to supplant their religion with his, but they would not listen. Yet I met many other types of missionaries as well. One went out into the villages with a spade and showed the people how to grow vegetables, how to bring in water and save it— not only demonstrating but doing. I met the engineering missionary who helped build a row of huts with proper sewage facilities. I met the farming missionary who showed the villagers how to raise better chickens and larger eggs with just a little extra reinforced feedstuff from back home. Most inspiring of all were the Christian groups who lived and loved their religion—the medical missionaries, both men and women. In the latter, the spirit of teacher, preacher, and healer was truly alive. One of these dedicated saints, Sir Henry Holland, built his own hospital from a feeble beginning half a century ago. He educated two sons as medical missionaries. Sir Henry Holland with his hospitals in Quetta truly ranks among the great medical missionaries of all time.

Then there were the Maltmans who gathered in some eleven abandoned waifs, fed and clothed them. Mrs. Maltman, the missionary's wife, taught the children to read and write, and the girls to cook and help in the kitchen, to sew and tend the younger brood. The boys were taught gardening, poultry raising (even though on a small scale), and repair work. They took jobs as house servants, gardeners, and errand boys. Between jobs, there was always a home and a meal. That was Christianity in action: "Of such is the kingdom of heaven." I felt humble as these youngsters addressed me in English and showed me around.

The Maltmans' mission was truly one of mercy. Their church back home had donated a station wagon, and bundles of clothes never ceased to arrive. Missionary Maltman told me of a traumatic disappointment he had had. He worked to send one of his young converts back to the United States for training as a missionary. After two years, the young man returned with what Mr. Maltman called the "I" complex. He had acquired a taste for an easier type of living, and he refused to work among the people who needed his services. The young man's goal now was to return to the United States with his family and to have his children educated there. Meanwhile, Mr. and Mrs. Maltman carried on with their adopted household of happy, healthy, wholesome children.

Mr. Ogg, a native of the United Kingdom, was not a welcome person on the streets of Mayalpur. He stood on the street corner with his Bible in hand, preaching. Frequently, he had to take cover for his life when hysterical mobs and deranged fakirs and medicine men ganged up on him. Apart from his evangelism, however, Mr. Ogg had valuable training as a chemist. His wife, also from the UK, had a medical degree and was a specialist in children's diseases. When her husband accompanied her on her visits to sick mothers and children, the men of the family stood by in case Mr. Ogg tried to baptize the child his wife was treating.

Both Dr. and Mr. Ogg spoke Urdu, and this saved them from many a beating at the hands of an excited, illiterate, misguided mob. With Christian perseverance, the way for the Oggs became easier. Dr. Ogg continued in faith to nurse and to heal, and Mr. Ogg went on preaching. He taught reading and writing, making suitable books and adapting Bible readings to the lives and needs of the people. As time passed, leading Muslims in the cities and villages lent the Oggs their support.

"Someone has to write simple, readable literature on tilling the soil, preventing disease, raising chickens, improving hygiene, and taking community responsibility," Mr. Ogg told me. "This information must be written within the people's vocabulary range. They are ready and waiting for it."

Such a project called for an informed representative, missionary, or diplomat, someone knowledgeable regarding the everyday needs of the people. It required someone informed regarding better ways of doing what the people are doing already, the little things the sum total of which is called living, as opposed to existing or vegetating. To know those little things, one has to live in the country, to observe, to share thinking, substance, and self.

Sir Henry Holland, the Maltmans, the Oggs, and many others are doing this work. This is the essence indeed of the people-to-people approach, the essence of Christian living.

· · ·

"I never think you are an American!" remarked my friend Miss Zamir one day. I asked her what she meant, but she only replied, "I don't know."

"Might it be the fact that I was not born in America?" I suggested. "My accent still retains a foreignness to America. And then I've travelled considerably, and I'm an older person. Perhaps I'm different from other Americans you have met."

"You take time to talk with us," she said. "You are not in a hurry."

Perhaps we Americans are overly anxious to get things done, to hurry from one activity to the other, to be thinking of the next activity before the present one is completed. "Foreigners are even in a hurry to go home when they have just arrived," Miss Zamir said.

Americans, she continued, were considered to be wealthy people. "We do not mind their wealth, but we do mind our having to accept American wealth, though we know that's the only thing to do. We need it. It helps us." She hesitated. "We common people lost much of the American aid through corruption. We might have had better roads, better sanitation, better schools. Now we know where we are going, and we need money to get there."

"What exactly do you need?" I queried.

Her answer was simple and certainly far from the abstruse reports that could be written on such a vital question. "Just three things," she said. "Food, medicine, and most of all, education!"

Though the struggle for food is as old as humankind, there are still too many hungry people in a world that can feed them all. Malnutrition is rampant, and it can be checked. Famine and disease still stalk the towns and villages of the great subcontinent. Disease was the concomitant of malnutrition. "America has found ways to prevent disease," Miss Zamir said. "America has medicine to combat cholera, malaria, typhus, typhoid, tuberculosis, dysentery—all of the diseases we have here.

"Sixty-five percent of the blindness we have is preventable," she went on. "Hundreds of thousands of human beings could be made happier with their sight."

"Where does education fit into this bill of needs?" I ventured.

"Right at the top," she said. "Teach my people to read, to communicate. Awake in them their latent potential, their incentive to discover, to learn, to challenge. My people can think, but they cannot read to accumulate information, to stimulate them into action. Help them to be literate; they are ready. Then they will raise their own standard of living and take their rightful place in the sun. Let us begin with compulsory education for all our children! That is not asking too much—three years of education for each child as a minimum."

Miss Zamir grew excited. "With food, medicine, and education, we can build houses, control flies, establish sanitation, halt leprosy. We can make playgrounds to take children out of the stagnant rain pools where buffalo wallow—a breeding place of disease. All of these problems we can and will solve, given food, medicine, and education."

Miss Zamir mused on, "I don't think we want you to help us with the things we can do ourselves. We would prefer to do them our way, at our own pace, not at yours. We do not want your culture; cultures are not for export. We have our own, and we want to keep it. We do not want your religion; we have our own, and it satisfies us. We want to determine our own future, for we are capable of doing it. We do not desire to be made in your image; our own is emerging, and we are proud of it."

She lit another cigarette. We sat in silence, broken by the *caw-caw* of the rooks and the shriek of the kite.

What Miss Zamir had been saying, I knew, was the stuff of which the new Pakistan is made. Pakistan can only go forward with fortitude to achieve self-determination. Pakistan *zindabad!* Long live Pakistan!

CHAPTER 14
AND SO THEY WERE MARRIED

My invitation read, "Begum Dari Mohammad Ali requests the pleasure of your company at the wedding ceremony of her son Zafarullah Mohammad, on December 1, 1959."

I was elated to be included on the guest list. I felt I had been honored. Zafarullah was an educator, and he was interested in education in my country, too. We had talked together frequently. He was a quiet young man of slightly over thirty, and I had not known that he was a bachelor until the invitation arrived. The bride's name was not mentioned in the invitation, for, as I learned, the groom's family made the wedding arrangements.

I took a rickshaw to the designated address, which was the home of the bride. It was five in the afternoon, and already the crowds had assembled around the house. Two young men greeted me warmly and escorted me to a room upstairs. There, two young girls took over and showed me to a chair. I was in the women's room; the male guests were escorted to another room.

Judging by the scurrying feet, the romping of children, and the general noise, there must have been fifty women and children in the room. I greeted the guests around me, and they greeted me, but the conversation was uncomfortably limited until two young girls sat by my side. They both spoke English. I must have looked out of place in my American dress, but the girls quickly put me at ease. Though I was the only one so attired, they thanked me for coming and graciously served me tea, nuts, and cakes.

I was not unhappy or ill at ease, for I met many charming young women. However, as two and a half hours slid by, I grew somewhat bewildered. There was no sign of the bride, nor any mention of a ceremony.

Eventually I pieced the story together. The bride was in her room with her sisters. She was attired, I learned, in a simple, everyday sari. The priest would arrive with a marriage contract. After reciting passages from the Holy Quran, he would read the contract to the bride and ask her if she was willing to take the man mentioned in the contract as her husband, under conditions specified. The groom, who had been previously interviewed by the priest, had stipulated in the contract the amount of the *meher*, or dowry, to be paid to the wife in the event that she should be widowed. When I asked my informants what amount might be considered, I was surprised to learn that it was some thirty-five thousand rupees, or seven thousand dollars. I suggested that such a large sum would work a hardship on any young man, but I learned it was not necessary to pay the meher. It was sufficient to make the promise in the contract.

With the contract came lavish gifts from the groom to the bride— beautiful saris chosen by the groom's sisters and mother; elaborate jewelry, including an ornate gold chain, worn around the waist; and a *tika* of gold set with precious stones as an ornament for her forehead. The groom also provided the bride with her wedding sari of bright scarlet. When the bride has signed the contract, she returns to her room, where her sisters help her don her wedding finery.

Accompanied by her sisters, the bride came to our room. She was conducted to the settee, where she sat between her two sisters. The excitement ran high. The bride's exuberant, ecstatic admirers told me every detail.

"Let's lift her veil and look at her," one voice said.

"She's young, she's pretty," said another.

"Her hair is all silver spread over," remarked another.

The bride's eyelids were closed, heavy with mascara. Her face was heavily made up with rouge and lipstick. She did not smile; she did not speak. She wore henna crisscrossed on her hands and feet. On the back of her hands was hennaed the letter *Z*, her husband's initial. Her dress was richly bespangled with sequins; she wore many, many gold bangles on her arms and four jeweled rings on her first finger.

What was to happen next? Until now, the bride had never seen the man who was to be her husband, nor had the groom seen his wife. They were to be seated together, both veiled, and each would hold a mirror in which they could see each other. At this time, the girls said, the groom would probably have to submit to the fun of the young people. They might remove his shoe, pull his hair from the back, and otherwise tease him. He would have to accept this treatment graciously.

After three hours, I felt I should take my leave, so I missed other parts of the festivities. Late in the evening, the bride and groom would go to the groom's home. There, the bride's sisters would meet the couple, asking the groom for money. At the same time, they would shower him with gifts of pots and pans and other kitchen utensils, furniture, rugs, and clothes, to set up his new home.

On the following day, I returned to the reception at the groom's house. A large tent had been set up on the compound. Again, crowds of women and children sat on folding chairs and on the ground, which was covered with burlap. The men were in another part of the tent, separated by a partition from the ladies' section.

We waited for two hours until the bride arrived, again in the company of her sisters. The groom was taken to the men's section of the tent. The bride was dressed in a completely new outfit, again heavily rouged and hennaed. Her eyes were still closed. My friends concluded that the mascara was heavy, and she was unable to open her eyes without effort. She was to return to her mother's house with the bridegroom, and there they would spend the first week of their wedded life.

The reception was elegant, with tea, fruits, nuts, potato chips, and candies. The bridegroom's mother and sisters were most gracious, hospitable, and kind. No one seemed to be in a hurry, so I did not feel uncomfortable when the sisters took time to describe the array of beautiful saris worn by the many guests. We then viewed the wedding gifts in the groom's house while he did the honors as host, attired in his gray *sherwani,* or frock coat, and gray *karakuli* cap. The bride remained silent and demure, her head bowed and her shoulders stooped as if she were doing penance. I did not feel that it was false modesty or that she was putting on an act.

I thought of the flower-bedecked church back home, the simple vows of love and faithfulness, the "Wedding March" from *Lohengrin,* the bonnie bride in her white satin gown and flowing veil. The contract and the variety of rituals in the arranged marriage and the love match carried the same essence, the bringing together of two persons. In each case, young people were starting life anew, with the blessing of God, and preparing to bring children into the world, nurtured in the name of God.

An arranged marriage or a love match—is it such a choice? The incidence of divorce in a Muslim family, with its tradition of the arranged marriage, is negligible.

•   •   •

My invitation to a Parsi wedding was another happy occasion. The lounge and the patio of the hotel were gaily decorated for the late-afternoon ceremony. An orchestra filled the hours of waiting before the bride's arrival. It was a gala time for the children, who had the run of the hotel.

My Parsi hosts described the saris. They surpassed imagination in the wealth of color and texture and in the originality of their stitching and design. I wondered about the eyesight that had been expended upon the appliquéing of thousands of seed pearls and colored beads on the delicate georgette.

The bridegroom was accompanied by two priests who stayed with him on the dais, flanked by rows of chairs to be occupied by the members of the immediate families. The young man was visibly nervous, but he good-humoredly accepted the remarks of the guests around me—we were seated directly in front of him—telling him, after the second hour of waiting went by, that the bride might have changed her mind and that we all had better go home. He waited, holding onto his bouquet of flowers for the big moment when the bride would appear at the door of the lounge, to be greeted by her father-in-law-to-be. He would place around her neck a necklace of pure gold and diamonds with a matching ornament for her hair. The groom wore tight, black velvet breeches, a short bolero-style jacket, a white blouse, and an intriguing, coronet-shaped hat with three peaks in front.

At long last, the chorus of the children and the beating of the drums announced the arrival of the bride. She wore a regal, white satin sari, studded with diamonds.

The ceremony was impressive. The priests chanted long prayers, solemn and sustained. They might have been in Persian, but none of my friends could translate them. The voices of the romping children in no way detracted from the solemnity of the occasion.

The prayers over, gaiety broke loose, and dancing and games followed. The bride and groom, arm in arm, circulated among the guests, the bride showing off her beautiful wedding gown and jewels. The bride and groom then withdrew to attend service in the local Temple of Fire, their place of worship, to return to the festivities later.

The happy couple had met at their place of employment. Both were secretaries. Theirs was a love match, with prewedding showers by the bride's friends, by her Girl Guide troop, and her coworkers. The accent was indeed occidental.

•   •   •

Elizabeth was an English nurse married to an officer in the Pakistani National Service. They had met and married in England while he was in training in London. Their baby was born at the home of Elizabeth's mother in England. Elizabeth was a blue-eyed blonde, attractive and sparkling. Tom, who used his English name, was dapper, intelligent, and a gentleman. They were deeply in love, and they deeply loved their boy.

Trouble began when Elizabeth came to Pakistan with her baby. She found it difficult to fit into a different culture, and she suffered. She adopted her husband's religion, Islam. She shared the family home. She sought to make friends with the sisters and their friends. She dressed in the sari, and at the request of her husband's family, she even wore a burkha when she was allowed to go on the street.

But two hurdles Elizabeth simply could not overcome. Her mother-in-law begrudged her eldest son's marriage to a foreigner, and that hurdle was insurmountable. Tom's mother outlawed Elizabeth. She did not and never could belong. Elizabeth had stolen her firstborn, the mother-in-law claimed. In her moments of distraction, the mother-in-law would vent her spite, fury, and anguish. She cursed the child in the crib and vowed that, even as Elizabeth had stolen her son, so would Elizabeth's son be taken from her.

Still another culture block marred Elizabeth's yearned-for happiness. When Tom returned from his ship, his first visit was to his mother. He had to give as much as half of his paycheck to his mother, for Elizabeth's place and needs were secondary. Such was the duty of the firstborn son.

Could these cultural differences ever be resolved? With the help of a psychiatrist and a separate apartment, Elizabeth worked around the problems. She interested herself in her little boy's education. She walked with him to school every day and picked him up after school. As she and Muzuam trudged home in the broiling noonday sun, she often wished that the rupees that were going to the mother-in-law might pay for a rickshaw or a bus ticket. But she had Muzuam, and he was a keen, bright, beautiful child.

Elizabeth listened to the stories of other foreign girls who were on the verge of marrying young Pakistani boyfriends. Some of them would return to England to wean themselves from the strain of the situation. She met others who were happily married, who had found the interests, satisfaction, and love they had anticipated. She met Dorothy, a designer of elaborate prints, who returned from a sales trip to the United States to find that her husband had married a second wife. It was a legal and culturally acceptable procedure. Not so to Dorothy! Dorothy felt she could not go back to her husband. She opened her little print shop to provide for herself and her boy.

Elizabeth concluded that her problem was hers to solve. She had the key to the solution—her love for Tom and her boy, Muzuam. The blue-eyed, blonde English girl, attired in her cerulean-blue sari, had overcome the problem of the conflict of cultures. So had Tom, who philosophically refused to allow cultural differences to destroy the happiness of three human beings. Muzuam now has a baby sister.

Marriage is, after all, in any country, what the married couple makes of it.

CHAPTER 15
LAHORE AND DACCA

I took my leave of the captivating drabness of Karachi to visit Lahore, a city some seven hundred miles to the north. It was mid-December, though the weather had not significantly changed when I left.

My first impression was one of sheer joy. A lady sat beside me on the bus from the air terminal, carrying a basket full of nasturtiums. She had brought them to greet some friends who had not arrived. Trees and flowers were plentiful around the hostel. The air was crisp. The horse-drawn *tonga* took the place of the rickshaw, and the horse ambled along in no hurry to get anywhere. The driver had a whip, but it seemed that all he was doing with it was steering his pony through the traffic, around cars, and between bicycles. He did not save his voice on the latter.

I perched on the back of the cart, finding some trouble in bracing myself against the floor, for fear I would fall off. I balanced myself back-to-back with the driver. The tonga had two wheels. I realized there was an art in using the tonga, which I had to learn. Wrapping my right arm around the back bar of the seat, I could not fall off, but both arms were now immobilized, so I dared not move. Yet, withal, I managed to visit office, church, market, bazaar, park, and friends. The tonga became my preferred means of transport. As the days went on, the world of Kipling's *Kim* came to life, and a model of his gun was a cherished treasure.

My companion was a young social worker who lived at the same hostel. She had studied at Stanford in California. Strange how small the world is!

The Old City down by the bazaar had an Old World atmosphere. Beggars followed us at every turn. "Mamma dead, Daddy dead; nothing to eat, Memsab." My Pakistani guide declared that a man standing at the street corner spoke to the boy and might well be his father. In the parks, around the memorials, by the mosques, the chant was the same.

My room at the hostel was bitterly cold. It led onto a grassy plot at the back of the main building. There was a verandah all the way around, so that the sun never reached the room to warm it during the day. There were heavy draw bolts inside and outside the door. The safety lock was difficult to manipulate, for my hands were very cold. I marveled at this faith in bolts and locks when at the back of the room, in the alcove that served as a bathroom, there was an outside door that could be opened at any time.

A servant came in the morning and left a jug of hot water. The hot water bottle leaked, but fortunately I caught the mishap in time. I took the little fur neckpiece from my suitcase, wrapped it around my feet, pulled the *razai* and my coat over me, and fought the freezing temperature. I could not understand how the girls in the hostel wore just their saris, sometimes a sweater, no stockings, and a pair of sandals. They were cold, but the cold did not disturb them. Perhaps I was making too much of it. Perhaps I should have let the cold alone and tried not to fight it.

I wanted to know about the blind persons in Lahore—that is, those who were not beggars. The two small schools for the blind took care of little more than a token of the blind population. I never had any trouble in speaking about blind persons; blind persons were everywhere.

During a discussion on the verandah of the hostel one day, a Pakistani woman said, "Your idea of having the blind children go to a regular school and have the assistance they need is a bombshell to us. We have always thought that blind children cannot be educated because they are blind."

"Not a bombshell," I said, "just a way of preventing another generation of blind beggars."

I talked with several young blind men. They wanted further education, but they were refused this privilege because of their blindness. They needed books. They could read Braille, and their English was quite understandable. They needed materials and paper. They wanted to be able to earn their own living.

I had tea with Mrs. Ramsan, a social worker. She told me about a blind man who had all his life made kites—kites that children love to fly, scrambling to the tops of houses, running down alleys, tangling kites with one another. Kite flying was a real sport. Because of a government regulation, tissue paper for his kites was no longer procurable. Did I think the man could get some paper? At the moment, he had to resort to begging. He resented the idea of taking his little son with him to beg, too, wandering up and down the streets. His pride and dignity were hurt. Could we get paper?

I wrote to my blind friends back in California. They launched a drive to help the kite maker, and thirty-six pounds of paper were sent to him. That would make a goodly number of kites!

My curiosity led me to Lalamusa, the site of the Village AID Program. AID formerly stood for Agricultural and Industrial Development. Now the program is National Development Organization (NDO).

My trip to Lalamusa took a whole day. Leaving early in the morning, I took a bus—a slow bus. It stopped at every village, and passengers came and went. The bus driver spoke a little English. I was alone on this trip, so I depended on the driver to interpret the countryside. I listened to the people. Women in the villages were much freer than in the cities. They laughed and talked with the men and with their children. It was evident that they were not wearing burkhas. The crowds and noise at each bus stop told me that the villages were not the peaceful little hamlets we find along the roads of America or Scotland. They were teeming with people.

The usual vendors of nostrums, Coca-Cola, and sweetmeats boarded the bus. I asked the driver if they sold newspapers, too. "People don't read," was his answer.

The bus stopped in front of the NDO office. It was the noon hour, and everybody had gone to his siesta. I sat in the concrete-floored waiting room to wait. The servant pulled a small table in front of me and served me a tray with tea. Such courtesy and kindness were the hallmarks of Pakistani hospitality, everywhere and at all times.

Mr. Youssouf showed me around the development. He showed me the tall stalks of sugarcane, the green beans, the immense beetroot, the large ears of corn, the fat turkeys—a project that could stand to be multiplied hundreds of times. Soil culture, rotation of crops, animal husbandry, and fruit growing were all studied in the project. The trainees returned to their villages after completing the course.

The fifty-acre plant more than justified its existence. Although entirely a government project, the program was assisted by American aid. It was truly commendable help.

I told Mr. Youssouf about some of the current projects for the blind in other countries. "We should be able to do something of that sort here in this country, but the idea is so new," he said. "We first must let it sink in."

Mr. Youssouf invited me to come to his house and meet his wife. She did not speak English, but she was courtesy itself. Their son and daughter were both at school. On their return, they made little speeches to me in English, which both of them were studying. We enjoyed tea and biscuits together.

It was time for me to go. We all crowded into the jeep and made for the railway station, for the last bus had already gone. I was in the compartment for women and children. The men came from another section to see that all was going well. The baskets and boxes, luggage and pets, all seemed to be stacked in our section. The flies were abundant, and the orange peelings were slippery under my feet. Children leaned over my knee, and I could not speak to them. More food was bought and passed through the window at each stop. Bedding lay everywhere—over the back of my seat and stacked on the seat at my side. If not the end of a perfect day, it certainly was the end of an exciting day!

•   •   •

It was less than an hour's flight to Rawalpindi, the new temporary seat of government until buildings at Islamabad were completed. Rawalpindi is an old fortress, with walls and embattlements reminiscent of the British regime. It is a comparatively quiet town. The tonga driver and his horse did not exert much effort during my sightseeing trip in the old part of the city. The delight of the trip was when my friend and I left the tonga and went down the narrow, winding streets to the old bazaars. I tried to identify the shops by the open stalls and boxes in the streets in front of them. There was a luggage shop where the artisan was stretching his leather over the frame of a suitcase. He carefully trimmed the corners, folded the leather, and sealed it down. Then came the chapati maker. He took his handfuls of dough, turned around and, without bending down, threw the dough on the side of the brick stove in the ground. He never seemed to miss. The bread cooked in the bricks. He then left the counter and, with a stick, turned over each of the chapatis to cook on the other side. The laws of hygiene may not have been observed, but the people had no qualms about buying the bread. I found chapatis tasteless, stodgy, and not to my liking, but tastes differ.

A surprise awaited my return to the boardinghouse. A fire burned in the fireplace, with a box of kindling and twigs alongside. Outside, roses bloomed in the garden beside chrysanthemums and lush shrubbery. The sun was warm when I caught its rays. In the late afternoon, the air was saturated with the smell of burning logs. Rawalpindi was indeed peacefully relaxing.

My school-day geography came alive on my trip to the northwest. The Khyber Pass, between Afghanistan and what at that time was called India, loomed large in the imagination of a Scottish student. Along its thirty-mile stretch, Scottish soldiers had commanded the forts and kept the door to India open. Here was the Khyber Pass, the lonely road that wound its way between the hills and ravines, with here and there a Pashtun tribesman with his gun strapped to his back and a brace of chickens attached to his belt. These tribesmen, nomads at best, lived by smuggling and barter. Some settled in the caves on the sides of the distant mountains where, it was said, rich Persian carpets covered the floors—rare art treasures, pilfered, stolen, or bartered. Life was cheap in these silent regions, cheap even today.

Busloads of tourists voiced their admiration of the long stretches of land reaching to the crests of the hills, with occasionally an oasis of green sward, a lake, or an encampment built strong enough to withstand marauders. Inside the encampments several families lived together. There were no windows in the battlements, only outlook towers with slits large enough to hold the muzzle of a gun.

Far below the road on which our bus was traveling, a caravan passed with more than fifty camels. The camels were loaded with furniture, chickens, food, and children. The men and women walked alongside the caravan. The camels were attached by ropes from one to the other. Dogs, goats, and donkeys brought up the rear of the caravan.

Along the road by the old forts were memorial tablets, recalling the companies of Scottish Highlanders who guarded the hostile territory. The eerie stillness of the land conjured up images of the feudal age, of forays and robbers, when the only recognized law was the right of strength and might. The whole scene was a panoramic no-man's-land of tribal warfare. Every newcomer was distrusted, and every stranger was a foe.

We reached the frontier of Afghanistan, but our passports did not take us further. The armed guards and the barbed-wire fences took the place of a friendly handshake. A pall of fear, distrust, and foreboding hung over the land where goodwill to all men had not yet penetrated.

•   •   •

As a bird needs two wings to fly, I was told, so did Pakistan need its two wings, West Pakistan and East Pakistan.[1] I wanted to meet the people in the East Wing, too. Dacca was my destination. A corridor of one thousand miles lies between the two wings; India keeps them separate. Since the partition of 1947, Muslim refugees have continued to stream into the East Wing, too. The population was dense, crowded into unsanitary quarters, with little food to withstand the rigors of tropical heat, high humidity, monsoon devastation, and poverty.

Forty-five million Muslim Pakistanis in this section speak Bengali. The capital is Dacca, not more than one hundred miles from Kolkata, the capital of West Bengal. East Pakistan used to be East Bengal.

To me, the people of East Pakistan had much more in common with the people of West Bengal than with the people of the West Wing, except for their religion. The Muslim League was the dominant consideration between the two nations, so we accept it.

I went completely askew in my interpretation of Dacca. I started to compare it with other cities. It fell, I thought, far short of the other cities of Pakistan. I had to get into Dacca's own shoes and see it as it was. It is an old, old city, climatically impoverished, for heavy rains wash away any semblance of sidewalks. Dusty roads surrounded by water that breeds every kind of insect, a still older section with many little streets like Lavatory Lane—this was Dacca. But on the winning side of the ledger, Dacca's people were courageous, confident, persistent, patriotic, and above all, warm and friendly. Their sense of humor struck me as particularly refreshing. A few of them had been in the United States, the country referred to by one man as "where you put up signs calling for Safety First, and then you drive like hell." There, in the United States, they said, the last poster that meets your eye as you take off in the plane is "Prepare to meet thy God."

The young students in university and college were alert, curious, and progressive. I spoke with them on three occasions. Their questions and arguments were such as I would have found in any American college, but their urge to do well, to act for the progress of their country, was more pronounced. They had, I felt, a consciousness of the part they were to play in the growth of their country and a self-dedication to the goal. They joked without bitterness about the gravy of important jobs and resources being concentrated in West Pakistan.

"But, you know," said one businessman, "it's the tail that wags the dog."

He was, I believe, talking for the fact that East Pakistan owns 75 percent of the world's jute. Its tea, its rice, bananas, pineapples, papayas, and mangoes are the world's best. But processing facilities are lacking; factories are now in the West Bengal region since the partition. The financial debacle of the last regime set East Pakistan back. Surrounded as it is by water and mosquitoes, disease is ever present.

The only way to cross the Padma, or Ganges, River was by boat. There were no bridges on our way north. Milling crowds swarmed everywhere, people from the refugee camps for Muslim immigrants from India. Somehow the refugees eked out a bare subsistence for themselves and their too, too large families. I wondered where education fit into this picture. Would blind persons ever have a chance for self-determination here, in spite of these colossal problems of disease, famine, flood, and malnutrition?

I trudged with my guide down the embankment to the lower part of the old city, over the dirt, dust, and refuse of the road, under a scorching sun. Children bumped against me, some of them just playing, others begging.

I felt close to the heart of Dacca. There was nothing offensive, even on the back streets. The lady who dressed my hair did it her way. A little fellow—all of the people seemed to be short of stature—showed us his handmade shawls and stoles, made of the finest jute fiber and silk, with exquisite embroidery. He spread a rug on the floor and sat on it as he displayed his merchandise. The bicycle rickshaw man took me where I wanted to go. The schoolteacher told me of his plans and his problems. The doctor and the dentist ran busy offices for little money. The office executives made their efficient contacts with the rest of the world. Government officials, facing the problems of the East Wing, took time to talk them over with us, citizens and visitors alike.

Dacca was alive. It had a life and character all its own. Its future of success and hazard was in good hands. I came to like Dacca.

NOTE

1. At its founding in 1947, Pakistan was divided into two noncontiguous wings, West and East, with India lying between them. After the Bangladesh Liberation War of 1971, East Pakistan broke away to become the independent nation of Bangladesh.

PART 3

SOUTH AND EAST OF THE HIMALAYAS

CHAPTER 16
SEEING THE TAJ MAHAL MY WAY

More red tape? More papers to sign? That was my first thought when the customs official at the airport in New Delhi asked me to step aside. If that was not a camera over my shoulder, what was it? "My Braillewriter," I said.

The other passengers had all gone. I opened the case for inspection.

"I was just curious to know what a Braillewriter is," the inspector said.

I unfolded my slate and proceeded to give the gracious lady her first lesson on Braille writing and reading. The demonstration took five minutes, and our conversation lasted fifty. She had time to talk, as she was going off duty. I always had time to talk.

After we descended from the bus at the city terminal, she hailed a taxi for me. I was on my way again with her good wishes, and she was on her way with mine.

There was frequently a bit of hesitation when I appeared at the door of a hostel, hotel, or YWCA, when the manager saw that I was blind. Did I need extra help? Could I look after myself? Could I get around on my own? As one question followed another, they began to answer themselves. After all, I had been journeying all alone. I was welcomed, shown my room, and given all the courtesies possible. Was it because I was an American? Perhaps. Was it because I was a woman? I think so. I was not a VIP. Of that I am sure.

Schoolteachers seem to have an affinity for one another. I met schoolteachers all around the world. Miss Joseph was a teacher from

Kerala, the state at the southern tip of India. She had served on a picket line when the democratic-minded people in that state paraded in front of their government building to protest the government's Communistic activities. For her actions, Miss Joseph had been taken to prison. She told me the saga of her imprisonment with her friends. They were not mistreated, but they did not get enough to eat—and how they missed their tea!

Miss Joseph and I went to see the city. She wore a soft silk sari. I do not believe I asked her the color, for I was absorbed by her parasol, which she said was white with large flowers. We went to the flower show on the grounds of the government buildings. She showed me pansies, geraniums, stocks, asters, roses, and jonquils in utter profusion— enormous blossoms, banks of them. I heard laughing children and friendly, garrulous mothers. None of the women wore burkhas. The air was heavy with perfume, the grass was damp and lush, the shade of the trees cool and balmy. To me, starved for flowers and grass and trees for the past six months, this was a paradise!

En route to the flower show, the taxi drew up at a street corner, and I was surprised to hear two people address me as I sat inside the cab. They wanted me to buy their American dollars for rupees. They explained that an American was in a hurry and gave them the dollars in payment for some transaction. They would sell them to me at a big bargain! I presume that someone had been taken in by these phony dollar bills; otherwise they would not have been selling them.

I spent two full days catching up with my mail. I posted a staggering nineteen pieces, including ten copies of the booklet *New Horizon in the Education of Blind Children,* which my colleagues and I had published in Karachi.

•   •   •

I removed my shoes and crossed the warm parquet surrounding the low, flat slab tombstone that stood on the place where Gandhigi was assassinated.[1] The ceremony was as solemn to me as it was to the hundreds of Indians who had come to pay homage to their *bapu,* their father, their Gandhigi, as they reverently and lovingly called him. Voices were hushed as we stood around the tomb, but from the sward below arose the song of the spinning looms and the laughter of children. It was not an atmosphere of loss but an atmosphere of life, a renaissance of spirit, of dedication to an ideal whose author would never die.

Visitors came from far and wide, some with donkeys, some wheeling carts, most of them walking, carrying their spinning wheels. They sat and spun in quiet contemplation as their master was wont to do. The fountains played all around. Children came in groups, some in processions from their schools, to pay homage at the holy shrine.

Gandhi was the savior of his people, the poor people of his country. He was the only teacher they had ever known, for he alone spoke to them and showed them the way out of their ignorance. To them, Gandhigi is now a wonder—beloved, admired, more than he ever was during his lifetime. The people had been his children. He glorified their simplicity, their purity, their peasantry. Now he was a legend. He was an inspiration to the youth as well as to those who had heard him speak, had followed him in his travels over the land, had learned from his lips the history of intolerance and hatred that led to the partition little more than two decades ago. Today they did not hate the Muslim empire that had been created. The mosques were open, and Muslims went there to pray. There had been too much bloodshed; people now sought to live in peace.

Yet I wondered about this idealism when I attended Sunday service at a neighboring church. The president of a small Christian college in the Punjab spoke to the congregation. The college had sixty Christian students and seven hundred non-Christians. The students were on strike, a strike that our speaker felt was meaningless and unnecessary.

"It is so easy for them to get little rugs and sit on the sidewalk," the speaker lamented, "demanding a new shed in which to park their bicycles out of the sun while they go to class."

The only real purpose of the strike, he believed, was to confer status on the strikers. "How can students be guided to do their own thinking," he asked, "instead of listening to forces from the outside that goad them to unrealistic action, revolt, and defiance?"

He went on to explain that most of the students came from the villages. They were the sons and daughters of illiterate parents. The parents' discontent may have been reflected in the unrest of the young people. The students represented the new India. The fact that the government provided modern classrooms and well-equipped chemistry and physics laboratories did not satisfy them. A bicycle hangar was more important than the classroom. Our speaker could only explain this strange standard of values as the work of outside influences. The students were being encouraged to riot for the sake of rioting.

Who knows? Unfortunately, social change seems fated to accept revolution in the name of progress.

• • •

I rode the regular passenger bus to Missurri, about seventy miles from New Delhi. The bus was crowded; children, dogs, and food were everywhere. We made frequent stops at bus stations, and at each stop more people crowded aboard, bringing more children, dogs, and food with them.

The noise at each stop was confusing, for I could not distinguish a word of the language. Beggars came to the door, as well as people selling cooked food, toys, and medicines. With a courteous "Memsab," I was asked like the rest to buy their wares.

My seatmate was Bashir, a fourteen-year-old student returning from sick leave. His English was excellent, and we had an interesting conversation. He wanted to know about American students, and I wanted to learn about student life in India. In two years, he would complete his bachelor of science degree. He was neither Communist nor anti-Communist, he told me. He thought his government was not all it could be, but he contended that a change had to take place in the people themselves. They would have to decide what they wanted and needed and not allow themselves to be influenced by promises, offers, and gifts.

Bashir was hard on his people. "Once they get a job," he said, "they sit." His father, an official in the government, worked until ten every night because of the inefficiency of his subordinates. "Too many hours spent in the canteen," he said, "too few with their files."

He told me to look at the cartoons of R. K. Laxman in the newspapers; they would give me an idea of the social order.[2] When he remembered that I am blind, he described a number of these cartoons. They mocked stupid expenditures for unnecessary lighting, displays, and show.

"President Nehru is all right," Bashir said, "but he is not the answer.[3] Only the people themselves can help their country. Nehru needs their backing and support. The people have to assume leadership and responsibility."

"What might be done about the problem of beggars?" I asked.

"Oh," he said, "build hostels for them and confine everyone who begs to one of the hostels. You would see the number of beggars decline immediately."

"Why do so many people beg?" I asked.

"They enjoy begging," Bashir said. "They like that life. They get by as footpath dwellers."

Bashir was hard on us Americans, too. "What did you think of the agricultural exhibition?" I asked.[4]

"The Americans overplayed it," he stated. "We do not want to see any more elaborate golden domes on buildings. We have plenty of those already. We need food and education for the masses. We need improvement in our standard of living."

He believed the Americans did not see the problems of the Indians, for they remained inside their compounds. "You don't find Americans on buses, taking rickshaws, standing in our crowds. They stay apart. They don't listen to us, so they don't understand us. They don't speak our language, so how can they speak to us? Only a few of us speak English to them. The educated Indian has turned Western, but 95 percent of us are Indian and want to remain so. This is my country. I would like to visit yours as you are visiting mine. I would like to visit America to see the background from which these Americans come, to compare it with my own country."

"What are you going to do when you graduate?'

"Go into government service, police service, or any job that comes along. I want to earn my living."

"What about the field of social welfare?"

"There is need for that but no future in it. I would not like it," he said.

Our conversation lasted the six hours of the journey, three hours apiece, for he had as many questions to ask of me as I of him. Yes, he was only fourteen; he would be fifteen in a few months.

On the way, Bashir described the passing landscape—wheat fields, sugarcane, nim trees, and margosa trees. I saw them all on my arrival at the delightful little town of Dehra Dun.

We got out of the bus at a jungle reservation, which we discovered was strongly fenced. The underbrush was thick, even at the edges. According to the bus driver, antelopes, deer, and even tigers were kept in reserves for protection when necessary. Farms and silos dotted the rest of the landscape. With water from five rivers, the earth is well nourished.

Dipping down some three thousand feet, we came to the Dehra Dun Valley. The valley is bounded on the north by the southern fringe of the Himalayas, by the Swalik Hills to the south, by the Ganges to the east, and by the Jumna River to the west. It is an unusually fertile spot with a superb climate and a wealth of flowers, fruit, and grain.

About midday, we stopped at a wayside hut to have some tea. I sat at a little table with two Punjabi ladies, a mother and daughter. Of course we talked about dress. They told me to come and examine their Punjabi costumes, with the knee-length kameez and the wide, ankle-length shalwar, like broad pantaloons. They wore their dupattas over the head and shoulders, not over the face. The magic word never failed. I was a schoolteacher, and we were friends.

I have often wondered if I would have had the presence of mind that these ladies had as the three of us went to the restroom. On the way to the tiny hut, with its hole in the floor and no running water, they took pains to describe, as delicately as possible, what I could expect. My foot did not go into the hole, and with the aid of my cane, I was able to keep my balance. There was no door, and the ladies discreetly stepped to the side.

"This must be different from America," they said as I thanked them.

What they lacked in facilities, they more than compensated for in graciousness and thoughtfulness. Could I ever forget them?

•　　•　　•

Agra and the Taj Mahal were my next venture. I consulted with an American travel agency near the Circle and found that the cost would be eighteen dollars. With my guide, I went to the nearby government travel agency and found that the fare was less than half the first quoted to me.

So, bright and early, I arrived in a rickshaw at the bus depot and boarded the large, lumbering tourist bus. The vehicle was full. I did not recognize the language of the crowd, which seemed to be all in one party. It turned out to be a group of Russians, both men and women.

Our first stop was a mosque, in front of which were many steps. The chief guide on the bus—there were two—came to me and said, "You are blind. You cannot see. You do not go into the mosque. You could have an accident."

I did not go into the mosque, but I knew I had to find some way to allay the guide's fears. When I returned to my seat, I clumsily sat down on the end of the *dhoti* of the gentleman beside me, pinning him to his seat.[5] My apologies opened a conversation. He was a Hindu from Madras. He was interested in the work of the teacher and preacher, Krishnamurti, and he was attending a series of his lectures in Delhi.[6] Would I like to go, too? As my knowledge of this great lecturer was confined to lectures I had read when he visited California, I was eager to attend. My new friend told me I would find many Americans at the meetings, held in a large tent.

In the meantime, we were on our way to Agra. I told the gentleman about my run-in with the guide and asked if he would let me take his arm, for I had risked coming without a guide on this occasion. I had no trouble after that. That was the second of the three times I was forbidden to do something because of my blindness.

As we approached Agra, it was not difficult for me to realize that we were in a Muslim world whose glory and grandeur were gone. The voice from a minaret, calling the faithful to prayer, sounded lonely in the midst of the ruins. Our guide described the glorious history of the Great Moguls, of Babar, of Hamayu of Jahungi, of Shah Jehan, the scions of the Mogul dynasty. It was hard to conceive that Akbar the Great was a contemporary of Shakespeare and Elizabeth I.

The beautiful Arjanan Bano was the wife of Shah Jehan. She died at the age of thirty-nine, bearing her fourteenth child. Grief-stricken, Shah Jehan had the Queen Palace built in her memory. The palace, or *mahal,* where the Moguls lived, stands in its semiruined glory before the approach to the mausoleum. Its size and splendor defy description. The high walls of the countless rooms were studded with precious and semiprecious stone—onyx, jade, lapis lazuli, and emerald. Some pieces of the original walls still remain, and some have been replaced. For the most part, only the empty settings tell of the invader's knife or the soldier of the Indian Mutiny some hundred years ago.

Still remaining are the exquisitely polished baths where rosewater and lavender once flowed. The palace was sprayed with water from the Jumna to keep it cool, and the pipelike drains throughout the rooms and terraces were far ahead of the plumbing in any Elizabethan stronghold of the same era.

Our guide lost himself in fantastic stories. He told us of the Peacock Throne, its gold, rubies, and emeralds stolen and lost forever in a shipwreck. He spoke of the Golden Chair, half of which might be in Teheran today. He wove these stories among the tales of *One Thousand and One Nights.* We were mesmerized by a blend of history and legend.

The Taj Mahal is indeed beautiful. I carried with me a small marble replica, and I studied its form as I listened to the guide's description and analysis. We walked among the long lily ponds and fountains. The thick petals of the water lilies were within arm's reach of the edge. No, they were not made by Shah Jehan. They were made at the request of Lord Curzon in 1931 to enhance the beauty of the mausoleum.

The broad Jumna flows by on the opposite side of the mausoleum. But the Taj Mahal itself is a thing of exquisite beauty. With my fingers I traced the filigree of the marble around the tomb—marble that was chiseled from solid stone into forms of intricate delicacy. The guide helped me trace the design with my upstretched hands.

Suddenly the guide stopped and placed in my hand a single,

half-wilted daisy. "There is a blind man, a beggar, sitting at the foot of the tomb," he explained. "Someone told him you are blind, too, and he gives you this flower."

I shook hands with the beggar in thanks. His heart was bigger than mine.

We descended into the lower part of the mausoleum. Seventeen feet below the tomb of the beautiful Mumtaz was the tomb of her husband, Shah Jehan. I smelled the oil of the guide's lantern and realized that no lights could or should enter the chamber below.

I walked all around the outside by the minarets, and on the terraces I felt the exquisite texture of the marble. In the warm rays of the sun, the marble was as soft as velvet to the touch. I felt in the presence of beauty, grandeur, and dignity. For the moment, I forgot about the blind beggar.

•   •   •

In Mumbai you slice off the end of a half-ripe coconut, put in a straw, and drink the milk inside. It does not taste like coconut milk; it is bitter, tart, and powerful. You drink coconut milk on Marine Drive along the front or by the edge of the water at midnight. You can hear the boats on the water and the lap of the waves on the shore. You come back to the Gateway and walk down the long steps to the water's edge.

Rich and poor, all Mumbai seemed to have come to the Gateway. I had to push through the crowds to get by. The city made me breathless. I seemed always to be pushing my way among beggars, businessmen, street hawkers, and hurrying shoppers. The government shops were richly stocked with silver, ivory, silks, and perfumes. The beach was pleasant; with my friend, I walked its full length.

The water of the Arabian Sea felt good on that hot Sunday morning. I was at home with friends in Mumbai—a brilliant young executive, his wife, and his mother. I was honored to be a guest in their home, to be welcomed as one of the family.

The young executive was blind. His blindness was no deterrent to his work or his success. Through his efforts, I saw how the social problem of blindness is being met through the work of farseeing, creative blind persons. India has an estimated two million blind persons, and that figure is conservative. A large but unknown percentage of these blind people are beggars. They sit on the sidewalks or crouch inside the doors of buildings, wailing dolefully for alms. There is nothing to be done for them except give them money. It is too late to salvage them. They are immune to training and rehabilitation. They are defeated before they start, second-class citizens because they are blind. This status has been society's verdict, and they have accepted it. It is not a tragedy to them, for they have never known anything else.

The tragedy comes when young blind men and women, capable of training and education, do not receive the opportunity to prepare for anything but a life of mendicancy. The National Association for the Blind seeks to provide them with such opportunity, to point the way to a new interpretation of the place of blind persons in society. The task is enormous in the face of tradition, lack of funds, ignorance, and public apathy.

With one of the young leaders in the movement, I was interviewed on the radio on an All India program. Our topic was "The Blind in Society." Not that I was qualified to speak on such a topic, after an all-too-brief seven months on the subcontinent. Yet, as an observer of some of the world's emergent nations, it was exciting to convey that blind persons on a global scale are seeking ways to participate in their countries' efforts to gain independence and self-determination. I had witnessed blind people working in home industries, placed in open industry, and training for specific jobs. The task was gigantic, but so was the beginning already made.

To see how the needs of blind children were being met, I visited four schools for the blind. The pupils were a pitifully small aggregate, considering the hundreds of thousands of blind children in the country in need of education. But again, these schools were a noble start. I received a warm welcome at every school I visited, for I had common cause with the teachers and the students. I was at home in the classrooms, talking with the children, listening to their reports in English and Gudjurat, a language I did not understand. The giggly little girls, the serious-minded boys, the studious, the indifferent, the lazy were there, just as they are in my own country.

The pupils asked many questions, translating to their fellow pupils when necessary. Three boys chuckled over the animal stories they read to me from their Braille readers. One bright little fellow addressed me on what to see in Mumbai. He was blind as I was, but we could each see Mumbai in our way.

The children sang. They made net bags and paper flowers. They played strange-sounding instruments, and I learned to like their music once I had heard it. The older children recited poems to me in English.

But why were not all of India's blind children receiving these opportunities? Perhaps it would come one day, when the idea of compulsory education, even in the first few grades, became a reality. Things are moving in that direction, but it will take a long, long time.

Will the world ever stay long enough at peace for us to establish a program of compulsory education? Barely 50 percent of the world's children receive an education today. Probably not even 1 percent of the world's blind children are so fortunate. Perhaps we might spare some tiny fraction of the price we will pay for that projected trip to the moon and turn it to the education of our children. For all children, blind and sighted alike, are our children. All of them have a right to education in this modern age of fast spending and faster transit. We cannot leave our children behind.

•   •   •

A great surprise awaited me one day in Mumbai. I made *Eve Weekly*. Here is what was written beside my picture:

> Dr. Mrs. Isabelle Grant
> Blind Schoolteacher, Counsellor and Administrator
> Currently on a tour through nineteen countries of the world, Dr. Mrs. Isabelle Grant, now in India, and totally blind as a result of glaucoma, is one of the most active persons I have met in a long time.
> Born in Scotland, Mrs. Grant secured a doctorate in comparative literature in the United States and subsequently taught in several schools in Los Angeles,

later becoming a counsellor and administrator in schools. During this time she married a well-known physician and combined the role of teacher and housewife at the same time.

When she became blind, she realized that she had two alternatives. One was to sit at home or enter a home for the blind and spend the remaining years of her life depressed and morose. The other alternative, the one which she accepted, was to step out and help other blind people in leading normal lives. In order to do this, she went back to the university and worked in the field of education of exceptional children, e.g., the blind, the deaf, the retarded, and the emotionally disturbed.

She is now a resource teacher for the education of blind children in a government public school which has both blind and sighted children learning side by side.

Tall, ladylike Dr. Mrs. Grant's talk is crisp and dynamic. On seeing her, one realizes the tremendous effort that she made in switching over from an active life of a person with sight into a more active life as a blind person.

Dr. Grant mentioned to me that a blind person reads in four ways and not one, as many people imagine. There is aural reading as when a normal person reads a newspaper to her. Then there are the Talking Books which are publications tape recorded for the blind. The third way of reading is through listening to records (not musical). The last way, of course, is the Braille, which is the slowest of all.

NOTES

1. Mohandas Karamchand Gandhi (1869–1948), known as the *mahatma*, or great soul, was the revered leader who helped India free itself from British rule through nonviolent resistance. He encouraged religious groups to respect one another and worked to improve the lives of women and the poor. Gandhi lived simply and wore clothing made from yarn he spun himself. He grieved the partition of India and the warfare between Hindus and Muslims. He was assassinated by a Hindu national, and the date of his death, January 30, is commemorated in India as Martyrs' Day. Gandhi's ashes are interred in a tomb in Delhi.

2. R. K. Laxman (1921–2015) is an Indian cartoonist and illustrator. His daily cartoon strip, *You Said It,* was published in the *Times of India.* A popular Indian TV series, *Ki Duniya,* is based upon his work.

3. Jawaharlal Nehru (1889–1964) served as India's first prime minister from 1947 until his death. He worked closely with Mahatma Gandhi as a leader in India's independence movement. As prime minister, he launched a series of programs to improve food production, develop industry, and build village schools.

4. The first World Agriculture Fair opened in New Delhi in 1959. Amriki Mela, the exposition's US exhibit, was built around the theme of "food, family, friendship, freedom." Displays included modern farm equipment, a dairy milking room, hybrid grains, and even a nuclear reactor that produced radioisotopes for agricultural use.

5. The dhoti is a long, white, cotton garment traditionally worn by Indian men in rural areas. It is held in place by a belt and may hang loosely to the knees or ankles.

6. Jiddu Krishnamurti (1895–1956) was a world-renowned lecturer, writer, and philosopher. He espoused no religion or political allegiance but believed that change in the world can come about only through change in the individual mind. His books include *The First and Last Freedom* and *The Only Revolution.*

CHAPTER 17
CEYLON AND THE SINGHALESE

S ri Lanka, known to the world as Ceylon, left me spellbound with its
exotic vegetation, its sounds, foods, and climate. The riot of color
I cannot surmise, but the warmth and kindness of the Singhalese
people is boundless.

Some eight degrees from the equator, the island of Ceylon has
a climate all its own. Of course it is hot, but its heat is tempered
by ocean breezes from all directions. Downpours with thunder are
almost a daily occurrence, and a blazing sun wipes up the water within
moments of its fall.

The old fort in Colombo is still British in language, commerce,
and atmosphere. Pettah, the old section of the city, was my choice. Its
crooked, narrow, cobbled streets, with two and sometimes three steps
up to the sidewalk, were quaint and sensible. Even in a waterspout,
the sidewalk remained dry. Awnings covered the fronts of the shops,
which were quaint as well. The hardware shop was a miniature, old-
time Klondike trading post, but Singhalese in style, not American.
The dry goods shop, with its shelves of saris and sarongs, smelled
like a clothes closet heavy with the odor of naphthalene balls. The
sound of the little Pettah shop was muffled, for it seemed to be full of
everything.

Pettah had a character all its own. Saint Lavinia was a hubbub of
industry, automobiles, and buses. The school I visited was built on a
cinnamon patch, flanked by rice paddies, fruit trees, and shrubbery.
New industry had taken over. I had an exciting afternoon in the

stadium, taking in a cricket match between the Royal Government and the Saint Thomas Colleges.[1] I screamed my head off, rooting for Saint Thomas, for my host was a Singhalese graduate of that Anglican institution of higher learning. He kept me posted on each development in the game, during the moments when he was not yelling, too. His charming wife, my hostess, was a little more subdued as she served us lemon juice to replace our dripping perspiration.

Hoarse and happy but soaking wet, we inched our way back to the bus. All Colombo seemed to have turned out for the match. While the match was at its boiling point, my excitement reached a pitch, too. All of a sudden, a huge wreath of artificial flowers fell into my lap. A rudely constructed box, covered with black cloth to simulate a coffin, was passed shoulder high through the stands; Royal was going to bury Saint Thomas! Other enormous wreaths were flung around, too. I wanted to keep mine as the most unusual souvenir of my global tour, but anticipating the consternation and confusion of the bewildered customs officer, I decided to forego that thrill. Quickly I rose and tossed the wreath to the shrieking fans across the aisle.

I was very much bothered by Ceylon's mosquitoes. I slept under a mosquito net, so I was safe from them at night. How I loved to lie and listen to their hum, knowing they could never get around the net that I tucked under the mattress all around. The bar of wood lengthwise over the bed gave me ample room to move around and assure myself that not a fraction of an inch of netting had worked loose. Had one little mosquito invaded my fortress, there would have been a battle royal to get it out and prevent an army from coming in. Precaution was paramount.

During the day and particularly in the cool of the evening, all the flying insects seemed to aim for my face. Had I smoked, I probably would not have been such a target. I do not smoke, so I had to bear the onslaught.

I loved the sounds of Ceylon. A morning symphony started just after four. Magpies dominated, and I could distinguish the soft warble of a sparrow above the noisy cuckoo and paddi birds. The cuckoo lays her eggs, I am told, in the nest of the mother crow for the crow to hatch. Fire-thief birds with trailing tails, cloth-thief birds, kingfishers, golden orioles, and robins all chimed in, with the *caw-caw* of the crow breaking in during a lull.

I admired the little blind boys in the school as they identified each bird by its song. We missed the graceful sweep of trailing tails as the thief-birds flew from tree to tree. But we followed their songs as they perched on the treetops or swooped up fast from the paddi fields.

The flowers were as exotic as the birds. I examined a dozen varieties of hibiscus, with huge blossoms that were like full bouquets in my hand. Oleanders, heavy with blossoms, lotus flowers, roses in profusion, jasmine, jacaranda, queen of the night, and temple flowers lavished their perfumes in the air, especially after a rain. The foliage was thick and lush. When I was not walking through moist, rich grass, I was ankle-deep in shrubbery and creepers. One banana leaf from the garden could well have served as a tablecloth. It was large enough for me to sleep on. Jambo trees with enormous trunks filled the foot of the garden. Mango trees, papaya trees, cocorusk trees, breadfruit—all grew within a stone's throw of the house.

I wanted to feel the weight of a breadfruit, so an enormous one, split because of its ripeness, was placed in my arms. Immediately I felt my arms covered with running ants. These were not the dainty little ants to which I was accustomed but large, thick fellows, scurrying between my fingers, over my elbow, round my arms. It was a sickening feeling, but it did not last long. We shook them off.

That was not as bad as the morning I stepped into one of the open concrete sewage drains that ran through the garden. I was really nauseated. I clung to the edge of a banana leaf, holding on, standing on one foot and not daring to move. A bucket of water was quickly on hand. I plunged my foot plus shoe into the bucket, then into another. It was all over after an agonizing five minutes, but I still wonder why these surface drains are left uncovered. I suppose they are open in case of overflow, but they are a nuisance to us blind people. Ever after, I was careful to probe with my cane!

The sago palm grows in Ceylon, and I am very fond of sago pudding. Sago flavored with juggery is a dish fit for the gods. Juggery is crystallized cane sugar, but in Ceylon it has an especially delicate flavor. Food was richly seasoned with cinnamon, cloves, ginger, or pepper, all of which grow on the island. Used alone or in combination, they were like adding nectar to any dish. Like any French connoisseur, I spread juggery on my bread and spiced it with selected condiments to suit my taste. Each concoction was unique, delicate, delicious.

To eat six bananas in succession was an ordinary feat! There were short ones and long ones, fat ones and thin ones, little, fat ones and big, fat ones, sweet ones and tart ones and thin-skinned ones. There were not quite fifty-seven varieties, but the number seemed to me not far short. As I finger the bananas here on the market, priced at twenty-five cents a pound, I think nostalgically of the paradise of Ceylon.

My Singhalese hostess, Clarisse, was an artist with her saris. She wore two kinds, a drape sari and a Kandian sari. The drape was the usual throw-over style, but the Kandian intrigued me. How could she arrange it to have this graceful flounce start at the front waist, dip to the left, then around the back with such dainty symmetry? Would she show me?

Dressed first in the little choli, or waistcoat, I stood by the bed. Clarisse showed me how to pivot around, leaving yards of sari on the bed, gradually folding myself into them. Then she showed me that, by keeping a handful of the sari carefully folded in the palm of the left hand, while the rest was being swathed around me, I could gently drop the folded material over my hips. She helped me secure the effect of an old-time "basque," as chic as it was difficult to manipulate. In the process, the six-yard sari always remained intact.

Then there was the "half-sari," which the young girls wore. One hung like a skirt without a bodice and was loosely draped around the hips, reaching to the floor. Made of georgette or silk, these saris were elegant and chic. My friend Clarisse was as smart as any of her saris.

We went to see the native dances. The music was haunting, and the four-foot masks were weird. After all, they were intended to ward off evil spirits.

I could not leave Ceylon without visiting a rubber plantation and the plantation where my tea was grown. On the way, I passed bullocks plowing the land or threshing the rice as they turned the big wheel, yoked together, dragging loads of vegetables. They were portly bullocks, for there was no shortage of feed for them.

Standing by a rubber tree, I felt the cut on the bark about three feet up the trunk. I ripped the crude rubber from the tree in strips until I had a sticky handful. The coolie alongside me was emptying the coconut cup of its gummy milk into his bucket. His job was to go from tree to tree, gathering in the sap. In a shed, acid is poured over the sap to make it coagulate. The lumps are pressed out with heat, processed, and made into sheets for export.

Continuing on our way, we rose to the tea plateaus. Rows and rows of small tea bushes, closely cropped, stretched between the irrigation furrows that kept the water from draining downhill. Women in saris and shady hats picked the two slender tea leaves with the node from among the tougher older leaves. They threw them over their shoulders into the baskets they carried on their backs. The leaves were then spread out on shelves covered with jute sacking, swept into a chute, crushed between rollers, soaked in water, dried in ovens, and put through sieves for grading.

I sampled the four grades of orange pekoe between my fingers. I had to confess that I could only gauge my preference through taste. Even the dust of the dried leaves is exported for certain kinds of tea.

I thought the people working on the plantations seemed happy, but theirs was a hot job. Even with their straw hats and sarongs, the heat was intolerable. The women liked their work, they said. I would now appreciate more my brew and my crepe soles.

Naturally I wanted to learn about education in Ceylon. Because of the British occupation until independence was acquired in 1947, there were government schools and a fair number of institutions of higher learning, many of them with religious support. I learned that an estimated 80 percent of the children of the island receive some standard of education, and between 10 and 15 percent of the country's blind children receive instruction. In comparison with other countries in the subcontinent and the Far East, these percentages are high, so the situation seems altogether favorable. Teachers receive instruction in local training colleges, many of them taking postgraduate work in the United Kingdom.

I found that a program of rehabilitation for the adult blind is in progress, slow indeed but moving. Opportunity for the blind in open industry is not yet provided; segregation of blind persons is still the accepted social order. Yet an association of the blind is becoming active, and the work of these blind citizens reflects the self-determination of the country. The future holds much in store for them.

The Department of Social Welfare is alert; its members talked freely about their goals for the placement of young blind men. I had the rare opportunity to speak with several of them. They were interested in their training and in their placement. They were also as interested in what was happening in my country as I was in theirs. Though they are blind, they want to see the world, too.

At the end of my visit, I sat in the airport, hugging a parting gift of three pounds of the most delicious tea ever a tea gourmet could imagine. I wondered how I was going to get all of it past customs. I was headed back to India.

NOTE

1. The Saint Thomas Colleges are several schools for boys in Sri Lanka. They were founded in the 1840s and 1850s and were originally affiliated with the Anglican Church. The College of Saint Thomas Mount Lavinia is located in Colombo and has branches in Bandarawela and Guruthalawa. The schools provide primary and secondary education based on the British system.

CHAPTER 18
FROM MADRAS TO KOLKATA

India is a nation of many countries, each with a personality all its own. To get any comprehensive idea of this great nation, I should have stayed much longer. The temptation was great, for my interest was high.

My impression of the northwest provinces was that of luxury beside abject poverty. The states of Gujarat and Mahrat left me with the impression of extreme affluence among the few and hunger among the many. Although I did not visit Kerala, I came in contact with several South Indians who whetted my curiosity about their region.

Madras

Madras did not seem to have the extremes of wealth and poverty that I witnessed in Mumbai and New Delhi. It is a harbor city, a center of education and culture, surrounded on its land side by fertile fields and plenty of water. Though it has pronounced European overtones, it savors of the Far East. Mumbai, its counterpart to the west, is distinctly western in outlook and manner.

After my visit to Ceylon, I found Madras to be a restful contrast. Its lovely buildings, its long stretches of beach, its Old World shops and its busy harbor had a calming effect on me. In Madras, I enjoyed stimulating teacup gossips with some unusually interesting women. One of them was an American who ran a nursery program. She loved her children, some from well-to-do families and some off the streets. All of them spoke Tamil as their first language and also knew English.

How did the average American woman compare with the woman from Madras? One woman I met was studying law at Madras University. She shocked her neighbors by wearing shorts. She and her friends, male and female, put on bathing suits to go swimming at the beach. That was going too far!

Another woman, who taught in a local men's college, was finishing her doctorate in hygiene and physical education. Another was principal of a girls' college, having taken part of her training in the United States.

Obviously, we were all of a kind—independent and focused on our work. But what were the other women of Madras doing? Were they all so career-minded?

Our conversation veered to the question of marriage. Marriages were still arranged; the love match was the exception. The bride did not choose her husband, and only in rare cases did she even see him before the wedding day. If the family was Buddhist, her relatives made wedding arrangements with the priest. The bride did not choose her wedding dress. It might be satin with gold brocade or something less expensive, but it was the gift of the groom's family.

The bride and groom were selected by families that had eligible members to be married off. The dowry and exchange of gifts were discussed as business arrangements. The bride had no voice in the affair, although it concerned her whole future.

The parents of the bride provided the wedding festivities, sometimes lasting for six days, with five hundred to a thousand friends and relatives of both families in attendance. People came from great distances and expected to be provided with room and board. They slept on the floor of the bride's house or under a canopy set up in the adjacent compound. They ate sitting cross-legged on the ground.

"Isn't it interesting how few divorces there are among these planned marriages?" remarked one of the teachers.

"All owing to the submissiveness of the wives," commented another.

I asked if similar arrangements were made if the families were

Christian. I learned that a Christian marriage in India was usually a love marriage. Vows were exchanged in the church, with little or no pomp and ceremony.

I asked about the status of the Christian in this country of so many religions. The discussion was revealing. Under the present regime, regional and national loyalties were paramount, and all things foreign were unwelcome. As Christians made up a very small minority, they were not often vocal. Extreme nationalists regarded them as intruders, particularly the Christian missionaries. Having just cast off the British yoke, these extremists feared a rising American influence. Wary of a cultural or political invasion, they distrusted Indian Christians.

The fear went further. When Christians assumed leadership in a philanthropic or social welfare movement, the movement was often suspect as a cloak for foreign imperialism or infiltration. I asked if this fear were nationwide, and none of my friends denied the possibility. Christians did not take the fear seriously, but they were careful not to antagonize anyone.

For me, it was a joy and an education to exchange ideas and compare ways of life without prejudice or frayed nerves. We met on common ground, we talked, and we went our separate ways in tolerance and understanding.

Yet I know I would have gone much deeper in our discussions had I been able to converse with people in their language. I felt the situation most acutely when I met children. I wanted so much to exchange greetings with them and to make friends. One little girl ran her hands up and down my cane. I had to ask her busy mother to explain its significance to her. It was her busy mother, too, who prepared the dessert of rose petals soaked in syrup, delicately perfumed. How I wish I could have talked with her!

Through my inquiries about the education of blind persons, I had the opportunity to visit two schools for the blind, one a church school, the other supported by the government. Both were excellent institutions. However, only a very small percentage of the blind children from the city and the surrounding countryside attended school. The schools were expensive to run, and money was scarce. One high-level educator told me there was a keen interest in extending the existing program, but knowledge was lacking, and there were few trained teachers to carry out such specialized work. I heard the same story everywhere: "We know something should be done, but we don't know what to do or how to do it."

Nevertheless, I felt that Madras was ahead of the game. I was privileged to visit a bicycle factory where fifteen blind men worked alongside their sighted neighbors. They did equivalent work and met equivalent or higher standards, according to the supervisor's report. Prior to placement, they underwent a brief period of on-the-job training. One man fitted wire spokes into place, and another put pieces of chain around the wheels. Sadly, I could not speak to them; I did not know their language. The supervisor interpreted for us, and that had to suffice. Blindness was not the problem between us; it was the lack of communication! I had to be satisfied with a cordial handshake while the supervisor did the rest.

Kolkata

West Bengal and its capital, Kolkata (or Calcutta), kept me guessing, bombarded with ever-changing impressions. Kolkata reflected the heterogeneity of all of India. It is a city of many tongues and many religions, of conflicting ideas about politics and nationalism, and it is polarized by extremes of luxury and destitution. How could I comprehend the indifference to the dead man on the street and the reverence for the Brahman bull that wandered across the path of the streetcar?

The hungry beggar on the street is not concerned with his country's contradictions; he needs food. The legions of hungry villagers are even less concerned with the gap between rich and poor, for they know less. They, too, need food. The population seems too enormous to feed and care for.

What is the life of the blind person in city and village? The endlessness of time is the endlessness of their condition. It has been, and it is. Time alone cannot change conditions, but people can.

Kolkata, a city of seven million, queen of the Bay of Bengal, is crowned by the majesty of the Victoria Memorial. It is the home of princes and maharajahs. The beauty of Paris, London, and Vienna fall short of Kolkata's exotic Asian splendor. The city is elegant with its array of single- and multispan bridges, its lush vegetation, its coco palms, and its swimming pools, or tanks. In tanks along the shady walks of the Maidan Park, women wash their saris and their dogs.[1] I could reach the water lilies that grew in profusion close to the edge and smell their freshness and fragrance. The hundreds of goats in Maidan Park were pets. Boys milked the goats on the streets and in the park itself.

On the sidewalk, insolent monkeys whipped their tails around my ankles. They darted across the street or scampered up the pillars of a verandah, prattling lustily all the time.

I patted the humped back of a Brahman bull as he squatted on the street. He was lean and bony.

"How do they stay alive?" I asked.

"People feed them," my guide told me. "They just wander on and on."

The pedestrian gets out of the bull's way; the bull does not step aside for anyone. The impatient foreign driver blows his raucous horn, but the bull does not stir. The Sikh taxi driver in his starched, trailing saffron robes and elaborate turban, which he was eager to show me, knew better than to try to get by. He waited.

I stepped into cow dung only once. It does not accumulate in the streets. The children pick it up and make it into cakes to use for fuel.

On the free day, lines of children with their mothers awaited the opening of the National Museum of Arts. I wanted to talk with them, but I had no words. I was with an English woman who had spent many years in India, but neither of us knew Bengali—if that was the language the children spoke.

On Thursday, we mingled with the crowds in front of the mosque. In this strongly Hindu nation, these hundreds of Muslims had the freedom to worship in their own way. I asked my friend to count how many women were in the crowds. She saw none around the compound of the mosque, but a few sat on the edge of the pavement along the street.

Before the mosque, children and adults swarmed around a bright red Himalayan cat. He was a brilliant red, said my guide, and the children were stroking his outstretched paw under the wiring of his cage. I did not attempt to reach him, for I could not get near enough to the cage through the hoard of people.

As I sat on the verandah of the hostel above the noise of the city in the late afternoon, my attention was drawn to the wailing of a cat close by.

"Oh," said my friend, "he cannot get at the lizards running up the wall. Their bellies are fat with savory, wriggly insects."

I believe I climbed more steps and entered more buildings in Kolkata than in any other city in India. I felt I was in the midst of a colossal mass of masonry. Many buildings erected by the British now served as government offices. I visited Christian churches of all denominations, each with a unique history, from the Scottish Presbyterian Church to the Barey Baptist. Each building was evidence of the contribution the British made to culture, art, religion, and government. But too few people participated in these cultural opportunities.

Countless tradesmen ran little shops along the sidewalks. A woman and her husband made rice cakes on a brazier, sending forth a pleasant fragrance of fuel and cooking. There were the barber, the cook, the dobhi with his washing, the pen-and-pencil repairman, the durzay with his sewing machine out on the street in front of his stall, the straw sandal vendor, and the basket maker. Often the stall served as a shop in the daytime and a home at night. With water, the faithful splashed the images and garlands of the sidewalk Hindu temple as they prayed. The temples and the worshipers lying prone before them blocked the way of the passerby.

Dirt was everywhere, and the city was overrun with cockroaches. Evil-smelling dirt clogged the streets and alleys. There was plenty of water available, but water and dirt did not seem to get together.

An American friend, Mr. Geffner, frequented a Kolkata teashop that seemed cleaner than the rest, though still it was not clean by US standards. One day the proprietor asked him how he could be more American and better off.

"If I were you," Mr. Geffner said, "I'd stop throwing dirt out in the street, and I'd start cleaning the pavement in front of the shop."

"My neighbors would laugh at me," the proprietor said. "We just do it this way."

"Try it," said his American visitor.

The proprietor gave it a try. Within two weeks, other shopkeepers on the street followed suit. The little shops were cleaned up and attractive, and they were still doing business.

One young Hindu had a sense of humor that I enjoyed. I asked him what he was going to do with his college degree when he completed his schooling. "I'll go into government work," he told me, "and be a crook like everyone else."

I went on a revealing ride one day. My American friend, a nurse, went to the hospital to pick up a baby whom she had left the previous week. Mary brought the baby back to the station wagon. "She is two years old," said Mary, "and was slowly dying of starvation in the refugee camp. She looks better now."

I asked to hold the child. She was the size of a six-month-old. Her little chest was cone shaped, and her stomach bulged.

"Like so many of the children here," said Mary, "she has rickets, and what else we don't know. There are seven other children in the family. When the milk arrived, she was always the last one to get any. There is a younger baby, too."

Mary spoke to the child in the few Bengali words she knew. "She's laughing at us," she told me.

Our young volunteer driver turned to us. "What is the future for these babies?"

"We can't ask for the future," Mary said. "Today is enough."

She went on to tell me about the child's family. "The father is about forty—an old man. His wife told me he's too old to work. 'But I'm forty, and I'm working,' I said. I thought I could get the father to start working on one of the plots granted by the government, raising vegetables. His wife just insisted that he is old, too old to work."

A person's actual age has very little meaning. Probably the husband had been poorly fed all his life. He had no education, and most likely he was ill. He was too old to work.

It was probably too late to make any changes for the husband, but it certainly was not too late to start making changes with the children. Could we control the number of children who were born? Family planning could contribute to family happiness. It could cut down on disease and improve nutrition. But the outsider could not implement such a policy. That was a matter for the people of India to determine.

Bert, the young driver of our station wagon, was a teacher from Canada. He and Mary, his wife, had decided to devote a year of their lives to serving the people in the refugee settlements around Kolkata. I thought of the discussions I had in Madras. Surely there was no imperialism in the hearts and minds of Mary and Bert. They were living their religion; they were helping the poor and needy who were God's people. They brought the loaves and fishes, the medicine and the love.

In Kolkata, I visited three schools for the blind. Most of the students either spoke or understood English. They wanted to know what young blind people did in America. What were their occupations? Were they accepted in open industry?

I marveled at the social consciousness of these young citizens. I marveled at their keen analysis of work with and for the blind in Kolkata. They sensed intrigue, exploitation, and personal aggrandizement by those who ran the agencies, all under the cloak of helping the blind. We concluded that this pattern was worldwide. It would have to be tolerated until blind people themselves could assume leadership in their cause.

These young people, whose average age was twenty, knew that education was the only way to equality. They wanted Braille books on all subjects. They wanted to know about foreign countries and how blind people fare elsewhere. One girl asked me how she could become a switchboard operator. She had read that there were many blind people in this occupation in Austria. Did I know any blind physical therapists? What training did they have? As a blind teacher, how did I handle clerical work?

We talked about integrated education of blind pupils in India, programs that allow blind pupils to go to the regular government school with assistance from a resource teacher. The students asked me what Indian cities I had visited and what I found there. The conversation went along for three hours, half of us sitting on the floor as we talked. When the discussion began to lag, it was revived with a cup of tea.

I learned that some of these blind youth had tried to get into industry, but they did not have sufficient training. Facilities for that extra training were not available. Two or three were attending college and would go back to the school for the blind to teach. I told them about the bicycle factory in Madras. I also told them of several training centers that I had visited, small though some of them were.

Would society ever learn that blind people could do more than make baskets and straw sandals, if given the training and opportunity? After all, sighted people need training for jobs, too. It's not asking for anything extraordinary!

I sensed no bitterness among these young people. They knew the social milieu that gave rise to their second-class citizenship. They also knew that they themselves were the only people who understood their capabilities and desires. They alone could bring about change.

They would do everything that lay in their power, but they needed help. Social prejudice in their country was very great. They knew that progress would be slow. Life-and-death problems needed immediate attention. Hunger, disease, and poor sanitation affected the nation as a whole. "Still," they argued, "we cannot wait until one problem is solved before tackling another!"

As I sipped my tea and listened to the crossfire, I mused that only yesterday we had not known one another. Today we were talking with the frankness of longtime friendship. Was it because we shared blindness as a common bond? I think that was only part of the explanation. These young Hindus had a sense of their obligation to society. They wanted to contribute, just as other people did. They knew they could do it if given a chance. As individuals, they were acquiring the spirit of self-determination that was sweeping their country. Let us give them time and the help they need.

•   •   •

My friend Margaret, a nurse, had spent forty years in India. Now she was back in Kolkata on a visit. One morning at the breakfast table, she talked with me about the problem of the blind. We agreed that there was little to be done for the older blind, either the men or the women. They accepted their status of mendicancy, and it had become a habit. Our concern then should be with the blind children, to prevent, if possible another generation of beggars. We talked about the possibilities in education but also of the insurmountable obstacles she had seen in her adopted country.

"Let's talk this over with Her Excellency, the governor of West Bengal," she suggested. Her Excellency was Margaret's friend, a woman she admired as no other on earth. Within a few days, we received a stately invitation.

The entrance to the governor's palace was imposing. Busts, urns, jardinieres—each was an elegant work of art. On the grounds, fountains sprayed mist in the cool breeze. The council rooms were hung with rich tapestries and adorned with golden-lion thrones. One held the throne of Tipu Sultan,[2] who imprisoned the British soldiers in the early days of the occupation, when Lord Robert Clive and Warren Hastings struggled for a foothold.[3] The sides of the throne were made of solid silver.

The long corridor leading to the reception room was flanked by guardsmen. Each wore the uniform of his particular tribe or district. One guardsman, amused at Margaret's description, removed his *topi* and placed it in my hands.[4] His uniform was white, and he showed me the brass buttons in a semicircle around his chest. His topi had an Indian crest in front and a tall, starched piece high up the back and hanging down to his waist. The crown part was swathed around his head. All of the soldiers were armed.

The secretary ushered us in, and Her Excellency greeted us. Tea was served with Bengal almond and coconut cakes. I was too excited to eat, but Her Excellency made us feel at ease with her warm hospitality, grace, and regal dignity. She thanked me for the booklet on the education of blind children, which I had taken the liberty of sending her. She also thanked Margaret for her book of poems, which she had sent to me some time previously.

With Margaret, Her Excellency talked about the vast problems she faced in her exalted position. The refugee problem was so discouraging, so enormous. How could she begin to do all that was needed?

Her Excellency told us that her father had had glaucoma and lost the sight of one eye. We talked about the plight of blind persons doomed to lifelong defeatism. Tuberculosis, famine, flood, disease, hunger—these were immediate problems. Education came next and would take time. Yes, every child, handicapped or otherwise, must have educational opportunity.

But hard work was in progress. Many conscientious persons were carrying on in the face of seeming defeat. One government minister, a physician by profession, saw between thirty-five and forty-five patients in his clinic before seven each morning and then went on to perform his official duties.

As we rose to take our leave, Her Excellency said I would be interested in her sari. It was lavender. She always wore a gardenia. She also wore two simple gold bracelets that she had received from her mother.

Her Excellency embodied kindness, dignity, and love. Her voice carried concern, hurt, and sadness for her people, brightened only by her willingness and ability to do all she could to alleviate their conditions. The visit was truly inspiring.

Margaret and I then visited the Council, where we heard representatives state their cases on the floor. Technical assistance, they said, was a prime need. India needed knowledge of fertilizers, selection of seeds, and industrial methods. The government should help now and step out when the people were ready to take over. And so the discussion went on.

In another discussion, we heard that leprosy [Hansen's disease] was on the increase. Too many children were developing the dread disease. People's attitudes about disease must change. Malnutrition had to be attacked, and the people must take their part.

I left the meetings with a deep admiration for the people working so earnestly against such relentless odds. They were facing their problems and legislating to solve them. They were not beguiled by starry promises from foreign intruders. They recognized that they needed help. They knew how to ask for it, but they did not wish to be bought. They were proud of their country and its independence. When they ask, we should be ready to give bread, not stones.

India's problems were too big for me to comprehend. I left with a feeling of sadness and inadequacy. The people had been kind to me and had taken me in as a friend. I had been in their homes and broken bread with them.

Many more of my people will travel in their country. I trust that others will understand India better than my opportunity afforded me. I trust that my people will offer the help that is needed. I trust that they will stop and listen until the pangs of hunger have been assuaged and all of the children are in school.

As students and friends, Indians will come to my country, and we shall open our doors to them. As we come to understand one another, may they set aside their notions of our ugliness, our dollar craziness and imperialism.

NOTES

1. Maidan Park is the largest park in Kolkata. It contains several playgrounds, a racetrack, several soccer stadia, and a cricket field called Edens Gardens. The park is also home to the Victoria Memorial, a monumental museum celebrating Queen Victoria and the history of India under British rule.

2. Known as the Tiger of Mysore, Tipu Sultan (1750–1799) is a hero in the history of Indian resistance to the British occupation. He ruled the Sultanate of Mysore from 1782 until his death. He was killed as he defended the Fort of Srirangapatna during the Fourth Anglo-Mysore War.

3. Lord Robert Clive (1725–1774) served as Commander in Chief of India under the British East India Company. His victory at the Battle of Plassey in 1757 gave the East India Company control of Bengal. Warren Hastings (1732–1818) became governor-general of Bengal in 1772. He was recalled to England in 1784 after accusations of corruption, but was acquitted at the end of a seven-year trial.

4. The topi is a simple, wide-banded cap that was worn by Mahatma Gandhi during the struggle for Indian independence. Generally known as the Gandhi cap, it was frequently worn by Indian officials and political candidates during the postindependence decades.

CHAPTER 19
BURMA AND THE WATER FESTIVAL

"What are you doing, Tina?" I asked as I heard the *flap-flap* of a cloth on the walls of my room.

"Trying to get the lizards down."

"Oh, don't bother, Tina. Leave them on the wall. They're safe there, and so am I. I'll keep my mosquito net up over the bed during the night, and they won't be running all over me."

So the lizards were not disturbed. But the mosquito net was very necessary, even in the afternoon in Yangon [formerly Rangoon]. Insects were everywhere. They hit me in the face, on the arms, and on the legs, for I never wore stockings.

Yangon, a fair-sized city of seven hundred thousand, was hot and sultry, set upon the huge, swampy delta of the Irrawaddy River. Torrential rains in the mountainous regions flooded the rivers, and Yangon seemed to catch all of the runoff.

My first impression of Yangon was that it was a rich city. It boasted a large harbor where ocean liners constantly loaded the tin, oil, jute, rice, and fruits that the country produced. The harbor and the elaborate hotels convinced me that there was money somewhere.

Here, as in so many other places, my first impressions proved misleading. When I talked with people who lived there, I learned more. They admitted freely their fear of Communist infiltration. They claimed that whole villages already were in Communist hands. The Chinese had come across the border, appropriating property and terrorizing the Burmese people. The government would have to exert more effort to combat the infiltration, if it could. But the people themselves were tired. The Japanese invasion during World War II had drained their strength. The land was still strewn with thousands of tons of metal debris left after the fighting. The Burmese guests at the hostel where I stayed were not afraid to speak out, but they felt powerless to cope with their country's problems.

The opportunities for blind people were severely limited. Blind pupils were not allowed to take the matriculation exam at the end of seventh grade, an exam that would qualify them for higher education. In segregated workshops, blind people caned chairs and made baskets and coal hampers. A few blind women used looms and made curtains.

I spoke with one young blind worker who desperately wanted to go to college. He was practicing his typing and working to improve his English. If he could not study in his own country, he would go somewhere else. I learned of a blind lad from the Christian Mission School who was studying in the United States. He would return and teach in the mission school. These young blind people knew what they wanted. They knew what they could do, if only they were given the opportunity.

While I was visiting the mission school, some young people from the city came to give the blind children a treat. They brought lemonade and sweetmeats, for it was festival time. It was indeed a kindly gesture, but as one of the older pupils remarked to me, it was further evidence of society's view that the blind were objects of charity.

•   •   •

Though a host of pressing problems seemed to crowd out the needs of the blind, I was heartened to observe that Burmese women were taking an active part in the social welfare of their country. I talked with several women who were involved in social welfare or held public office. I had observed a similar awakening among the women of India. I imagined the growing impact these intelligent, dedicated women will have on Asia's subcontinent. They have it in their power to revolutionize education and social welfare. Perhaps it is not a vain hope to look forward to the day when women will offer blind persons the consideration they merit as human beings.

Compared to families in Pakistan and India, Burmese families were relatively small. A family of five or six children was considered large. The literacy rate was fairly high in the cities, reported at 70 percent. However, literacy was far lower in the villages, and the blind were not included in these figures at all. Of the thousands of blind children in the country, I was told that only about three hundred attended school—and that was a liberal estimate.

An average coolie earned seventy to one hundred djats a month, about twenty dollars in US currency. According to the women I spoke with, that salary could support a family. With its fertility, its water, and its sunshine, the country could produce plenty of food.

My pronunciation of Burmese names and words was often the cause of hilarity. I had considerable trouble with names. It seemed incomplete to call a friend Mrs. U Nu. Names such as Oo Ba, Po Ko, Po Cho, and Day O made me think I might have trouble with the Burmese language! I was corrected on my pronunciation of the word Yangon, too. As I was led to understand, the name of the capital is pronounced Yang-on.

Burmese women are often artistic. They showed me many kinds of *ketchin*, or handwork. They did hand embroidery and made jewelry of their own design, all exquisite to the touch. I listened to their descriptions of their star sapphires; they must have been very pretty.

•   •   •

The Burmese New Year's Festival took place during my stay in Yangon. My introduction to this late-spring celebration came as I rode in the bus from the airport. Despite the stifling heat, the windows of the bus were tightly shut. Suddenly I heard the shouts and laughter of children as bucketful after bucketful of water splashed against the bus windows. The bus driver spoke little English, and all of the passengers were Burmese, but eventually I disentangled the explanation—"Water Festival."[1]

Instead of depositing me in the center of the city at one of the large hotels, the bus driver indicated I should stay on the bus so he could drive me to my hostel. He rushed me up the front steps just as a bucket of water was unleashed upon me. He then brought up my suitcase.

My hostess, an American woman, explained that the festival celebrated the New Year in the Buddhist calendar. Today was Children's Day. The festivities would last all week, and I would be in the thick of them, so I would have to watch out for more dousing. Some people carried umbrellas, and the more courteous water throwers allowed them to stay dry.

I went downtown in the hostel car, and we rolled up all the windows and smiled benignly at the bucket-wielding children. Rounding a corner, we realized it was not a bucket this time but a hose that showered continuously—a smart though mean device!

The following day, I took a cab to the city, for I had to arrange a change in my visa. Leaving the office, I reached the bus in safety. As usual, I proceeded to put a paperclip in my passport to help the next clerk find his place in the mass of documents I carried. I had forgotten to raise the window and for my neglect was treated to an unwelcome shower. I was an easy target. I only hoped that the water was clean!

That day was Grown-Ups' Day, and the adults had even more fun than the children. In the evening, I attended the parade with its humorously decorated floats. Jazz overshadowed Burmese melodies, much to my disappointment, but young Burma was enjoying a wonderful night on the town, the final eve of the celebration.

New Year's Day was a solemn occasion. The festivities moved to the pagodas.[2] With two friends, I joined the crowds. We climbed the steep hill to the main pagoda, which my friends explained had a cone-shaped dome. Saffron-robed priests came in groups, each carrying his begging bowl. At the approach to the enormous temple, we were asked to remove our shoes. The ground was hot and muddy, for on this special day the pilgrims showered the Buddhas with water as they chanted their prayers. I still do not understand why water was thrown on the Buddhas. Water on us mortals was meant to wash away the sins of the past year and cleanse us for the new year to come.

We visited an unusual temple. At the entrance was a market, with stalls where vendors sold everything from feed to cloth, from hardware to enormous brass gongs and an endless variety of bells. The noise swelled as families arrived with picnic baskets, cooking braziers, sleeping mats, and enigmatical bundles. My friends and I sat in the midst of them on the slimy cobbled pavement and ate a snack of fruit.

The temple was a cool relief from the heat of the other seven pagodas outside. Young people threw water over the images as they smoked their cheroots. Older people chanted audibly, throwing flowers and water. It was a motley gathering, the well-dressed and ostensibly rich elbowing their way among the beggars. The reverence of the chanters was stifled by noise.

The celebration drew people of all creeds to the pagodas. About 5 percent of Burma's people were Christians, and an estimated 13 percent were Muslims and Hindus. The majority were Buddhists and animists.

A few people at the festival took notice of us as visitors and readily approached us to talk. As they spoke English, they gave us an interpretation of the festivities. They showed us around and were most hospitable.

After a while, we descended the hill, found our shoes, and hunted for the car. The stir and confusion reminded me of a baseball game in which our team had won. This was a religious festival—Burmese style.

•   •   •

Easter Sunday fell the following week. I attended a sunrise service in the compound of the local Christian high school. The morning was chilly, dewy, and fresh. We had a half-hour walk from the hostel. The road was perfumed by the early scent of flowers, grass, and trees. It was quiet all around. We took our seats on benches in the open. The hush was broken only by the flight of a bird overhead or the warbling of others as they began to awaken.

As the dawn broke, so did the bird chorus. The birds emulated the trumpets and the organ that had been brought for the occasion. No Easter was ever more glorious than that celebration by a handful of people in far-off Burma. The birds raised their paeans of praise to the skies. Alleluia!

Sing we to our God above,
Praise eternal as His love.
Praise Him all ye heavenly host,
Father, Son, and Holy Ghost.
Alleluia!

The verses of the Gospel according to Saint Mark, read in Burmese, then in English, were warm, reverent, and hopeful. The benediction and the Nunc Dimittis were borne aloft, echoed and reechoed by the organ, the trumpets, and the birds, in complete triumph.[3]

NOTES

1. Throughout Southeast Asia and parts of China, the New Year is celebrated by a festival that involves ritual cleansing with water. During the Burmese Water Festival, or Thingyan, revelers boisterously douse people and objects. Held for four days, usually from April 13 to 16, Thingyan also includes music, dance, puppetry, and parades with decorated floats.
2. A pagoda is a graceful tiered structure used during religious worship in Theravada Buddhism. Pagodas are so much part of the Burmese landscape that Burma is called the Land of Pagodas.
3. The Nunc Dimittis, or Canticle of Simeon, is a traditional evening prayer used in many Christian denominations. In Latin, the words *nunc dimittis* mean now dismissed.

CHAPTER 20
THAILAND, THE FREE LAND

My usual procedure on arrival in a new city was to inquire about guided tours. I then would select the places I wanted to visit for more extensive study. My tour through Bangkok filled me with curiosity. Unexpected, lively, romantic, and Eastern, Thailand is a very rich country. Its people are alert and progressive. They are world travelers, and world travelers come to visit their country.

Bangkok might well be called the Venice of the East. Everywhere I went, I was either on the water or crossing over bridges. And everywhere there were Buddhas! Sleeping Buddhas, reclining Buddhas (one of them eighty feet long and studded all over with precious stones), an emerald Buddha with a cloak around his shoulders.

Bangkok seemed always to be on parade. There were processions of priests in saffron robes with their little bowls. They ate and smoked while in procession, much to the amusement of my Burmese guide.

But where were the beggars? By now I took the presence of beggars quite for granted.

I was told there weren't any beggars on the streets of Bangkok. "The beggars go to special homes for the destitute," my informant explained. "Fruit and rice and dried fish are plentiful, so under normal conditions, no one goes hungry."

I lived on bananas, mangoes, and sticky rice. I took the floating market ride up the river on an old barge crowded with Thai people going to market. Three girls, travelers from the United States, also joined us. I had a Thai guide who neatly explained the traffic on the river. The houses on the bank stood on stilts. Steps led up to the doors. The children, with their little bare bodies, played in the mud and in the water at the foot of the steps. They shouted, *"Lai, lai!"* ("Float, float!") to us as we went by.

Little boats were moored at the foot of the steps, should the owner of the house want to do some marketing up the river. Women piloted these small craft as often as men did. Laundry, personal hygiene, cooking, selling, attending to the little spirit houses in front of the dwelling—these were the daily occupations of the townsfolk who lived over the water. The spirit houses, which resembled little birdcages, kept the good spirits inside the houses and the bad spirits outside.

As a matter of course, bananas and sweet cookies were passed around for the barge passengers. Our excitement reached a pitch of hilarity as the American girls read off the names of the shops along the bank. Basket maker, dentist, and then doctor—and close by was the coffin factory, with open coffins standing on end in full view of us as our barge passed by. We thought the arrangement was most convenient!

I disembarked with my guide at the central fruit stand right in the middle of the river, and we toured among the savory-smelling cafés. One shop reminded me of a dime store, with porcelain, brassware, trinkets, and artificial flowers on display.

The walls of the Temple of the Dawn were rudely encrusted with broken pieces of porcelain in the form of flowers. I had great doubt as to the beauty of such rude efforts, and I noticed that the other visitors did not seem to be enthusiastic about the novelty, either.

In contrast, I enjoyed the sound of the temple bells. Only the faintest breeze came up from the water, but it was enough to set the hundreds of bells around the temple in motion. The sound was like soft music carried on the wind, a sweet tune rather than a tinkle. I stood and listened while the swelling crowd of tourists inspected the souvenir stalls. The music was delightful above the hum of the city, now louder as the wind hit the brass tongues of the bells and set more of them ringing against one another.

I was forcibly awakened from my reverie by the raucous blast of a nearby radio. Elvis Presley's voice smothered the bells. It was time to move along.

A visit to the royal barges transported me to a world of legend, as though I were carried into the Arabian Nights. I walked precariously on the catwalks between the barges. I imagined what they would be in all their finery and adornments, sailing down the river on royal procession days or escorting royal guests through the city. The royal palaces had many remarkable features, including the jumping-on platforms for mounting elephants. Anna Leonowens's room in the palace of the King of Siam was preserved, as well as the room where she played with the royal children.[1] Naturally, the Coronation Room and the Queen's Waiting Room were splendid. As there was only one coronation chair, the queen had to wait outside. After such excitement, I was reluctant to go back to museums, lectures, and more Buddhas.

• • •

I sat with my guide, a young Thai student, both of us cross-legged in front of the emerald Buddha. I listened with joy to my guide's story of the great Buddha. He explained the joy that Buddhism brought to his life. He was satisfied that he had found his elixir of life in his religion.

At the door to the temple, he pointed out the poor box, explaining how his people take care of their poor. Reverently he handed me a Buddha charm as I dropped a coin into the box. The charm was an unexpected surprise.

This lad from the travel agency was a student of political science. He was earning money to travel abroad. I was deeply moved when he asked me to meet his sister, a charming young girl studying to be a teacher. Both of these delightful young Thais spoke English well enough to interpret their country to me. I could not even say good-bye to them in Thai.

No visitor goes to Bangkok without exploring the silk shops along the boulevard. A young Thai girl who was boarding at the hostel became my guide for that day. "You must see Jim Thompson's place," she said.[2] "That is where all the American women go."

I was a little dubious, for I was counting my bahts, but at least I wanted to visit. The temptation was just too great.

• • •

Unwillingly, I broke away from my gadding around to attend to business. I wanted to know what was happening in the schools of Bangkok. I was not surprised when a school official informed me that 92 percent of Thai children attend school up to the third grade. They have access to basic education to combat illiteracy.

"Education is compulsory," he said. Teachers had to be certified to teach in the government schools, and many had obtained higher education abroad. The university in Bangkok was extensive, thorough, and forward-looking.

"What about blind children?" I asked.

I learned that there was a private school in Bangkok. It did good work, but it did not come near meeting the needs of the blind children in the city. It did not even attempt to reach those in the villages.

"There is much blindness among children," said one social worker.

"The cause," said a pediatrician, "is malnutrition, lack of vitamin A, and chronic dysentery."

The explanation puzzled me, considering the amount of fruit and vegetable production and the tons of fish brought into the harbor.

Volunteers raised money for the school for the blind with racing programs and card parties, and these funds were supplemented with some allowance from the government. With an estimated six thousand educable blind children in the country, fewer than 250 were in school. There was plenty of room for expansion of the program.

There are very hopeful stirrings. Some young blind persons are working in industry, and others are employed in a workshop. "We have much to do for our blinds here," said my young informant. "We lika know what you do!"

•　　•　　•

A trip to the Angkor Wat and the Angkor Thom was next on my list. The visited required a flight from Bangkok to Cambodia. It was a strange experience. Ordinarily I traveled alone, having arranged to meet a guide on my arrival. Yet, to my knowledge, there were only Americans on the flight north. Their doubts about my ability to function alone were ludicrously obvious. The American men tried to be helpful. Would the stewardess come and help me with my seatbelt? Would she help me get off the plane?

"What are you doing here?" one American woman asked me. Her question took me aback, but I smiled graciously and told her I was going to see Angkor Wat. Perhaps I am fortunate that I did not see the expression on her face.

I was the last passenger to leave the waiting room of the air terminal. I told the ticket clerk that I would appreciate having one of his passenger assistants show me to the bus.

"Okay," he said. That was all. I had the services of a porter—exactly what I needed.

The Americans had already boarded the bus when I arrived, and they were waiting to start the tour around the Wats. When we arrived, the chief dispatcher came to me and said, "Lady, you are blind, no?"

"Yes," I said.

"You cannot climb these steps. There are hundreds of them." I learned later that was a gross underestimate!

"Could you please find one of the servants or helpers from the hotel to be a guide?" I asked.

"That will be easy." The dispatcher apologized profusely on his return. He brought a guide, a young student who spoke only Cambodian and a little French. My luck was with me, for I had twenty words of French. I ended up with the best guide on the tour. He made me climb more steps than anyone else in the group. The stone was worn, and the going sometimes was tricky. On one flight of steps, I encountered a two-inch-wide step, followed by an unexpected broad strip. The softness of the sandstone and the erosion over the centuries caused the irregularities. All the effort I expended to see this wonderful Angkor Wat, or principal temple, that had been unearthed from the jungle gave me mute evidence of an advanced civilization of the midtwelfth century.

We listened to the chief guide's story, but my guide added much more from his study of Indo-Chinese history. He let me trace with my fingers all the Buddhas around the place. Many had had their heads cut off, and others had fire serpents hanging from their mouths. With the help of my guide, I traced the pictures of pelicans; of chess boards and chessmen; of birds in groups of three, five, or seven, which seemed to be the sculptors' lucky numbers; of serpents with three, five or seven heads entwined around the Buddha. My guide described some of the friezes that I could not reach, even though I stood on the ledges. They were covered with gold leaf but were faded by the region's tropical rains.

My guide gave me a "National Geographic account" of the history and excavation of the Wats and showed me traces of Greek art in the friezes. He explained how the conflicts between the Brahmins and the Buddhists could be traced in the subjects of the sculptures.

I examined the statues until my hands were mercilessly scratched and scored. We had such a good time!

Before we parted, my guide plied me with questions. He got a liberal education on what it takes in my country to get a degree from the university, what a high school teacher has to do to get certification, and how much it would cost him to spend a year in the United States. Our French proved totally adequate.

I was sorry to leave Thailand. It had lived up to its name for me, a name that means "Free Land." The old kingdom of Siam once stretched far into Cambodia. What Thailand has lost in territory it has gained in freedom. Its people reflect the satisfaction that comes from effort, effort on behalf of their country and themselves.

CROOKED PATHS MADE STRAIGHT

NOTES

1. Anna Leonowens (1831–1915) served as governess to the wives and royal children of Siam's King Mongkut from 1862 to 1867. Her 1870 memoir, *The English Governess at the Siamese Court,* is a romanticized account of her adventures. The 1951 Rodgers and Hammerstein musical, *The King and I,* is loosely based upon Leonowens's story.
2. Jim Thompson (1906–1967?) was an American designer and entrepreneur who helped restore silk weaving as a lucrative cottage industry in Thailand. His Thai Silk Company, established in Bangkok in 1948, made Thai silk popular throughout the Western world. Thompson disappeared while on vacation in Malaysia in 1967, and the mystery has never been solved.

CHAPTER 21
MALAYSIA: PROGRESS AND PLACEMENT

My plane left for Malaysia at two in the morning. It was hot and steamy and sultry in the non-air-conditioned airport. The mosquitoes were biting my ankles and my arms. It was agony. There must have been fleas, too, judging by the bites. Would that plane never come?

I was not in a receptive mood when an attendant at the desk came to me and asked, "Old lady, you have baggage?"

Yes, I had baggage, but I was no old lady! Misapplied epithets can wreak havoc on one's aplomb at two in the morning, even though one is quite aware of a night porter's limitations with a foreign language.

In vain I tried to drown my indignation in a glass of papaya juice. I nursed my wrath as I decided that perhaps the attendant mistook my white cane for that of an old woman. Probably he did not know that I was blind—not old!

I was on my way to Kuala Lumpur, Malaysia [formerly Malaya]. The passengers were impatient. I sat on a bench, rubbing one leg against the other to scratch the insect bites. An American woman sat beside me, and we engaged in conversation.

"Everything is so pretty here," she said.

"You mean the scenery?" I asked.

"No, I mean the things you buy, the silk and jewelry."

I was curious. What had she found that had aroused her admiration? She was bursting to tell me. "While my husband and I were in

Darjeeling, we noticed an exquisitely beautiful necklace in the shop of an old Hindu."

"Please describe it to me," I said.

"It was a rope of star sapphires and other precious stones, pearls and amethysts, and the chain was of gold."

"It must have been very pretty," I said, thinking I might have the opportunity to feel such a delicate work of art. It was not available, for it was in her suitcase. I was sorry.

"It must have cost you a small fortune," I volunteered.

"Well," she replied, "the old man wanted a hundred dollars for it, but my husband beat him down to forty dollars. It's a beauty."

"But the government regulates the prices of everything in India," I said.

"Oh, yes, you can't go above a certain price."

So to make the sale, the old Hindu had to take a sixty-dollar loss, I thought. And that for a necklace that had all those precious stones in it! No wonder, I considered, that Americans are not the best-loved people abroad these days. If the necklace was worth one hundred dollars, and that was the legal price in India, the husband should have paid the price. It was little enough for such an elaborate necklace, which would probably have cost at least five times that amount in the States.

The plane was announced, and I picked up my belongings. I had a satanic hope that the gems would turn out not to be real (hardly possible under the circumstances) or that the customs officials would make her pay duty on the full value of the necklace.

•   •   •

At Kuala Lumpur, I felt the first twinges of fatigue. On my first day, I woke at three in the afternoon, thinking that it was nine in the morning. My watch was still running; the time was correct.

With tea, crackers, and cheese, I was quickly on my feet again. Crackers and cheese! Yes, the old English influence was still alive here. With my Chinese-Malaysian host and hostess, I felt at home. The climate was delightful, the trees refreshing and shady. We packed a lunch and basked on a tarpaulin by the side of the brook in Templar Park outside the city. We spent an afternoon such as I had not enjoyed since a similar picnic in Yosemite. There were business activities, cars, funny rickshaws that I liked, buses, and people all around me.

Kuala Lumpur was a busy place. Factories were busy, too, but people inside them had time to speak with me. Each of the shops was like a little market.

Blind persons, too, were busy. There were blind stenographers, switchboard operators, plastic workers, packers for the Glaxo Pharmaceutical Company, sorting and verifier machine experts, comptometrists, and teachers.[1] They worked side by side with sighted persons and were held responsible for equal output in quality and quantity. An association for the blind was constructively active, and the government cooperated with the leaders in rehabilitation, placement, and education. I observed that the philosophy of the school and the rehabilitation center was not one of providing custodial care for blind persons but of creating opportunity and independence.

Many young blind people were in training for mechanical work, for agriculture, for commercial work. They made sturdy and much-needed coal baskets, furniture, plastic chairs, and artistic basketry in coir and rattan. A Braille press punched out the dots to create books. Readers were on hand to help students when they needed material read aloud.

About two hundred of the nation's estimated forty thousand educable blind children were in school. It was a small but commendable start! How I admired the teachers in the schools for the blind! One teacher might have children from Borneo, Sarawak, and the islands of the Far East, all speaking different languages, added to the others who spoke Malay, Chinese, English, or all three.

Schools for the blind are expensive to run, and they take the children away from their homes. With the development of teacher-training programs, the possibility lies ahead of opening the public schools to the blind children in their home villages. Trained teachers could provide the assistance they needed due to their blindness.

•   •   •

In Kuala Lumpur, Christians worked beside Muslims and Hindus. Chinese and English were everywhere. Three languages dominated: Malay, Chinese, and English, and most of the people were trilingual.

On this rich, compact peninsula, the Federation of Malaysian States, with a population of better than five million, I felt nostalgic and homesick. After the hardships of the subcontinent, this land felt too similar to home. But my nostalgia soon wore off. I was having too good a time with groups of blind persons, young and not so young. They were eager to exchange ideas, discuss problems, and share experiences.

It was refreshing to see girls out in business, working and earning alongside the men, free from the confinement of the burkha. In the schools, the girls took their physical education exercises wearing shorts! Young men and women enjoyed parties together in the garden or on the lawn as the breeze carried off the heat of the day.

The Far East has been likened to a great sleeping giant, slowly awakening to the realization of itself. I sensed that power in the people of the Malaysian Federation. The wealth, resources, and production of this vast, densely populated area of the world have been exploited by the West, but the picture is changing. The West will always have a part in production and profit but now with the full acquiescence of these emerging countries. Malaysia is a leader in self-development as well as in the assumption of its own management by its own people.

NOTE

1. The comptometer was a key-driven adding machine somewhat resembling a typewriter. It was first manufactured in 1889 and was widely used until the late 1960s. By pressing combinations of keys, the operator could add, subtract, and perform a variety of complex calculations.

CHAPTER 22
SINGAPORE AND SAIGON

Shopping in Singapore all but drove me frantic. There were so many things I wanted to buy but couldn't, and so many things were so cheap I thought I couldn't afford not to buy them. I wanted jade. I wanted brocade. I wanted ivory—anything and everything of ivory. The teak ornaments were of rare beauty and form, exquisite to the touch. I wanted those inexpensive camphor-lined chests. I wanted those fine linen tablecloths, smooth as silk, hand-drawn and hand-sewn. I wanted satin tea cozies, satin robes, heavy satin pajamas with gold-embroidered dragons. But I ended up with some handkerchiefs and the memory of wonderful days spent wandering in the luxury of the Singapore shops.

I listened with rapt attention to stories of the Japanese occupation. Friends described months spent in the Death Cell, where men, women and children were thrown together when they refused to say the things their captors wanted them to say.

Now, in peacetime, my friend and I ate bananas as we rode in a bicycle rickshaw around the esplanade. We heard the soft music of the water lapping close by and the more distant music from the dance halls in the city. The balmy magic of the evening was punctuated by the toot of a ship's siren in the harbor.

For the first time, I ate shark's fin and called for more as the waiter brought me a hot, wet towel to wipe my hands. The food was much more savory when I ate it with my fingers! Thunder and torrential rains did not upset us; we waited for two or three hours until the storm passed over. Time was not a problem for anybody. We just ate some more while we waited.

Singapore fascinated me. Elegant, rich, and modern, it is a gigantic crossroads of the world. By air and water, Singapore is the place where the East and West truly meet.

•   •   •

Saigon reminded me of Paris, perhaps because the hotel in the side street where I was living was French in its furnishings and jalousies. The restaurant had a French menu and French-speaking waiters, but the owners were Chinese.

The name Saigon is the French corruption of Tai Tong, meaning "large harbor" in Vietnamese. Viet means "country of the south."

Vietnam was not clean; I was constantly slipping on refuse in the streets. As I waited for my guide at the hotel door, I was accosted by innumerable beggars asking for alms in pidgin English. They seemed to be old hands at the game, for they refused to take no for an answer and hovered until I sent them on their way with a coin. Some peddled wares that they placed in my hands. They seemed to understand the significance of a white cane.

With my guide, I visited the offices of education and asked about their programs. "Education obligatoire" had not yet been established, for there was not enough money to send all of the children to school. Between 50 and 60 percent of the country's children were in school, most of them in the cities. As usual, the villages were shortchanged in terms of education.

It was a joy to talk with these Vietnamese educators. Theirs was a hard job. They had clear goals, but they had to be pleased with small progress. It might even be ten years before compulsory education would be a reality—compulsory through the first three grades. The teachers with whom I spoke were forward-looking, ambitious, and intelligent, but they were frustrated for lack of funds, equipment, and training. Those three needs went together.

I felt a silence, a reluctance to talk about the threat of communism in their country. The people of Saigon knew the situation in northern

Vietnam. They knew that the southern country could fall prey to the menace, and they were doing what they could to stem the tide. But the country was poor. The people in the villages were hard-pressed for help of any kind, and the help of the Communists would seem all to the good. Schoolteachers though we were, we did not have the answers.

• • •

The world loves a wedding. Christine's wedding was performed in high Vietnamese style. The Roman Catholic cathedral in Saigon was decorated with white flowers for the occasion. Two hundred guests attended the ceremony. Christine drew all eyes, dressed in her white satin wedding gown and flowing veil, and carrying an enormous bridal bouquet.

The ceremony was subdued yet impressive. Its music filled the bright summer morning. It ended with congratulations and snapshots as friends and relatives gathered around the happy bride and groom. Even passersby from the street joined in admiration around the young couple.

Vietnamese fashion, the reception was held in the evening, in the compound of the local school. The evening was hot, but that didn't discourage a large crowd from gathering even before the formal reception began. Well-wishers drank to the health of the bride and groom with everything from Coca-Cola to champagne. The bride had changed to a pale blue silk evening gown, which she said suited her dark hair. She wore flowers, and the dress had a train. The groom was in formal dress with a boutonniere. It was a most happy occasion.

At eight o'clock, the doors of the reception hall opened. The festival began with grace and a song. English, French, and Vietnamese intermingled, and no one was left out. Everyone sat on folding chairs at the tables, decorated with mats and flowers. Children, so many of them, ran everywhere, but they too settled down when the serving began.

First came shark's fin soup with fish stomachs. The little bowl with a saucer beneath it was well filled. Then came a small piece of chicken, highly flavored, served in the same bowl. By then I was ready for dessert. But I was mistaken; there were twelve more courses to come, interspersed with four more soups!

A helping of chicken soup was poured into the bowl. Rice and curry came next, followed by asparagus soup with crabmeat. Highly seasoned vegetables followed. My little bowl was filled to overflowing with the new dishes and the remaining portions of previous ones. A spoon, chopsticks, and fingers were my utensils. More exotic dishes followed, but my appetite gave out. Such delicacies reached too far beyond the limits of the simple menu of toast, boiled eggs, and boiled fish that was my prescription.

Dessert followed, and the bowl was no longer necessary. The dessert was a slab of gelatin made with agar, flavored with sugar and fruit juice. It was eaten with the fingers like a candy bar. Vanilla meringues, rice cakes, and sugared fruits followed in luxurious succession. It was a sumptuous feast, provided by Christine's immediate family, fit for the most demanding epicure. Eating lasted for hours.

The wedding gifts were stacked high on tables at the end of the hall. The bride and groom could not possibly have handled all of them. Arm in arm, knowing no bounds to their happiness, the pair went around the tables, shaking hands with the guests and thanking them for coming to the reception and for their gifts. Songs, jokes, and dances followed as spirits ran high and the bottles low. The party went on and on.

•   •   •

But my mind turned to more prosaic matters. I was interested chiefly in the education of the blind children of Vietnam. The estimate of twenty-five thousand blind persons in the country was considered an understatement. Of these, about six thousand were children of school age. There were two small schools for the blind, with fewer than one hundred pupils enrolled. Some of these pupils actually were adult men working on basketry and broom making. They sold their wares when and where possible, and begged when and where possible as well.

Equipment for the schools was in short supply. The government helped all it could. It provided housing for the pupils at the two schools and paid the salary of a teacher at each one. Catholic sisters and servants helped in the programs. Custodial care was the first consideration, and the educational program came haphazardly.

The need was great for a teacher-training program, for an expanded program to include many more blind children, and for a constructive, sound plan of education. I noted that one of the schools had been in existence for fifty years, yet the skeleton of a program served only a handful of blind boys. A local association raised funds through donations and social affairs—a pittance indeed in the face of the need to educate six thousand blind young people. There had to be another answer.

CHAPTER 23
THE NEIGHBORLY FILIPINOS

By the time I touched down in the Philippines, it was evident to me that I was tired. By now museums no longer lured me. Churches and church organs did not awaken excitement. At just the wrong moment, I heard an announcement over the loudspeaker: "Flight to Los Angeles, Number 123, boarding at Gate 4." Was I really so close to home?

In midsummer, Manila was steamy and sticky. Rain came down in buckets; thunder filled the air. Taxis were hard to find. This was the scene of the fighting that had cost so many American lives during the war. I was in the land of Corregidor! I thought of our boys in the prison camps, cooking rats in empty cans to eke out an extra morsel beyond their meager rations of rice. I imagined them nibbling blades of grass in the prison compound, starved for green vegetables.

But the war was over. Manila was now a beautiful city with long marine drives. It boasted imposing government buildings and fancy hotels, restaurants, and dance halls.

My weariness was only temporary—or perhaps it was temporarily dispelled. About thirty teachers were holding a workshop at one of the local schools, and I was invited to participate. Those were three glorious days. We talked, drank tea, ate cookies, then talked some more. I learned so much from these Filipino teachers. Their classroom problems were the same as ours in the United States. But with their restricted budgets, what could they do?

Most of the teachers in the group came from the villages. They told me that only 70 percent of Filipino children attended school. How could they pull the other 30 percent into their classrooms, which were already overcrowded?

Then we talked about the education of handicapped children. The picture was discouraging. Of the more than eleven thousand blind and partially blind children on the islands, fewer than one hundred were in school. I had seen this pattern in all of the countries I had visited so far. Blind children were only included in plans for education on the most restricted scale—a scale too limited really to matter. Because of their blindness, these children were thought to be uneducable. Generally they were considered capable only of making baskets with their hands, as if handwork did not also involve intelligence. Blind children were being molded according to a stereotype of hopelessness and helplessness. Voluntary welfare agencies were growing up around them. The blind children, if by chance they left or were made to leave their homes, were dependent upon these organizations. No leadership could emerge from such captivity, for leadership springs from opportunity. A new generation of blind children had arisen from the previous generation of blind persons, as helpless as the last, and so it had been since the beginning of time.

"Our people do not believe in educating the blind," explained the director of a social welfare agency. "Our families take care of their blind members."

Traditional custodial care was the accepted pattern. If a blind person was employed at all, he worked in a workshop—"sheltered," of course, for blind persons needed to be looked after. The sheltered workshop was the haven of safety for the blind worker in his middle years, an asylum where the winds of fortune did not blow upon him. He did not even have to pay the forty-centavo bus fare to take him to and from his workplace, for a free bus picked him up. He was not asked if he would like to go into open industry and do exactly the same job he did in the workshop. He might have a wife and family at home, yet he was denied the opportunity to compete with his neighbor in the factory—for he was blind.

The worker in the sheltered workshop was physically blind, but society made him mentally blind as well. There was nothing he could do about it, not yet. He was defeated before he tried, defeated by the hand that claimed to be helping him. It was an age-old pattern, a pattern that led the people entrusted with their country's social welfare to do a better and better job of what should not be done at all.

I knew there was another way. Blind persons could be given a voice, the right to make decisions that directed their lives. They could meet the challenge to equality with sighted men and women. They were persons with the same drives and desires as all human beings. On the basis of their blindness, they had been deprived of their rights by sighted people who knew nothing of the limitations or potentialities of blind people.

The idea was not new. "If we do not see to it that our blind children get an education like the rest of the children, how can they ever amount to anything?" asked one of the teachers in the discussion group. "If they do not get a primary education, how can they get the chance to move on to higher education?" And so the idea went on, gathering momentum.

We all took part in the discussion. The teachers forgot that I was blind; one day, I knew, they would forget that their own blind students were blind. They concluded that no magic was necessary to teach blind children. Blind children were only children who would read with their fingers instead of their eyes. They would use different techniques perhaps, but what two children are alike? They were children with the rights of other children, and citizens with rights conferred upon them by the country of their birth.

This conviction of equality of the individual was deep-rooted in all of the countries I observed. What was different was the way in which this equality was being carried out. Cultural patterns, stages of progress, and methods varied. Nations were requesting help to achieve opportunity and equality for their citizens. They also sought guidance to educate and train blind persons and to train teachers.

A new day in the life of the blind was breaking. These teachers from the village schools of the Philippines promised the dawn of that new day.

PART 4
HOMEWARD BOUND

PART 3

CHAPTER 24
SCONES, BUTTER, AND RASPBERRY JAM

In all its formidable majesty, the Cuantus Electra winged its way southward over the equator. Steady and swift, she scarcely throbbed in her well-charted air lane high above the clouds.

This was the overnight flight, but no one slept. The hostess made the usual check of the passengers' names. My neighbor in the double-seated side of the plane was Thomas Parnell. We both settled down to coffee and biscuits and silence.

Thomas Parnell! Thomas Parnell! The name was taking form. No, it couldn't be. How could he be down here on the other side of the world? People just don't meet like that! But as midnight approached and nobody slept, my curiosity, or my garrulousness, got the better of me.

"Excuse me, sir," I said. "I heard you give your name as Thomas Parnell. Did you ever by chance go to the San Pedro Harbor School in Los Angeles?"

Such a foolish question, I thought, but it was too late; the question was out.

"Yes," he said, "I did."

"Then you *are* Thomas Parnell!" I said.

"But I don't remember you," he answered.

"Do you know Caroline Brown?"

"Yes, I do, very well."

"Do you know Janet Young?"

"I married her sister."

"Her name was Elaine, wasn't it?"

"Yes, but I don't remember you. I've gone over all the teachers I can think of, and I just don't remember you."

"All right," I said. "Let's go in at the main door on Gardner Street. Pass the student body office and go into the room in the corner, Number 114."

"Gosh sakes, you are that little blond teacher!"

"That was twenty-five years ago."

"But how did you remember me?"

"I don't know, Tom, but two things have helped. Schoolteachers remember names. The name Tom Parnell was familiar. I probably called your name dozens of times in history class. But something else, I think. Your accent. I caught a shade of something familiar. You had come from New Zealand directly to Harbor High School. You had a New Zealand accent. I was struggling with my Scottish accent, so we had something in common. You still have that New Zealand overtone, and I'm sure that's what I caught."

From that point till four in the morning, there was no sleep and much coffee. Tom told me how he had made history in the POW camps of the Philippines. Now past forty, he had seen much of the world since the days he served in his country's defense. He was on his way to visit an old buddy.

In my quarter of a century as a teacher in Los Angeles, this sabbatical was only my second year away from the classroom. The other was the year of my eye operations before I lost my sight. I thought of all that had happened since those days in the classroom when Tom would arrive tardy, without a pass or a pencil. Only a schoolteacher is privileged to have such moments of delight, recognizing a former student far from home.

We touched down in Darwin in the chill of the morning, dazed for want of sleep. We welcomed the invitation from the airline official who offered to take us through Darwin in his jeep, as he had an errand to run.

Just eight hours ago, we had left the tropical heat of Manila on the northern side of the equator, to be plunged into the numbing cold of winter. I could not adjust to the change. I pulled my big coat around me and pushed my hands into the sleeves.

I listened as our jeep driver told us about this quaint little city far in the north of Australia. He described his work with the II. Tom raised no question about the II, but I needed to know what the initials stood for. International what?

"What does II stand for?" I asked.

"Australian Airlines!"

I really was in Australia, where a basin is a bison and there is no difference between tape and type or race and rice without the context.

I knew I was in Australia for another reason, too. I had cherished a beautiful corsage of gardenias and roses, a gift from a friend in Manila. I had kept it in its carton to save its freshness and fragrance, hoping to wear it in Brisbane. But flowers are on Australia's forbidden list; they might be carriers of plant diseases. My lovely corsage was consumed in the incinerator.

•   •   •

In Brisbane the next morning, I found myself in a new world. My hostel, which offered bed and breakfast, might have been in London or Edinburgh. The snug little dining room seated several guests, most of them women. The guests passed around butter balls and marmalade, and then came the morning rolls. I had not tasted such rolls in many a long year. Next came the sausages and fried eggs. The tea was infused in a cozy-covered pot. No tea bags! The telltale stray tea leaf escaped the filter and slipped into my cup.

After the meager diet I had been forced to follow for the past eleven months, this food was like manna from the skies. I got acquainted with milk again! My gastronomical desires knew no bounds. Yet I could not eat. I felt as though I were sitting down to a dinner, already satiated.

My room, too, seemed overwhelming. It was crowded with carpets and furniture, a great change from the cement floors and springless charpals and straw mattresses to which I had become accustomed. The bed was warm and inviting under its load of three wool blankets, an eiderdown, and a hot water bottle. I sat on the edge, trying to pull myself together after nearly a year of wandering. I was at home again.

Early in the morning, I found the maid on her knees, polishing the slick floors of the lobby. When I came to leave this delightful home, I gave the hostess ten shillings to thank the maids for their service to me. "Oh," she said, "that is too much!" The taxi fare was fifteen shillings and nine pence. After the knats, rupees, anas, bahts, and pesos that had been my currencies for so long, it was comfortable once again to work with shillings and pence.

If I was at home in the bed and breakfast, I was equally at home with the Australian friends I made, both blind and sighted. Their Scottish and English heritage was reflected in their homes, their work, their education, and their children. Creative, hardworking, forward-looking, they knew where they were going. They wanted the best for their children in education, they fostered their cultural interests, they loved to work, and they loved to play. They provided education for all of their children, blind and sighted alike. Programs were carefully planned and flexible enough to meet modern needs. Blind persons worked in open industry as well as in workshops, according to their wishes and needs. I was a guest on a radio program, talking about some of my observations during my journey.

Obviously, the first allegiance of the Australians is to their mother country, but they are looking across the Pacific to the United States as never before. They know our magazines, and they want to know us better. We can make this possible. I can help with my exchange of tapes. I listen to their voices, and they to mine, across a nine-thousand-mile expanse of ocean. We need to know Australia better, for it stands for freedom, too.

•   •   •

I was unwinding slowly after the rigors of heat, humidity, and semistarvation. Sydney was a tonic. I was back in a European- or American-style metropolis—busy streets, suburban trains partly underground, businesses, and buses. A bustling harbor linked us with the rest of the world. The weather was raw with rain and squalls, but I drew in long breaths to revive my depleted energy.

My friends invited me to join them on a trip to the Blue Mountains. High above the city, the air was colder still. Ice glazed the water, and the brush was moist and springy. Thick foliage slapped across my face, making my cheeks tingle.

We walked briskly to keep warm. My feet and hands were numb, for my circulation seemed sluggish. The Australian girls stepped right along, and I refused to trail behind. We stopped to identify the trees by their leaves. We picked up red devils—pieces of twigs that lent themselves to being dressed in the little, red flannel jackets we bought at the curio shop in the woods. Red devils were the spirits of the Blue Mountains.

The birds had a grand time that afternoon. The long, sustained whistle of the whistle bird was answered by the soft tinkle of the bell bird in perfect harmony. I listened to see which was answering which.

Sydney's Greenwich Village offered a Little Bit of Sweden, a Parisian restaurant, or a restaurant with a Swiss chalet atmosphere. The choice was mine. The rain outside and the crackling of the fire added to the local color.

My Sydney shopping tour was a great success. My friends knew exactly where to go in the big city. I wanted furry animals for my two little grandsons. I settled on an imposing, upright, long-tailed kangaroo with its baby joey sticking out of its pouch and a flat-billed, furry platypus that invited stroking. Would I care to have them packed? I saw myself unpacking the parcel every time I passed through customs until I reached home, and I had no intention of doing that! I took a shopping bag and placed the animals so that their heads stuck out at the top. I slung the bag on my left arm alongside my typewriter, Oscar, the bag with my passport, and the rest.

By now my belongings assumed enormous proportions. The animals spoke for themselves, and no customs officer ever questioned me about them. I must have looked like a walking menagerie.

My shoes gave out. The heat had cracked the leather, and the rain did the rest. I bought a pair made in Australia, not imported. The shoemaker said the pair I bought would last me all my life. They are so sturdy, they probably will.

•   •   •

Australian education followed the European tradition—thorough, basic, and fundamental, with no frills. Teacher training was likewise sound. I was told that all blind children attended schools for the blind, with the possible exception of a few aboriginal children. Preparation for the higher education and employment of blind young people showed how similar their problems were to our own. One instructor bluntly told his pupils, "You may think it is bad enough to be blind, but just wait till you see what is ahead of you in society. The greatest limitation of blindness is the sighted. We must change the attitude of society toward the blind." His solution as an educator was to give his students the best preparation possible, so that they could meet an indifferent society on their own merits.

I observed this spirit of independence and understanding of their own problem in a group of young blind persons in Sydney. After completing school, they had formed an association to present their case to the public through their active participation in community life. They were setting up their own businesses and promoting legislation that would assist them and the community as a whole. They realized the need for leadership from within their own ranks.

I was the guest of a similar group of young blind persons in Melbourne. This group had outgrown the philosophy of cradle-to-grave custodial care prevalent in so many institutions run for the blind by the sighted. They were alert to the goals of a well-wishing, do-gooder society that would perpetuate a modernized medievalism—sheltered workshops, homes for the blind, and specially designed, repetitive jobs. They wanted the challenges of equality and competition. They wanted the right to fail, should that be the outcome. In the outlook of these young Australians, I felt the infinite possibilities of this new country, with its scant population of twelve million in a land the size of the United States.

The cold was exhilarating, and wherever I went, the people were friendly and hospitable. I rode buses into the uplands, where the crisp winter sun and the wind up the canyons filled me with new life. My friends and I stood on the edge of the cliffs and listened as our voices ricocheted back and forth across the ravine, then died away in the distance. The birds responded noisily to one another, or were they calling to us?

An aboriginal man outside the teashop high up on the mountain proudly displayed his dexterity with his boomerang. He sold us his native wares from his tiny shop across the road. Four o'clock tea was a treat, with all the scones and raspberry jam I wanted, and delicious cupcakes with sweet butter.

My Fair Lady was playing at Her Majesty's Theater near my hostel. The cast was partly British, partly Australian. I easily identified the actors' nationalities from their accents. The house was sold out, except for one seat where the view was partially obstructed by a pillar. That suited me. I was accorded the utmost courtesy when I arrived at the box office and they saw that I was blind. At intermission, an usher asked if he could escort me to the bar. My seat was changed, but the acoustics remained excellent. *My Fair Lady* in the Australian accent sounded unfamiliar to me, but I enjoyed it to the fullest. I was aware at once of being at home and yet away from home.

•　　•　　•

On Sunday morning, the hush of the Sabbath was broken by the chimes of the neighboring church. They seemed to be playing every psalm tune in the Scottish psalter. I listened. I was back in my childhood in Scotland, repeating the words of the old songs with the chimes: "All people that on earth do dwell ..." "Oh God of Bethel by whose hand ..." "How excellent in all the earth ..." "I to the hills will lift mine eyes ..." Here, far toward the Antarctic, Scotsmen had brought their faith, their hope, and their love. They had built a nation for their own and for others to enjoy.

I felt very close to the Australians. It seemed a long time since I was deep in the tropics, near to India's coral beaches, yet it had been little more than a month. This was my country, too.

Following the directions of the secretary of the hostel, I found the church easily. Crossing the street, I had the aid of a kindly gentleman who stopped on his way to his own church to help me.

"Never mind, lady," he said. "There is no blindness in heaven!"

I was so amused I could not think of an answer, except to thank him for his assistance. As he took leave of me, he added, "And I'll see you there!"

The chimes continued to play as I was shown to a pew. *All people that on earth do dwell*, I thought. How many of these people had I met since I started this safari, which was now drawing to a close? Who were they? British, French, Italians, Greeks, Turks, Jordanians, Lebanese, Egyptians, Pakistanis, Indians, Singhalese, Burmese, Thais, Cambodians, Malays, Vietnamese, Filipinos, Australians. Nearly all of us believed in a supreme being, professing each in our own way. Muslim or Hindu, Christian or Buddhist, all of us were free to worship as we chose. How we worshiped did not matter.

I made still another tie with Melbourne. Mini, my blind teacher friend from Athens, had asked me to visit her brother and his family in far-off Australia, if I happened to go there. With typical Australian courtesy, the telephone operator helped me locate Mr. Maurice Papadakis. He was an executive in an automobile plant. His first gesture was to invite me to meet his family and have dinner with them.

Mr. Papadakis and I met at my street corner. We took the bus home, for his car was not available. We were deep in conversation about our experiences in Athens when the gentleman to my left interrupted courteously. "Excuse me, lady," he said, "but you must come from the north of Scotland. I'm from Beauly." My home was less than fifty miles from his.

I was puzzled. Had the environment revived the old Scottish element in my speech? Had I unconsciously reverted to the Doric?

Here was another sample of Melbourne friendliness. I was obviously a visitor, and far from an imposing one at that, for my hand-washed dresses, my now somewhat battered hat, my far-travelled overcoat were anything but prepossessing. One thing I knew: the rain and the wind, the sleet and the oatcakes had invigorated me as no tonic ever could have done. I felt as though years had dropped from my life. My energy seemed boundless.

Save for the condition of my finances, I was again ready to go on. Even that unfortunate condition was of short duration. Knowing the wayward propensities of their mother where money was concerned, and sensing that my traveler's checks must be running low, my daughter and son-in-law had three hundred dollars awaiting me. I breathed more easily as I traipsed on with my platypus and my kangaroo, Joey.

The best was yet to come in Melbourne. In the company of Mr. Papadakis's two daughters, Athena and Kyrie, I made a pilgrimage to James Cook's cottage in the middle of Fitzroy Gardens. The day was bitter cold, and we all wore coats and wool mittens. We ate Cadbury's chocolate to keep warm. The girls laughingly told me that my nose was red, that it matched my wool gloves. We kept behind the trees as much as we could to break the wind. The South Pole seemed not very far away!

The tiny, two-story house had been removed from Yorkshire, England, in 1934, stone by stone and brick by brick. Every piece had been marked to ensure placement in its original location when the house was reconstructed. Even the plants and creepers were brought from Yorkshire. The curator told us that an obelisk had been erected in Great Ayotte, Yorkshire, to indicate the transfer of the cottage to Victoria. Inside are the Lares and Penates of the Cook family. Though born in Morton, Yorkshire, the captain lived in this cottage for the greater part of his life. The curator allowed me to touch Cook's tall seaboots, papers, and bed, the mantel shelf adorned with ornaments, the small fireplace with its firedogs and andirons. Then up the narrow staircase we went to the sleeping quarters. Chairs, tables, and other furniture were just as they had been brought from England. The lean-to at the back of the house was the stable, with just enough room for a horse and cart.

This relic of the past, almost as far south as habitation was possible, had a deep significance for me. In my old family home in Scotland, as far back as I could remember, there was a cherished volume, *Captain Cook's Three Journeys around the World, with a Sketch of His Life*, published by George Routledge and Sons, the date not being given. On the flyleaf was a statement, "First Prize for Arithmetic, and Grammar, and Second Prize in History Awarded to William Dean, at the annual inspection of the Kinneddar Public, 1884." Though I recalled my father holding up his prize with an exhortation to us, the insert in that book was a sufficient reminder to us that our arithmetic, grammar, and history could not fall below par. My father liked that book. Though he was not a seafarer himself, his three brothers were all captains of schooners that sailed the world over. We children had fingered the opening pages as children often do, and the first five had become loose and lost. But Captain Cook's story had remained with me. I recalled the log of the *Endeavour* and Captain Cook's entry of April 19, 1770: "Saw the land extending from northeast to west from the *Endeavour*'s decks and christened it Point Hicks after Lieutenant Hicks, a member of the crew." The life of this intrepid seaman, scientific explorer, and skillful navigator had always been a link of understanding between my father and me. In the cottage, I was paid tribute to my father's memory.

•   •   •

To me, New Zealand is wrongly named. If there weren't already a Nova Scotia, it should have been called New Scotland. Auckland reminded me of Aberdeen. It was a beautiful city, busy and businesslike. The people were well educated and proper. Everybody worked, and nobody went hungry.

I made new friends among blind and sighted alike and visited them in their homes. We exchanged ideas on everything from the new birdcage hairdos (of which I knew nothing, having been away from occidental culture for so long) to the pros and cons of the welfare state (of which they knew so much, and I so little). I visited fine academic schools. I also got a glimpse of the life of the Maoris, whose rough-hewn boats and rafts were built to withstand the fury of the South Pacific. The Auckland bookshops were veritable treasure troves, the flower shops were fragrant with chrysanthemums and violets, and the tiered parking lots were ultra-modern.

The young reporters who interviewed me for the women's column of the Sunday paper knew their profession, but they were reluctant to believe that I had traveled so long and far. My host and hostess corroborated my story, explaining that I had been with them in Rome.

I felt completely at home in the land of the tiki, the kiwi, and the fern. But it was time for me to leave.

CHAPTER 25
THE LITTLE SCHOOLHOUSE

It's a long, long way from New Zealand to Hawai'i. I spent six hours on the plane from Auckland to Fiji and eight hours flying from Fiji to Honolulu. How distorted our sense of distance has become when hours are the measure of a long journey! I thought of sailing from Auckland, but although I had slowed down considerably, I did not have the patience to spend weeks on an ocean voyage. I was excited at the thought of arriving home. Any speed less than five hundred miles per hour was marking time.

Nevertheless, I wanted to visit Fiji. The plane landed at Nandi on the island of Vitalev, and suddenly I was back in the tropics. The hotel proprietor was somewhat hesitant to accept a blind person as a guest, but finally he agreed to give me a room for the night. As a group of air force personnel was due on the morrow, I would have to leave in the morning.

That evening, a display of native dancing was held not far from the hotel. My guide spoke very limited English, but I asked my questions through gestures. I wanted to get close to the dancers and see them in my way.

I had no difficulty. Their nose rings intrigued me. I thought their long earlobes, stretched to the point of discomfort, were a high price to pay for beauty. The music sounded weird to me; the instruments were very unusual to my Western ears. I learned that these were professional dancers who entertained visitors to the islands when called upon.

Suva and Lautoka were my next stopovers. Suva, with its shops, hotels, and teacher-training college, was a visitor's paradise. Lautoka is less frequented by foreigners, so it is much more native.

I took up quarters in what appeared to be Lautoka's only hotel. The attention of the servants and waiters reflected a British atmosphere. My Fijian guide, one of the servants who spoke a little more English than the others, was very friendly. I told him I wanted to visit the schools, of course, for I was a teacher. He also agreed to accompany me to the native huts so that I could get a better idea of native life.

On a Sunday afternoon, when the children were not in school, we walked far down the road to where the huts stood. My guide introduced me to one of his friends. They explained the intricacies of how a mud hut is built, how the straw is put on the roof, and why the shape is round. They told me why the cooking stove is placed in the middle of the hut. The huts seemed to be arranged without any pattern or symmetry. There were no sidewalks, and we made our way wherever we could get a foothold.

In no time at all, I found myself at the center of a circle of children. We harmonized with "Good morning, how do you do?" and "Good afternoon," for that seemed to be the extent of their English lessons. They certainly understood more than they could say. The younger children would ask questions in Fijian, one of the older children would pick out a question and interpret for me, and thus the conversation went along. After I visited a few more of the huts, I said good-bye to my retinue. Through my guide, I told them that I had to go but that I would see them on the following day.

My guide and I went shopping in Lautoka. We met more Fijians. We talked about their work, their children, and the blind people of the islands. Yes, there were many blind people, they told me, but they just stayed at home. One young man spoke up and said that he knew of a blind boy who went to school in Auckland, New Zealand. Some blind people worked in the sugarcane fields, some worked at copra or copra oil. Some packed bananas or pineapples. They earned too little, I was told.

My guide and I were supposed to be looking for a figurine of a little Fijian girl and boy, but I was more interested in the conversation. We could not find the figurine I wanted, so I bought the model of a Fiji policeman with his shorts and sun hat, and another of a not-too-authentic girl with her fuzzy hair. These purchases were conversation pieces. I was happy to sit around and talk with the Fijians.

Next morning, I called the local taxi driver and engaged him for the day. We set out for the village school. The driver wanted to take me to the "better" schools. I asked him what they were.

"Oh," he said, "the Catholic schools and the Muslim school."

"No," I said, "we will go to the village school."

We drove along the road past the hut encampment and stopped close to the school's entrance. There was no sidewalk, and a ditch separated the schoolyard from the road.

A perfectly charming young teacher saw me from her classroom and came out to greet me. She spoke excellent English and was a graduate of the training college at Suva. She told me she was not in native dress; she wore a Western-style blouse.

"How many children have you in your class?" I asked.

"At present I have 108 pupils. I am giving an English lesson. Will you please enter?"

After a moment's hesitation, she suggested that I meet the principal and offered to take me to him.

There were only two teachers in the school of 176 pupils, the teacher I had met and the principal himself. He taught a class of sixty-six, in addition to handling his duties as principal. He invited me into his classroom, and the children rose as I entered.

Mr. John, as he gave me his name, asked if I would speak to the children. This would be a good opportunity for them to talk with someone from a foreign country.

There was silence for a moment. Then very quietly, I said, "Would you like to hear about my school and my children?"

A chorus answered, "Yes, sir!" and that broke the ice. I explained that though they could see me, I could not see them. Did they know what the word blind meant?

"Yes, sir," came the chorus again. Mr. John urged us to continue, and we went on for a whole hour.

The discussion turned to the clothes my children wore compared with their dress in Fiji. Mr. John suggested that one boy and one girl come to the front of the room. They came without hesitation. The children were free and courteous, though at times they all wanted to talk at once.

The boy who came up front told me his name in answer to my

question. Then I asked how tall he was. "One yard and two feet," he told me. He explained that he and all of the other boys were wearing *sulus*.[1]

To the little girl, I said, "How old are you?"

"My age is ten years," she answered. She wore a print dress that any little American girl might wear. Her hair was braided in short, stubbly braids.

This class was the older group. "Will you come back tomorrow and talk with the other class?" the children asked. Unfortunately, another visit was impossible, for tomorrow I had to leave.

The English lesson was over. The children thanked me in unison and clapped their hands gleefully as Mr. John and I left the room. That visit was two hours of pure joy!

I was genuinely sorry I could not return, but I had a plane reservation for noon of the following day. I did not dare risk taking the bus again. On the outbound trip, the little jitney had broken down, and I was stranded in a straw hut waiting room at the side of the road with a group of fellow passengers, not one of whom spoke English. Another bus came along some time later, but no one seemed to be in any hurry.

For my trip back to the airport, I employed my taxi driver again. I arrived in Kandi to find that my plane had been delayed six hours. To return to the Lautoka children would have been foolhardy. In plane travel, it pays to be on the spot. So there was nothing to do but wait. I settled my impedimenta on the chair beside me—Joey the kangaroo and the platypus, my miniature menagerie having been considerably augmented with Maori and Fiji dolls. It was not a comfortable wait, for the day was hot and unpleasant. Perhaps I could doze off; everything would, I thought, be safe enough.

I felt a hand on my shoulder. "I see you have still four hours to wait. I am an officer on duty here, and I am going home to dinner. Would you care to join my wife and me?"

Such hospitality, such thoughtfulness, such kindness! I accepted the invitation and spent the rest of the waiting time in the most genial of company. The officer was English in background but worldwide in interests. My story was interesting to him, too. For me, this was just another crooked path made straight.

NOTE

1. The *sulu va taga* is a wraparound skirt-like garment worn in Fiji by both men and women. The sulu may be decorated with intricate designs. For formal occasions, it can be worn with a tailored shirt or blouse.

CHAPTER 26
POSTSCRIPT: IN RETROSPECT

So I came to the end of the crooked paths for one year—paths that really were not crooked at all but just the way life is. We think they are crooked; we fear that they are, when, of their own accord, they straighten out as we step along over them. Some were strewn with flowers. Some had big potholes. But even around the potholes there was a way. Some paths led down dangerous, eroded gullies; others led up the mountains to places where strange birds answered one another's calls in a June midwinter. I trod some paths barefoot, for the ground was hallowed to the people and therefore to me. But all paths were lined with friends, some of another race, color, and creed from mine. We were alike in our differences. They helped straighten out the paths for me. I wonder, looking back, if I helped straighten out any paths for them. I would be content if I had done so, even in a very small measure.

At the end of every straightened path, I had a sendoff from friends that was warming, exciting, and genuine. Sometimes a bevy of schoolteachers, church friends, or community friends saw me off, or a delegation from the newly formed blind association. A rose was pinned to the lapel of my coat—roses are luxuries in Karachi. My typewriter and my Braillewriter were carried to the plane, and my arms were filled with packages of biscuits or bottles of dysentery medicine—for one cannot always run to a drugstore.

One dear friend made me a blue choli, the little jacket-like blouse worn under a sari. I had a red one, but she thought I needed a blue one. It came with special buttons, attached to one another by a silver chain.

At three o'clock on a bitter cold morning in Lahore, friends came to bid me *choda hafiz* and good-bye, clad in their thin cotton saris, sandals, and sweaters. I shall never forget that freezing air, nor the broken footpaths, nor the three enormously high steps that led up to the air terminal office. Nor shall I forget the lovely, fragrant corsage of gardenias and red roses that I carefully guarded in its box on my knees during the flight over the equator, only to have it confiscated at Darwin. I will never forget the crooked paths that led me to explore Fiji, down the dirt road to the mud hut village and the happy classroom of nearly seventy little Fijians—the Fiji Islanders of tomorrow.

As takeoff time arrived at Hawai'i, I was serenaded by a group of young people, sighted and blind, singing their alohas. Their voices merged with the hum of the motors and disappeared in the breeze. My tears fell on the perfumed leis around my neck and draped over my arms.

As the jet swept down to its landing strip in San Francisco, I had fallen into a daze of ecstasy. Was it the joy of being back home? Was it the joy of having walked all these crooked paths made straight? Or was it the joy of stepping out of that plane, wearing the same old beige, velour felt hat with the ribbons, the same tan coat, albeit both of them the worse for wear from weather and wind? I landed in San Francisco fifty-two weeks from the hour of my departure.

The most crooked path of all was one of my own choosing, the recounting of my long safari. My blind friends urged me to tell the story. Young blind people were especially insistent. If an old lady could do it, they said, then they too could do it in due time. My sighted friends also insisted that I tell my story. They were reluctant to believe that I had made the complete circuit of the globe. They said it could not be done, even after I had done it. How could she have done it, they asked one another. She is blind. What did she see? Nothing!

So my story is filled with nothing, the nothingness seen by any blind person anywhere, seen by the millions of blind persons in the world today. Nothingness plus opportunity turns into a real something, if this story has any message whatever to give.

•   •   •

To write this story, I had to struggle with Braille notes that did not make sense. With the heat and humidity of the tropics, my Braillewriter had become rusty, and many of the dots did not come through. With the loss of one dot in the Braille cell, a word can become unintelligible. Furthermore, the mechanism was out of gear, and dots ran into other dots. The humidity also softened the paper almost to pulp, and dots became illegible. My notes were sparse to begin with, for I needed the space in my suitcase for clothes, not paper. I sent some notes home by surface mail, for airmail was too expensive. I am sure the package of Braille pages found a niche at the bottom of the ship's hold, for the dots were all but flattened.

This path was terribly crooked until I discovered that one decipherable word was often enough to bring back an entire conversation, a tea party, an argument, or a talk. I shuddered again under the shower of insects from the curtain on that rainy day. Again my foot slipped into the drain. Once more I sat on the gentleman's dhoti.

I returned to a full-time teaching job. I love teaching, and I gave it all that I had. I love to see children grow in grace, knowledge, and understanding—and have fun at the same time. After the school day's work was ended, I often spent a relaxed half hour with my memories and my typewriter. I wrote on Saturdays and on a few vacation days, if I wasn't reading a Braille magazine up in the air or riding a Greyhound bus or scrubbing my kitchen floor. I composed on my typewriter with my Braille notes on my lap. At times I typed serenely along with my typewriter on stencil and had to backtrack several pages and compose again. If the telephone rang, I might forget the last word I had written or even lose the trend of my thought.

Everything conceivable happened to my typewriter. The ribbon twisted or the paper fell out, and I lost the last line. I typed over the same page twice. I forgot to number some of the pages. When I wanted to change words and phrases, I inserted personal notes to my reader, such as: "Go back two pages to happy and write felicitous."

I was sometimes ready to give up—this path was just too crooked. Then one day a letter came from a young blind Pakistani. I had talked with him at length, though not enough. The letter read:

Dr. Mrs. Grant, Madame:

It is with a sense of profound gratitude that I am writing you this letter. I lost contact with you since your departure from Pakistan. It was mainly through your persuasion and guidance that the Blind Association came into existence. It will not be optimistic to believe that you have not forgotten your friends here. We shall need your help and guidance in the noble mission we have undertaken.

You will be pleased to know that the Association has started functioning. We are trying our level best to awaken the blind of this part of our country. The very establishment of our Association has infused a new spirit. We are at present busy with the membership campaign.

We will try to keep you informed about the various activities. Please try to send us the annual reports of the associations of the blind in your country, and any other literature which may be of help to us.

With best wishes and kind regards,
Yours truly, Bashir

To Bashir I owe the conclusion of this story, the straightening out of the most tortuous of the paths. To him I owe my rededication to the work of trying to make life a little more pleasant for those blind persons less fortunate than I am. Only by the grace of God do I live in America, and they in less-favored countries. But for the grace of God, I would also be a beggar. I simply ask where I can serve.

AFTERWORD

When Isabelle Grant returned from her round-the-world journey, she resumed her teaching duties at Washington Irving Junior High School. However, the people she met on her travels were braided into her life. When she wasn't teaching or writing *Crooked Paths Made Straight,* she was exchanging letters with acquaintances in Pakistan and India. Over the years, her print and Braille correspondence burgeoned. In 1972, the *Sacramento Bee* reported that she wrote in seven languages to some eight hundred blind people around the world.[1] She encouraged blind people to learn Braille and typing, to seek competitive employment, and to organize—always to organize! She was convinced that the only way blind people would ever stand as equals among their sighted peers was through the power of collective action.

Late in 1960, Isabelle visited the tenBroeks at their home in Berkeley. Years later she described how she presented Jacobus tenBroek with a compelling new idea. "'Dr. tenBroek, what we need at this point is an international federation of blind persons over the world. The blind need it, are ready for it, and are asking for it.' The answer came without hesitation. 'All right, Isabelle. Go right ahead and start it and we shall be behind you.'"[2]

Ablaze with plans, Isabelle was eager to return to Pakistan and the other emerging nations. In September 1962, ten weeks after her official retirement, she set off for Pakistan on a one-year Hayes-Fulbright Fellowship through the US Educational Foundation. The fellowship covered her travel expenses and provided $2,300 for food and accommodations. Her purpose was to train Pakistani educators to teach blind children, continuing the work she began when she conducted her workshop with teachers in Karachi in 1960. She won a second Fulbright Fellowship in 1963 and went back to Pakistan for yet another year.

In addition to training Pakistani teachers, Isabelle sought out blind people who had leadership potential. She was especially eager to develop leaders among blind women. The situation for most blind men was bleak, but women had even fewer opportunities. In parts of the world where a woman's only role was to marry and have children, a blind woman had no place. Considered ineligible for marriage, she was a lifelong burden on her relatives. She ate the food that was left after more valued relations had eaten, and often she was hidden away as a family disgrace.

One of Isabelle's earliest protégés was Fatima Shah, whom she met sometime in 1960 during her first visit to Pakistan. A physician by training, Shah had slipped into hopelessness and isolation after she lost her sight. She was astonished when Isabelle Grant, totally blind herself, arrived in a rickshaw to visit her. She asked Isabelle how she managed to travel by herself. "I'm not alone," Isabelle replied. "I have Oscar."[3]

Swept along by Isabelle's enthusiasm, Shah wakened to a renewed sense of purpose. She found other blind women and men and inspired them with her new sense of hope. Only a few months after her first meeting with Isabelle, she founded the Pakistan Association of the Blind. Under Dr. Shah's leadership, the organization worked to create new opportunities for Pakistan's blind children and adults.

In 1964, Isabelle Grant's dream of an international organization of blind persons came to fruition. Isabelle helped establish the International Federation of the Blind (IFB). Jacobus tenBroek served as its first president, succeeded by Fatima Shah. Over the years, Isabelle Grant served as treasurer and board member. She also edited *Braille International Magazine,* the IFB's quarterly publication. Available in English, Spanish, and French Braille, the magazine connected its readers with one another as part of a rising worldwide movement.

Delegates from twenty-five nations attended the first convention of the IFB, held in Ceylon (today's Sri Lanka) in 1969. "We, the blind of the world, are [seeking emancipation] from custodialism, second-class citizenship, and the stereotype of inferiority and ignorance, all because of traditional misconceptions regarding blindness," Isabelle Grant told the assembled delegates. "Blind persons have only one way to go—onward and upward, under their own steam, under their own power, using their own abilities and strength."[4]

The IFB was not the first international organization that attempted to promote the cause of the blind. Founded in 1949, the World Council for the Welfare of the Blind (WCWB) brought together delegates from agencies that served blind persons. Most of these agencies were run by sighted people who spoke on behalf of their blind clients, viewing them as people in need of care and protection. The IFB, on the other hand, was run by blind people and empowered the blind to speak for themselves. Considering their philosophical differences, it was inevitable that the two organizations had an uneasy relationship. Isabelle frequently found herself caught up in a political maelstrom as the IFB and the WCWB fought to be heard by governments, religious groups, and international consortia.

• • •

Isabelle Grant was convinced that education was essential in order for blind people to take their rightful place in the world. To become educated, they must have access to an abundant supply of Braille books. Back in California in 1964, Isabelle flung herself into a fresh project. An international postal treaty allowed Braille materials to be shipped overseas free of charge if they were packed in cartons weighing less than fifteen and a half pounds. Isabelle solicited used Braille books from schools and individuals across the country and sent them abroad.

Friends within and outside the National Federation of the Blind responded with enthusiasm. From Austin and Des Moines, Cincinnati and Phoenix, boxes of Braille books arrived at Isabelle's Los Angeles home. Storage was an immense challenge, as Braille books are far larger than their ink-print counterparts. In Braille, a novel such as *A Tale of Two Cities* might fill five large volumes, each measuring a foot square and two to three inches thick. A Braille textbook might come in twenty or more such volumes. "What if the front porch of my apartment does look like a secondhand dealer's establishment, with immense cartons stacked to the ceiling of the awning?" Isabelle wrote in 1965. "The cartons are ripped open, books matched, repacked in small, easily handled parcels, wrapped in tough butcher paper, and tied with tough twine, labeled, stamped according to postal manual regulations. The project has called for the renting of a garage and the hiring of a truck for transportation to the post office. Quite a job! Quite a chore! But shucks, retirement is a myth, anyway!"[5]

Wherever possible, Isabelle responded to specific book requests from teachers and students. The requests ranged from books on mathematics, psychology, and the sciences to novels and poetry. English dictionaries were in great demand, as were books on agriculture. By the fall of 1965, Isabelle reported that she had shipped five thousand cartons of Braille books and magazines to forty-eight schools overseas.

To help her with the work, Isabelle recruited a small army of dedicated volunteers. The NFB raised money for cartons, twine, and the rental of a truck to haul boxes to the post office. Federationists also contributed Braillewriters, slates and styluses (devices for writing Braille by hand), and packages of heavy Braille paper.

Isabelle also planted the seeds of similar programs in other parts of the country. When she visited longtime friends Ray and Diane McGeorge, she persuaded them to start a used-book project in Colorado. "She was utterly charming," Diane McGeorge recalled. "She had an incredible gift for getting people to do what she wanted. You just couldn't say no to her."[6]

•　　•　　•

Although he never had Isabelle Grant's zest for travel, Jacobus tenBroek shared her commitment to improving the lives of blind people throughout the world. In all of her ventures, she had his unshakeable support. "I was ready to take off for the second year in Pakistan," Isabelle wrote in a short article on the founding of the IFB, "when Dr.

tenBroek, accompanying me to the airport, said: 'You remind me of a lone eagle flying off around the world.' 'Not a lone eagle,' I replied. 'For I have always the Federation behind me.'"[7]

In the fall of 1967, Isabelle set off on another yearlong expedition, this time focusing on ten nations in Africa. The American Brotherhood for the Blind (today the American Action Fund for Blind Children and Adults) provided two thousand dollars for her airfare and other expenses. As always on her travels, Isabelle avoided luxury hotels. She preferred to stay in hostels and inexpensive guesthouses where she could meet and mingle with the local people.

Isabelle sent periodic updates to Dr. tenBroek, but he wanted much more systematic information. "I assume you have considered the problem of reporting fully and in detail upon personalities and conditions you find in the various countries, and that you have decided it is impossible to do this while you are hitting the road so hard," tenBroek wrote to her on January 15, 1968. "Let me urge you to arrange for appropriate pauses in your travels and investigative activities so that you can send me complete reports. It will be utterly impossible for you to do this in adequate detail after you complete the whole trip and return to this country. Indeed, I am absolutely certain that the only feasible way of doing it is taking two or three days at the end of your visit to each country and setting down everything you have discovered."[8]

Early in March 1968, Isabelle wrote to Dr. tenBroek, describing a visit to a village of the Matabele tribe in Southern Rhodesia (today's Zimbabwe). "Going from hut to hut, handling the spears, shields, beer jars, kaffir corn porridge bowls, and speaking with several of the Matabele and Shona tribesmen through an interpreter were just too much to keep to myself," she enthused. "The tribesmen were much more interested in the fact that I, as a blind woman, was out traveling alone. They were entranced by my folding cane. Their blind remain in the huts, or sit and beg, or receive food to keep themselves alive, from their fellow tribesmen. The blind children are just there, and nothing is done about them."[9]

In another letter, written from Kenya on March 19, 1968, she stated that conditions were "sometimes very, very difficult from inaccessible roads, torrential rains (for this is the tropical belt), the constant threat of malaria, and anything from dry toilets to non-potable water.... This is not America. It is not even America two hundred years ago."[10] She was enduring these rigors at the age of seventy-two, a time in life when most of her peers had settled into comfortable retirement.

Far more disturbing to Isabelle than physical hardship was her encounter with apartheid, the rigid separation of the races imposed by the government of South Africa in 1948. "I found in South Africa I had to learn how to speak, when to speak, and when not to speak," she wrote in *Africa Passbook*, her as yet unpublished memoir of the trip. "As the days and the weeks went by, I learned how apartheid worked and did not work."[11] After overhearing the racist remarks of a group of Afrikaans women, she wrote, "I shuddered to think of man's inhumanity to man—but I had more to learn. I had better not explode—just yet."[12] In an article called "Quotes from My Letters," she wrote, "In South Africa and in Rhodesia I was unhappy, uncomfortable, afraid. I have nothing in common with segregation of people, and apartheid to me is inhumane, does not face facts, and is absolutely discriminatory."[13]

In the midst of her African travels, Isabelle received tragic news. Jacobus tenBroek, her beloved friend and mentor, died of cancer on March 27, 1968, at the age of fifty-six. For Isabelle, the loss must have been devastating. Yet she carried on with her journey and her work.

•   •   •

Back in California, Isabelle renewed her efforts to send Braille materials overseas and to awaken interest in the international blind community. She spoke to the Lions, the Rotarians, and the Kiwanis. She talked to school groups and ladies' aid societies. She addressed government officials and international aid organizations. Often for her speaking engagements she wore a traditional Pakistani costume, visible proof that she had traveled the world and identified with the people she had come to know.

Isabelle's Braille notecards were filled with reminders of stories to share—tales that must have amazed and delighted each new audience. "Lizard Story" referred to the incident in Burma when she entered her room to find a servant busily knocking lizards from the walls. Another favorite was "Cobra Story," which occurred during her visit to a school for the blind in Malawi. A voice shouted, "Jump!" and Isabelle jumped just in time to avoid stepping on a deadly snake.

The stories Isabelle told demonstrated that blindness need not prevent a person from living a fulfilling and even adventurous life or from making a contribution in the world. Once this truth was in view, she urged her listeners to help build opportunities for blind people in the United States and abroad. Her Scottish accent was charming. Her stance and expression exuded confidence. Her passion was irresistible.

After tenBroek's death, Isabelle remained deeply committed to the National Federation of the Blind and its mission in the United States. When she was in the country, she attended the organization's annual national conventions. She also took part in the conventions and other activities of the NFB's California affiliate. "She was especially interested in blind youth," remembered Michael Hingson, who met her at a convention when he was in his teens. "She'd tell us to set goals for ourselves and follow our dreams."[14]

One young woman who absorbed Isabelle's message was Joanne Fernandes. In 1966, when she was nineteen, Joanne met Isabelle at an NFB national convention. Joanne was interested in international work, and Isabelle showed her that blindness was no obstacle. Three years later, when she and her husband planned to spend several months in India, Joanne asked Isabelle for the names of blind people she might contact. Isabelle gave her a list of names and urged her to help start an organization of blind people during her stay. "Her passion was infectious," Joanne recalled decades later. "When we got to India, I started looking people up." She discovered a promising leader in a blind man named J. L. Kaul, who had established a workshop that provided employment for blind women. "Life was hard for blind men, but blind women in India were at the very bottom of the social heap," Joanne explained. "Isabelle had a very special concern for them and did whatever she could to support them."[15] Joanne Fernandes and J. L. Kaul founded the National Federation of the Blind of India, an organization that remains active in the twenty-first century.

•   •   •

On December 8, 1971, a member of the California Assembly, Eugene Chappie, sent a letter to Oslo, Norway. The letter was addressed to the nominating committee for the Nobel Peace Prize. "Gentlemen: I am writing to request your consideration of Dr. Isabelle L. D. Grant of 801 Redcliff Dr., Davis, California, as a nominee for the Nobel Peace Prize. Dr. Grant, a retired blind schoolteacher, is known not only here in California but throughout the United States and in many parts of the world for her work for many years with the people of Pakistan. I urge you to give her every consideration in your deliberations, for she is a most worthy person for this high award."[16] The nomination was spearheaded by a longtime friend, Leticia Sheffey of Bishop, California. Sheffey had lived for several years in Lahore, Pakistan, and had firsthand knowledge of Isabelle's work. Rep. Harold T. "Biz" Johnson of California's Second Congressional District made the formal nomination. It was supported by Sen. John Tunney, also of California, and by a varied and enthusiastic group of government officials, educators, and members of organizations of the blind.

"She chose to work in South Asia and later in Africa because there most of the people of the world live and the need is the greatest," Leticia Sheffey wrote in her eloquent letter of support. "As long as there are people, and as long as she can help them and uplift them, she will do so. To her this is a privilege, not without its hardships, tears, sacrifices, work, and challenges, but nevertheless a privilege, a joy, a love.... Of the blind, she says, 'Blind people are on the march throughout the world, and, like the dawn, you cannot hold them back.' Neither can one hold back Dr. Grant."[17]

"I don't want any of that tear-jerking stuff written about me," Isabelle told a reporter for the *Sacramento Bee* who interviewed her about her nomination. "No syrup. Just say that I worked for a new attitude toward the blind by the sighted, and that I am trying to convince blind people—including women—that they can do just about anything if they will get out and do it." She added, "I am indeed touched. But of course I haven't a whit's chance of getting it."[18]

As it turned out, no one was awarded the Nobel Prize for Peace in 1972, and the prize money went back into the general fund. Still, the nomination was a high honor indeed. It was public recognition of

Isabelle's ongoing work with the blind, an acknowledgment that her work had value for all of humanity.

The Nobel nomination was one of many accolades that Isabelle Grant received in appreciation of her work. At the national convention of the National Federation of the Blind in 1964, she was presented with the Newel Perry Award, the Federation's highest honor. On March 2, 1971, she received a commendation from President Richard M. Nixon "in recognition of service to others, in the finest American tradition." At the 1972 convention of the IFB, she was awarded a silver medal by the parliament of the city of Paris.

Apart from such large-scale public recognition, and perhaps even more deeply cherished by Isabelle, were the personal letters that flowed in from those she had helped and inspired during her travels. Among her papers are hundreds of letters, some in print and others in Braille, from blind women and men around the globe. They thanked her for books and typewriters she had sent and for scholarships she helped them obtain. Some thanked her for helping them pursue studies in the United States. Nearly all of them thanked her for extending the hand of friendship, for believing in them so fervently that they came to believe in themselves.

•   •   •

Despite her advancing years, Isabelle Grant remained vibrantly energetic. In August 1976, she wrote to a friend, "Please tell them that I seem never to have slowed down, that I am still going strong in spite of my fourscore years, just completed.... I am still on the job, having since last December been in Yugoslavia, speaking at the first conclave of the blind women of the world; then in Greece, a return visit; then in Helsinki, Sweden, the UK, and then the two-week convention of our own NFB. I also made a two months' journey through four countries in South America."[19]

Nevertheless, her heart was beginning to fail her. Early in June 1977, she was hospitalized for a minor heart attack. She returned home amid plans to address the United Nations in July. She did not live to make the trip to New York. She died in her sleep on June 25.

Isabelle Grant was gone, but the work she began went forward on its own momentum. By the time of her death, sixty nations had joined the International Federation of the Blind. Within each of these countries, blind leaders fought for the rights of the blind to receive an education, to live independently, to work, to contribute to society. More and more blind students studied beside sighted classmates in integrated classrooms, taught Braille and the use of the long white cane by teachers Isabelle Grant had trained. Raised with a new sense of their rightful place in the world, those students went on to inspire the next generation.

After decades as uncomfortable allies, the IFB and the World Council for the Welfare of the Blind merged in 1984 to become a new international organization, the World Blind Union (WBU). With headquarters in Toronto, Canada, the WBU had 190 member nations by 2012, representing an estimated 285 million blind and visually impaired persons throughout the world. As the voice of the blind, it speaks to governments and international bodies on issues concerning blindness and visual impairments. In conjunction with the International Agency for the Prevention of Blindness (IAPB) and the International Council for the Education of People with Visual Impairment (ICEVI), the WBU works as a member of a coalition called the Vision Alliance. The WBU has worked with the United Nations to ensure the rights of persons with disabilities and pressed for many articles that specifically include the rights of people who are blind or have low vision. It advocates with the World Intellectual Property Organization (WIPO) to ensure that books in formats accessible to the blind can be shared among countries. It sponsors leadership-development opportunities for blind women and provides scholarships for blind students. A scholarship fund for blind women in developing countries was established through a bequest by Isabelle Grant in memory of her daughter, Hermione Grant Calhoun.

One of the many achievements of the WBU is the preservation of the free international postal privilege for the mailing of Braille books and other materials for the blind. It was this international treaty that made possible Isabelle Grant's massive distribution of Braille books, the program that started Braille libraries all over the world.

Surely Isabelle Grant would rejoice at the achievements of the international blind community. She would be thrilled by the technological advances that have opened a wealth of opportunities to blind people in education and employment. And surely she would insist that the work is not yet done, that the blind of the world cannot rest until they have achieved full equality and won the respect that all human beings deserve.

Dr. Isabelle Grant fought for the rights of the blind, but her work has far wider implications. She was a humanitarian in the truest sense. "In my work I have learned to know and understand people of all nations and all religions," she once explained. "The common denominator to all this is human relations. I guess you could say this is my religion. I can't think of anything more important to the future of peace."[20]

NOTES

1. The *Sacramento Bee*, July 2, 1972.
2. Isabelle L. Grant, "IFB: Story and History," draft article for *Braille International Magazine* (1974), Isabelle Grant Collection, Bancroft Library, University of California–Berkeley, Carton 5.
3. Shanaz Ramzi, "Dr. Fatima Shah: Showing the Way," http://groups.yahoo.*com/group/FRIENDS_of_UP/message/8027*, retrieved 3-6-2012.
4. Jean Murphy, "Dr. Isabelle Grant: Fighter for the Blind," *Los Angeles Times* (1969), Isabelle Grant Collection, Bancroft Library, Carton 5.
5. "Books, Books, Send Books!" (1965) Unlabeled newspaper clipping, Isabelle Grant Collection, Bancroft Library, Carton 3.
6. Diane McGeorge, personal interview, November 29, 2012.
7. Isabelle L. Grant, "IFB: Story and History," draft article for *Braille International Magazine* (1974), Isabelle Grant Collection, Bancroft Library, Carton 5.
8. Letter from Dr. Jacobus tenBroek to Isabelle L. Grant, January 15, 1968. Isabelle Grant Collection, Bancroft Library, Carton 1.
9. Isabelle L. Grant, "White Cane in Black Africa," *Braille Monitor* (March 1968).
10. Lou Ann Blake, "Dr. Isabelle Grant—Teacher and World Traveler," *Braille Monitor* (March 2007).
11. Isabelle L. Grant, *Africa Passbook*, unpublished manuscript, Jacobus tenBroek Library, p. 63.
12. Ibid., p. 64.
13. Lou Ann Blake, "Dr. Isabelle Grant—Teacher and World Traveler," *Braille Monitor* (2007).
14. Michael Hingson, personal interview, October 30, 2011.
15. Joanne Fernandes (Wilson), personal interview, December 17, 2012.
16. Letter from Eugene Chappie to the Nobel Peace Prize Nominating Committee, December 8, 1971, Jacobus tenBroek Library.
17. Letter from Leticia Sheffey, Jacobus tenBroek Library.

18. "Dr. Isabelle Grant Is Nominee for Nobel Prize," *Sacramento Bee* (July 2, 1972).
19. Letter to Judy, August 17, 1976, Isabelle Grant Collection, Bancroft Library, Carton 3.
20. Lou Ann Blake, "Dr. Isabelle Grant—Teacher and World Traveler," *Braille Monitor* (2007).

Printed in the United States
By Bookmasters